THE ESSENTIAL MARCUSE

Herbert Marcuse

The Essential Marcuse

SELECTED WRITINGS
OF PHILOSOPHER
AND SOCIAL CRITIC
HERBERT MARCUSE

Edited by Andrew Feenberg and William Leiss

BEACON PRESS, BOSTON

Beacon Press
25 Beacon Street
Boston, Massachusetts 02108–2892
www.beacon.org

Beacon Press books
are published under the auspices of
the Unitarian Universalist Association of Congregations.

10 09 08 07   8 7 6 5 4 3 2 1

This book is printed on acid-free paper that meets the uncoated paper
ANSI/NISO specifications for permanence as revised in 1992.

Text design by Yvonne Tsang at Wilsted & Taylor Publishing Services
Composition by Wilsted & Taylor Publishing Services

Library of Congress Control Number: 2007922268

Credits

"Remarks on a Redefinition of Culture" first appeared in *Daedalus*, 94:1 (Winter,
1965). © 1965 by the American Academy of Arts and Sciences. Reprinted with their permission.

"Heidegger's Politics: An Interview with Herbert Marcuse" first appeared in the
Graduate Faculty Philosophy Journal, 6:1, published at New School University. Reprinted with their permission.

The following pieces appeared in Marcuse's books published by Beacon Press, with
permission to reprint granted by the estate of Herbert Marcuse: "Repressive Tolerance," "A Note on Dialectic," "The Foundations of Historical Materialism," "Sartre's
Existentialism," "Freedom and Freud's Theory of Instincts," "Philosophical Interlude,"
"The Affirmative Character of Culture," and "Nature and Revolution."

CONTENTS

INTRODUCTION
The Critical Theory of Herbert Marcuse

The Education of a Revolutionary Philosopher

Origins

Herbert Marcuse was born in 1898, eldest son of a Berlin merchant. The Marcuses were Jewish but this was largely a matter of indifference during his childhood, a time of rapid assimilation. In fact Marcuse used to joke that on Friday evenings one could hear mothers calling out "Siegfried, Brunehilde, Shabbat!"

Marcuse's adolescence took place in the period leading up to World War I. Germany was pulled in opposite directions by contradictory tendencies during this time. As in England where Victorian rectitude was beginning to give way to a freer, more experimental attitude toward life, so in Germany spiritual turmoil was rife especially among the youth and the artistic community. Meanwhile business prospered and, just as Marx had predicted, the working class expanded rapidly in numbers and political assertiveness in lockstep with the success of capitalism. It was no doubt impossible to foresee where all these tendencies would lead. Where they did in fact lead was to war, the greatest, most destructive war in human history up to that time.

The pointless cruelty of this conflict remains as its lasting memorial. In the trench warfare tens of thousands of soldiers were sent directly into machine gun fire. Ordinary young men were treated as mere cannon fodder by arrogant military leaders who had not yet understood that war could no longer be fought as before against modern technological means of destruction. Between 1914 and 1918 an incredible nine million people were killed and an additional twenty-three million injured. Yet no one looking back on the conflict has been able to explain convincingly why it had to take place.

In 1916 Marcuse was drafted into the German army. He was fortunate in being assigned to a rearguard unit and so did not see fire. But he suffered the disillusionment that was the main spiritual consequence of the war. Europe could no longer brag about its high level of civilization now that its appalling barbarism was apparent for all to see. In Germany, the traumatic loss of faith embraced the entire political system, not only the governing parties but also the socialist opposition that had supported the war enthusiastically at the outset. By the end, with millions of working people dead on all sides, it was clear that this was worse than a mistake, that it was a profound betrayal of everything for which the socialist movement stood.

It was too late for the official socialist party to gain the trust of skeptical youth. Like many other young people Marcuse was radicalized by the war and turned to the left splinter groups that split off from it. However, his enthusiasm was moderated by an experience at the end of the war that gave him pause. Revolution broke out in Munich and the military command lost control of the army in Berlin. Elected to the revolutionary soldiers' council in the capital, he watched with dismay as the rebellious troops reelected their old officers to lead them. From this experience he drew the conclusion that the most radical of the new left groups, Rosa Luxemburg's Spartacus League, was doomed to defeat. German workers were not ready for revolution.

After the war, Marcuse attended the University of Freiburg. While there his teachers included the founder of the phenomenological school of philosophy, Edmund Husserl. He graduated in 1922 with a doctoral dissertation on novels about artists in conflict with society.

Marcuse's approach in this thesis was strongly influenced by the early literary criticism of György Lukács. Lukács, a Hungarian who wrote primarily in German, was an important figure in the cultural world of Germany in this period. His early pre-Marxist writings expressed a kind of desperate utopianism that appealed to Marcuse and many others who experienced the war as the end of an era. Lukács applied Georg Simmel's idea of the "tragedy of culture" in a theory of the novel that emphasized the conflict between the energies of the individual and the increasing weight of social conventions and institutions in modern society. The individual is rich in potential for creativity and happiness, but society threatens to confine the "soul" within empty "forms."

In novels in which the protagonist is an artist, the conflict of art and life in bourgeois society exemplifies this theme. Overcoming or mitigating this conflict was to remain Marcuse's great hope, reappearing in his mature work in the concept of imaginative fantasy as a guide to the creation of a better society.

After completing his studies Marcuse worked for several years as a partner in an antiquarian book store in Berlin. The turn to a literary, or in this case a quasi-literary, career was not unusual for the sons of Jewish businessmen. Cultural aspirations were standard equipment in this rapidly rising stratum of German society. But all was not well in Germany. As he worked in his bookstore, the young Marcuse felt a profound dissatisfaction not only with the chaotic postwar status quo in Germany, but with the philosophical currents of the time, which failed to address the meaning of the events he had witnessed. A society capable of the monumental stupidity and inhumanity of European capitalism deserved to be overthrown. But by whom? And with what alternative in view?

The Attraction and Failure of Marxist Socialism

The answer seemed obvious to many young people of Marcuse's generation and background: Marxist socialism. In the nineteenth century, Marx had formulated his theory in the context of the reality of a new capitalist-industrial system, one in which men, women, and children alike were forced by the threat of starvation to work as much as eighty hours a week in dangerously unhealthy factories for pitifully small wages. When labor unions formed to improve wages and working conditions, the system responded with arrests, murder, and violent intimidation. The socialist movement in Europe and North America that sprang up in response advocated seizing the "means of production"—

the factories and natural resources—from the hands of their capitalist owners and operating them under the direction of the workers.

The ideological basis of the brutal exploitation of labor under early capitalism was the theory of so-called free markets: the individual worker was free to sell his or her labor to the factory owner, or to decline to do so; the capitalist was free to offer whatever level of wages he wished, irrespective of the needs of worker and family, and also to have sole control over working conditions at the factory. Moreover, the owner had no responsibility for the deaths or injuries the workers might suffer, and the workers' families had no claim on compensation. There was no moral or ethical basis to the relation between worker and owner, no sense that the disparity in wealth and social power between the two sides was anything but a "fact of nature," no recognition that this disparity in power and wealth corrupted from the outset the very notion of freedom that it pretended to celebrate.

These were the historical circumstances in which Marx formulated his theory in the mid-nineteenth century, and to a great degree those conditions had not changed much by the 1920s. After making some gains in the late nineteenth century, the working class was reduced to desperation and poverty once again in the aftermath of the First World War. With some exceptions there was still no adequate "social safety net." Violence and intimidation directed against labor unions, and especially against union organizers, both by corporations and governments, were still common.

Marx's ideas still seemed relevant for there was a sense that things had changed little since Marx's day. For many, the notion that the capitalist-industrial system was irredeemable was an evident fact, and so for them the idea of replacing it root and branch with a radically different socioeconomic order was alive and well. The means of achieving this new order was to be socialist revolution by the oppressed working class once conditions were ripe, industry developed, and capitalist leadership of society discredited.

These seemed to be precisely the conditions prevailing in Germany at the end of World War I, and yet the revolution had failed. The socialists and communists offered no convincing explanation for that failure, hence no hope of better success in the future. They continued to rely on an economic interpretation of Marxism that did not correspond with the spirit of the time. Marx, who subtitled his major work, the three-volume *Capital,* "a critique of political economy," often presented his thought as a rival economic theory of industrial society superior to the established theories in both explanatory and predictive power. But for many of those who had been through the war and its aftermath, the idea of an economically motivated revolution missed the point. The crisis of German society was at least as much spiritual and cultural as economic. A new concept of revolution was required by this unprecedented situation.

The spiritual chaos was a breeding ground for artistic creativity. No longer optimistic about socialist revolution, Marcuse was excited by various revolutionary aesthetic currents emerging in this period, but they offered no realistic prospect of moving the masses. Meanwhile the political situation in Germany gradually degenerated in the long prelude to the Nazi takeover.

It was in this context that in 1927 Marcuse read a much discussed book by Husserl's former assistant and successor, Martin Heidegger. In *Being and Time,* Heidegger transformed Husserl's phenomenological method into a remarkably delicate instrument for investigating the most basic human experiences and commitments. This book changed Marcuse's life. It seemed to promise a way out of the dead end of traditional Marxism, a way forward to a new concept of revolution. Marcuse returned to Freiburg to take up his studies again, this time with the intention of entering the German university system as a professional philosopher. To understand his excitement, it is necessary to explain phenomenology briefly in both its original Husserlian and its Heideggerian versions.

Husserl and Heidegger

The early twentieth century was a time of fantastic cultural innovation in science, art, literature—and philosophy as well. William James in America, Bergson in France, and Husserl in Germany all struggled to break with the dominant assumptions of the philosophical tradition in pursuit of a more "concrete" grasp of life.

Husserl, for example, proposed a return to "the things themselves," by which he meant a philosophy of immediate experience. This marked a break with the main schools of neo-Kantian thought in

Germany, which were primarily concerned with epistemology, the theory of knowledge. The overestimation of science called forth a reaction that appeared justified in the wake of the war. The question of science receded before a crisis of civilization that demanded an explanation of an entirely different sort. Husserl provided the method that would be employed for this purpose by phenomenologists and existentialists such as Heidegger, Sartre, and Merleau-Ponty.

Husserl called his approach "phenomenology" because he was interested in describing as accurately as possible the "phenomena" of experience. Consider, for example, our perception of an object such as a table. As we walk around it, we see it from different angles. Each perception is a presentation of the self-same table, but each is different.

We assume normally that the perceptions are held together by the "fact" that they are all attached to a real table out there in the world. Husserl did not entirely disagree, but he argued that this assumption made it impossible for us to appreciate the actual process of organizing perspectives and holding them together in our consciousness. To gain an understanding of the mental process in which consciousness perceives the table in and through its perspectives, we need to suspend the "natural attitude" and attend to the "immanent" structure of experience.

What is then revealed is the "intentional correlation" of acts of consciousness with their objects. What appears on the one side as an act such as knowing is essentially bound up with an object, the known, and so also for seeing and the seen, remembering and the remembered, and so on. From the phenomenological standpoint acts of consciousness create meaning in experience. The multiple perspectives on the table come together as what we call a "table" and constitute it as such.

Husserl's phenomenology led him beyond these initial considerations to a startling paradox. We usually think of consciousness as "in" the mind. In our everyday common sense understanding, the mind is an object in the world that is connected somehow to another object, the body. According to this objectivistic model, we explain our encounter with objects, such as the table, as an interaction between two things in the world, light rays striking the retina. But, Husserl claimed, this causal account does not get us to experience itself. That requires the suspension of the natural attitude with respect to mind and body as well as things.

Today we might explain Husserl's insight in terms of the difference we sense between a robot detecting the presence of the table and moving aside, and a human consciousness of the table. The robot operates very much like the objectivistic model of perception, but it has nothing we would want to call experience. Indeed it needs none and neither would we humans if we were simple creatures of reflex without a world.

Husserl concluded that experience is not a state of a mind-thing or brain, relative to human limitations, but an independent and irreducible realm of being he called "pure consciousness." Pure consciousness is a "field" coextensive with the world of objects in which those objects take on their meaning. So radical was Husserl's claim to the discovery of this new realm that he argued that God himself cannot grasp objects immediately but must perceive them perspectively just like humans. In sum, there is no "view from nowhere"; all encounters with reality are in principle first person encounters from out of a specific situation in the reality that is observed.

So far there is little about phenomenology to excite a young revolutionary intellectual. But Heidegger applied Husserl's method in a new way that bared not just ordinary perception but our human existence as persons. This proved a rather more interesting enterprise. Heidegger began by criticizing Husserl's continual reliance on the language of consciousness. The subject of experience is no kind of mind, even in Husserl's modified formulation. Rather, it is an existing individual, a whole acting self, essentially engaged with a world of objects it encounters in use. Meaning emerges in these encounters.

The intentional correlation now holds together human being and world in a unity Heidegger called "being-in-the-world." Note that "world" in Heidegger's sense does not refer to nature but rather to something like our notion of a "world of the theatre," a "Chinese world," or the "way of the world." There can be many such worlds, none merely subjective or private, but none absolute and unique either. These worlds are each a meaningful context of action rather than the sum of existing things. Significantly, "world" in this sense cannot be understood without reference to an acting and understanding subject whose world it is.

Heidegger went on to argue that our way of being in the world is fraught with tension. The things of experience are not simply "out there" waiting for us to find them. For them to be "revealed" as meaningful, we must be drawn to them, preoccupied from out of our concerns. Worlds are thus a function of the future we project for ourselves and the salient objects that emerge on our path to that future. But we are not absolutely wedded to any one future, to any one world. Insofar as we are persons, we are necessarily in a world, but there is no ultimate reason why we must be in this particular world rather than another one with different meanings and structures.

This indeterminacy is a source of metaphysical anxiety, a kind of existential doubt. There is a gap between self and world into which questions can slip. We are capable of interrogating our world and ourselves. This is no mere accident of our being but is our essential defining characteristic. It is a necessary precondition for having a world in the sense of an organized whole of meaningful experience rather than a mere sequence of reflexive responses to particular situations.

This precondition is related to the still deeper fact that our experience always leads back in some sense to ourselves. Our experience is, precisely, ours. Or rather, *my* experience belongs to *me* and is inseparable from *my* being. I cannot exist outside of the world of experience, and experience is marked by its relation to me as a subject and actor. Experience has "mineness" about it. As for Husserl, so for Heidegger the first person standpoint is interpreted as the opening of a realm of meaning.

Heidegger went on to argue that these phenomenological truths are obscured in average, everyday experience. Ordinarily, human existence is sociable and conformist. This "inauthentic" relation to self and world tends toward a leveling down and forgetfulness. Individuals neither doubt nor affirm their own experience but act according to what "they" normally do. They say this, they do that, and so say and do I. I forget that I am a questioning being, a being to whom experience belongs personally and inseparably.

This is not wholly bad; socialization takes place through participation in "the they" *(das Man)*. But "authentic" individuality is also possible at moments in which the individual becomes conscious of the limit death places on life. In such moments the individual can become aware of his or her individuality beyond any and all mindless conformism. In the light of death true action can give meaning to life as the individual lays claim to his or her own existence.

This account shows how far Husserl and Heidegger had traveled from the consensus of their day according to which the main task of philosophy was to ground the sciences. In fact, despite important disagreements, both Husserl and Heidegger hold that individual experience is an ontological foundation more basic than the nature of natural science. Knowledge in all its forms is derivative not merely in the sense that its claims are validated in experience, but more fundamentally, in that the very act of making claims presupposes the subject's belonging to a meaningful world. Both Husserl and Heidegger thus deny that a naturalistic explanation of reality can account for the totality of being. There will always be a vital remainder, the very fact of a meaningful world revealed in experience. Marcuse accepted this heritage of phenomenology and challenged the hegemony of science in modern culture and its practical basis, which he called "technological rationality."

Marcuse's "Heidegger-Marxismus"

One can see from this very sketchy description of Heidegger's complex theory why he came to be called an "existentialist" despite his rejection of this title. Like Kierkegaard and Nietzsche he promised philosophical insight into the most fundamental problems of personal life. Heidegger's work, Marcuse wrote at the time, "seems to us to indicate a turning point in the history of philosophy: the point where bourgeois philosophy transcends itself from within and opens the way to a new 'concrete' science."[1]

Marcuse applied this "concrete science" to understanding the passivity of the working class in the revolutionary situation at the end of the war. What is more, the idea of authenticity suggested a way of completing Marxism with a new theory of revolutionary consciousness. Traditional Marxism had failed because it relied on the motivating force of economic self-interest when in fact revolutions are not made for simple economic reasons. Marcuse now had a far more powerful instrument for analyzing the "radical act" in which individuals "exist" through transforming their world.

In 1928 Marcuse became Heidegger's assistant as Heidegger had been Husserl's. He published a series of essays that drew critically on Heidegger's thought and attempted to synthesize it with Marxism. Marcuse's fundamental objection concerned Heidegger's basic concept of world. Heidegger had attempted to uncover ultimate structures of the world as such, leaving the particulars of specific worlds to the side as sociological details. When in the later parts of *Being and Time* Heidegger did refer to these details, he raised them to a higher plane by identifying specific worlds with national communities of meaning, carriers of tradition.

Marcuse argued that in so doing, Heidegger obscured the divisions within communities. Indeed, from a Marxist standpoint, class divisions are ultimately more significant than nationality since modern capitalism destroys tradition and replaces it with a society based on self-interest. Authenticity in this situation becomes a matter of seizing the historical moment along with one's class in the affirmation of human possibilities against the deadening routines of the existing society.

While working with Heidegger, Marcuse went on to write a second thesis on Hegel that was to qualify him to teach in the German university. This thesis, entitled *Hegel's Ontology and the Theory of Historicity*, was published in 1932.[2] It is a remarkably rich and complex interpretation of Hegel strongly influenced by Heidegger. But it also departs from Heidegger in addressing the issue of history primarily in terms of Hegelian and Marxist notions of labor as the human power to *produce* worlds.

In Hegel's text labor is for the most part only loosely and metaphorically related to actual work in the usual sense of the term. Labor is understood as the act of negating the given reality in the creation of objects or institutions that reflect various aspects of human reality. But despite the vagueness of Hegel's reference to labor, Marx made the most of it and saw in him an important predecessor. Marcuse's appreciation of this Marxist take on Hegel is implicit throughout his thesis, but he gives it a Heideggerian twist.

This is plausible because labor also plays a role in *Being and Time*. An initial analysis of tool use forms the background to the notion of being-in-the-world. And as Marx would enthusiastically appropriate and narrow Hegel's concept of labor, so Marcuse would adapt Heidegger's concept of worldhood to mesh with his own Marxist approach. The world created by labor is in fact the Heideggerian world of experience awaiting and preparing the authentic act of the human subject whose world it is.

Marcuse's interpretation of Hegel was also influenced by Heidegger's theory of history as is apparent from the Heideggerian term "historicity" in his title. Heidegger established the central significance of time in the constitution of worlds. It is the reference to an anticipated future that gives order and meaning to the present. But Heidegger worked out his theory of temporality most fully in relation to the individual human being and failed to explain clearly and persuasively how history is constituted at the collective level.

Here Hegel and Marx offer an important complement and corrective to Heidegger. For them the future is a collective project that emerges from social tensions that themselves reflect different projects borne by different social groups. The progressive projects realize potentials in the present that reflect developing human capacities. This notion of potential became the basis for Marcuse's later theory of the "two dimensions" of society, the dimension of everyday facts and the dimension of transcending possibilities that lead on to higher stages of historical and human development. With this reinterpretation of Hegel, Marcuse prepared his new concept of revolution adequate to the crisis of twentieth-century German society.

Astonishingly, this interpretation of Hegel came close to anticipating aspects of Marx's own early unpublished writings. In 1932 a previously unknown text emerged from the archives. These *Economic and Philosophical Manuscripts* revolutionized the image of Marx. Here in 1844 Marx argued that capitalism was not simply an economic system. Capitalism alienated workers from their essential nature as creatures capable of building a world through labor that "objectifies" their needs and powers. But this world does not belong to them. Instead it is appropriated by the capitalist and turned against its creators, perverting their whole existence into a debased struggle for survival. Marx attacks the destruction of the "human essence" in an economic system that reduces the worker to nothing but the abstract capacity for "labor-power"—abstract because in the early factory system labor was stripped of all particular qualities of skill and creativity and was measured solely in quantitative units of time.

In this text Marcuse discovered a Marx who was more than an economist, who spoke to the contemporary crisis of modernity as a whole. What is more, he found remarkable similarities to his own rather creative interpretations of Heidegger and Hegel. In a number of passages

Marx makes surprising claims that distinguish his concept of nature from that of the natural sciences and bring it closer to the phenomenological concept of experience. Marcuse did not have to stretch the point in treating Marx's affirmation of the unity of human being and nature as an intentional correlation of subject and object, a kind of being-in-the-world. What is more, like Husserl and Heidegger, Marx grants this experiential unity a supreme ontological significance. But unlike these phenomenologists, Marx's version of being-in-the-world has a radical historical character. He argues that the objectification of human faculties through labor under socialism creates a humanized nature in which we can finally be at home.

Marcuse emphasized these aspects of the *Manuscripts* and made of this early work of Marx the culmination and turning point of his own phenomenological education. His lengthy review, which can be read among the selections in this book, is the basis of his later thought.

The Decisive Break

We have now followed Marcuse up to 1932, a crucial year during which the political situation in Germany became increasingly threatening. Socialists and Communists were still deeply divided just as the right came together around Hitler. In the elections of 1933, the Nazi party emerged with over a third of the vote and powerful allies who gave it total control of the government. Then suddenly it was announced that the widely revered teacher, Martin Heidegger, was to be the first Nazi rector of the University of Freiburg. Marcuse had not seen it coming and the shock sent him reeling.

There has been much discussion of Heidegger's fateful decision to join the Nazi party. Was his philosophy itself a National Socialist doctrine? Was Heidegger guilty of anti-Semitism not only in his official capacity but more significantly in concealed references in his philosophical writings? Was *Being and Time* a dangerous book?

The answer to these questions is not obvious. Heidegger was by no means alone in making the leap from ivory tower indifference to misguided political enthusiasm. Nietzscheans and Kantians, even Thomists, rallied to the Nazi banner.[3] The post–World War I crisis affected everyone in Germany, not only young leftists like Marcuse. Many in the academy turned to the right rather than the left for a solution.

The right drew its strength from the widespread sense of the exhaustion of the heritage of the Enlightenment, indeed of Western culture itself. Perhaps his students knew that Heidegger shared such sentiments, but this by no means identified him as a Nazi. The further leap from fairly routine culture-critical pessimism to Nazism required the belief in a new era of authoritative traditions and leaders. And one could hardly qualify as a Nazi without condemning the Jews, considered as carriers of corrupt modernity, and supporting their expulsion from normal social intercourse. Apparently, these were not views reflected in Heidegger's lectures and conversations before the rectorship.

The Heidegger "case" cannot be decided here. Deep ambiguities in Heidegger's abstract formulations facilitated the misunderstanding that led to Marcuse's remarkable invention of his so-called *Heidegger-Marxismus*. Indeed, so obscure and difficult are Heidegger's radical new ideas that after the fact it was also possible to see in them the sources of his disastrous political turn.

But it is significant that Heidegger had four Jewish students who were later to become prominent social philosophers of liberal or leftist persuasion. Hannah Arendt, Hans Jonas, and Karl Löwith all found themselves in the same position as Marcuse, shocked by their teacher's sudden political commitment and bereft of normal career prospects. That his Jewish students could have been so thoroughly mistaken about their teacher suggests that his thought was not as deeply tainted as many contemporary critics have argued.

The whole German world was falling apart but Marcuse had a more personal problem: he needed a job. He appealed to his old teacher Husserl who obtained for him an interview with Max Horkheimer, the head of the Institute for Social Research. The Institute was a group of academic Marxists who possessed some exciting new ideas and, just as important in this historical juncture, an endowment. These Marxists had applied their method to the study of class attitudes in Germany. The results worried them so much that they moved their money and operations to Switzerland before the Nazi seizure of power. Thus they were not only interesting interlocutors for the unorthodox Marxist Marcuse, but also possible employers.

In 1933, Marcuse moved to Switzerland to work with the Institute in exile. From there, the Institute moved to Paris and eventually to the

United States where Marcuse remained for the rest of his life. The Institute's famous "Critical Theory" and Marcuse's contribution to it are described in the next section.

Marcuse and the "Critical Theory of Society"

Explaining Critical Theory

Marcuse is identified with a group of German thinkers known collectively as "The Frankfurt School" because they were all affiliated at one time or another with the Institute for Social Research that had been founded at the University of Frankfurt in 1924.[4] In addition to Marcuse, the most prominent members of the school were Max Horkheimer and Theodor Adorno. In recent years Walter Benjamin has been recognized as another important member.

The Frankfurt School was one of the main components of the early-twentieth-century trend called "Western Marxism." This phrase refers to Western European thinkers who were heavily influenced by Marx and whose interpretation of Marx's work differed notably from the version propagated in the Soviet Union.

The Frankfurt School defined its own unique version of Western Marxism during the 1930s, when its members were in exile from Nazi Germany and already scattered across the rest of Europe and as far abroad as the United States. The label they gave to their version was "the critical theory of society."

In an essay published in the Institute's house journal in 1937, entitled "Traditional and Critical Theory," Max Horkheimer defined the "critical theory of society" as:

1. "a theory dominated at every turn by a concern for reasonable conditions of life";
2. a theory which condemns existing social institutions and practices as "inhuman";
3. a theory which contemplates the need for "an alteration of society as a whole."[5]

Nowhere in this essay does Horkheimer explicitly identify critical theory with Marxism, but toward its conclusion the theory's Marxist roots become apparent:

Thus the critical theory of society begins with the idea of the simple exchange of commodities.... The theory says that the basic form of the historically given commodity economy on which modern history rests contains in itself the internal and external tensions of the modern era; it generates those tensions over and over again in an increasingly heightened form; and after a period of progress, development of human powers, and emancipation of the individual, after an enormous extension of human control over nature, it finally hinders further development and drives humanity into a new barbarism.[6]

The first sentence in this passage is a faithful rendition of the essential ideas in the most important writings of Karl Marx, who had opened his main work, the first volume of *Capital* (1867), with an exposition of commodity exchange. Its closing statement reflects the specific perils of the time in which it was written when European fascism held sway in Germany and Italy and was beginning to menace all of civilization.

In that same year and in the same journal, Marcuse published his counterpart essay, "Philosophy and Critical Theory." His emphasis was on the fundamental human values that ground the project of critical theory. These values, such as freedom, had been well explicated in conceptual terms in the tradition of Western philosophy, but for the most part philosophy seemed incapable of envisioning how they might actually be realized in social life. Marcuse summarized the commitment of critical theory to this task. Critical theory is identified by:

1. "concern with human happiness, and the conviction that it can be attained only through a transformation of the material conditions of existence";
2. "concern with the potentialities of man and with the individual's freedom, happiness and rights... [F]reedom here means a real potentiality, a social relationship on whose realization human destiny depends";
3. "the demand that through the abolition of previously existing material conditions of existence the totality of human relations be liberated."[7]

Once again, although the name of Marx is not explicitly invoked, his spirit pervades these passages.

But critical theory was much more than recycled Marxism. The need for a new foundation for the critical theory of society was dictated by the times. Circumstances were very different from those that inspired Marx. First, on the left of the political spectrum, there was the Soviet Union, "officially" a socialist regime ruled by a government answerable to the workers and paying homage to Marxian ideology. Second, on the right wing, there was the fascist movement, already ruling two European nations and threatening to spread police-states everywhere, flaunting an officially sanctioned program of racism, anti-Semitism, political murder, and the brutal repression of civil liberties.

In different ways both represented something new in the modern Western political tradition, a "totalitarian" ideology in which the state claimed the power to transform and oversee every aspect of social life — work, family, religion, culture, education, politics, and economy. Both also claimed to represent an international movement that would soon sweep away the existing forms of life in other countries. By the latter half of the 1930s there was little doubt that warfare among nations on a terrifying scale was being prepared.

For the members of the Frankfurt School, themselves among the early victims of the terror and repression that would soon spread far more widely, this was the concrete situation calling for a renewal of the critical theory of society. Both of the new developments required a response — although, based on what was known at the time, the threat from the right appeared by far the worse of the two.

To be sure, Soviet Marxism was converting Marx's humane and ethical vision of progressive social change into the repressive ideology of a totalitarian state. But the full extent of this betrayal was not yet evident. The Frankfurt School responded to the early signs by emphasizing the centrality of the concept of human freedom (including political freedom) in the socialist vision, and by criticizing the reduction of Marxist thought to a set of crude formulas.

The threat from the right appeared to be the more serious for a number of reasons. First and foremost, it had arisen in powerful Western nations, nations that were heirs not only to the most modern industrial technologies, but also to a long tradition of European culture based on the most important human values—enlightenment, science, rationality, individual and political freedom, universal education, equality, tolerance, democracy, and the rule of law. These values had been accepted by the partisans of socialism and incorporated into their own vision of a better future in the expectation that socialist revolution in the advanced European countries would realize them even more fully.

But in fact the very nations that had appeared to be "ripe" for the transition to socialism now appeared to be regressing, not advancing, and in the process they undermined the progressive achievements not just of modern democracy but of the preceding four centuries.

Second, the fascist movement was still growing in strength, and if it should succeed in conquering Europe and North America, then all hope of a better future would vanish indefinitely.

It should now be clear why Horkheimer and Marcuse, in the passages from their 1937 essays quoted above, described the critical theory of society as they did. They were reaffirming, not just the genealogy of the theory itself, but its commitment to both the continued need for social transformation toward democratic socialism, on the one hand, and to certain fundamental values of the Enlightenment tradition, on the other. In the longer run this was a fragile duality. After the Second World War, Horkheimer gradually came to believe that these twin commitments were incompatible, and that only the second of them should be defended. Marcuse, on the other hand, continued to believe—until the end of his life—that the two were inseparable.

But there was a third element in critical theory, not yet discussed, one which was shared by Horkheimer and Marcuse, although almost certainly more strongly by Marcuse, namely, the "utopian spirit" which, from the beginning, was a core element in that theory and its moral basis.

Utopia, which means both "no place" and "good place," is one of the oldest traditions of thought in the modern West. The idea originated in a seminal work entitled *Utopia*, penned in 1516 by the English statesman and philosopher Thomas More. For the next three hundred years, a series of books of a similar nature appeared envisioning a more perfect society. Most of them were influenced by More and followed his format, including detailed and fanciful descriptions of the daily life routines in their imaginary societies. In most of them too, one finds another of More's sly tactics, a critique of society as it then was, disguised as a merely descriptive account of a way of life that supposedly actually existed in some concealed, far-off location across the seas.

The great turn in the utopian tradition occurred during the nineteenth century with the coming of industrialism. Until then, the political economy of the good society was usually described by utopian writers as a form of communitarian agrarianism, that is, a farm-based economy with progressive social relations, including equality of possessions and work obligations, enlightened penal codes, peaceful relations with neighbors, universal education, satisfying craft labor, and (sometimes) more equal gender relations and democracy.[8] With few exceptions, these were not "rich" societies although they all made provision for basic needs; the main point is that they were more just, more humane, and more enlightened. But now, with industrialism, for the first time it appeared that the society of the future could be all these things and far richer too, since now everyone could be freed from one of the main curses of earlier times, endless, backbreaking labor.

These themes found their way into that part of the tradition of social criticism that promoted an explicit vision of socialism or communism. Marx was well aware of these utopian speculations but he was skeptical of ethically inspired depictions of the future. Unlike most of the utopian writers, he believed he could show not only the need to transcend the unjust society in the name of something better, but also how to accomplish that goal. In effect, he argued that what was required was a far more exact account of how the prevailing society functioned, because the secret of its future lay buried in its present. In Hegelian fashion Marx argued that once one understood the precise nature of the changes that capitalist-industrial society had forced upon its predecessors, it would be possible to understand the forces growing within that would doom it in the future.

Those changes were the following: free-market relations and the commodity form of production, and their impact on human labor; the factory system, sweeping together diverse populations into larger collectivities; the collapse of older social class formations into just two polarized classes, capitalist and proletariat; and finally, the existential foundations of the revolutionary character of the proletariat, the class that would abolish itself in the process of unseating the capitalists from power, the class that—unlike all its predecessors—would not reestablish political domination to serve its own interests but would instead bring to an end all class relations in human history.

Marx presupposed the truth of the utopian tradition—that a more perfect society was not only desirable but also entirely possible—without drawing a blueprint. We have from him only the marvelous epigram for the guiding principle of the future society, "from each according to his abilities, to each according to his needs." Russell Jacoby has labeled this way of thinking "negative" or "iconoclastic" utopia, a longing for a better future that is deeply felt but refrains from even hinting at its social topography.[9] And it is precisely this style of utopian vision that both Horkheimer and Marcuse explicitly referenced in their essays on the critical theory of society.

The Utopian Theme in Critical Theory

Expressing himself in the cautious and indirect language that he adopted in his period of exile, Horkheimer wrote of critical theory:

> One thing which this way of thinking has in common with fantasy is that an image of the future which springs indeed from a deep understanding of the present determines men's thoughts and actions even in periods when the course of events seems to be leading far away from such a future and seems to justify every reaction except belief in fulfillment.... But in regard to the essential kind of change at which critical theory aims, there can be no corresponding concrete perception of it until it actually comes about.[10]

Marcuse also linked the idea of utopia to the human capacity for fantasy. In his "Philosophy and Critical Theory" he refers to the famous set of three questions, which Kant had posed at the end of his *Critique of Pure Reason:* "What can I know? What should I do? What may I hope?" Marcuse comments:

> What critical theory is engaged in is not the depiction of a future world, although the response of fantasy to such a challenge would not perhaps be quite as absurd as we are led to believe. If fantasy were set free to answer, with precise reference to already existing

technical material, the fundamental philosophical questions asked by Kant, all of sociology would be terrified at their utopian character. And yet the answers that fantasy could provide would be very close to the truth, . . . [f]or it would determine what man is on the basis of what he really can be tomorrow.[11]

At the time when they wrote such lines, Horkheimer and Marcuse would have had the reality of their own circumstances clearly in mind: they were among those who had fled for their lives from a regime that would have arrested, tortured, and killed them either for their thoughts or their ethnicity, or both. As the darkness of fascism descended over the land of his birth, Marcuse reduced critical theory to its barest essentials:

> In replying to the question, "What may I hope?," [fantasy] would point less to eternal bliss and inner freedom than to the already possible unfolding and fulfillment of needs and wants. In a situation where such a future is a real possibility, fantasy is an important instrument in the task of continually holding the goal up to view.

As we shall see,· Marcuse never wavered in his adherence to this standpoint. His faith in fantasy was closely connected to beliefs about art that predated his turn to critical theory and survived the disappointments that led his closest colleague, Max Horkheimer, to abandon it at the end of the Second World War.[12] That unwavering commitment to utopia, to the possibility of a better future, is a defining feature of his life's work and the most striking aspect of it that clearly sets him apart from the other principal figures identified with the Frankfurt School, with the possible exception of Walter Benjamin, who died at the beginning of World War II.

Although the Institute for Social Research was eventually reestablished at the University of Frankfurt in 1951, the heroic period of the Frankfurt School was over. The gap between Marcuse and his former colleagues is evident in discussions held in 1947 as to when and how to restart the Institute's main publication, the *Journal of Social Research*, which had been suspended during their period of exile. In this context Marcuse drafted a programmatic document for Horkheimer in which he proposes that the theory must be adjusted to current circumstances and become more closely tied to practice, that is, to explorations of how the dream of the better future might be realized.[13]

This untitled document argues that after the war the world of nations is split into neo-fascist and Soviet camps, and "what remains of democratic-liberal forms will be crushed between the two camps or absorbed by them." Further, it remains true to the vision that a society of free persons can only result from the actions of a "revolutionary working class" because "it alone has the real power to abolish the existing relations of production and the entire apparatus that goes with it."

The document acknowledges that the working class of the time is not ready to play this role because its own needs and perceptions have become "habituated" to the structures of the existing capitalist society. Thus traditional class antagonisms are frozen in place, and one cannot imagine any longer the possibility of a revolutionary consciousness arising spontaneously in the working class, as Marx had assumed it would. Therefore Marcuse draws the "logical" but to us rather startling conclusion that all this "has confirmed the correctness of the Leninist conception of the vanguard party as the subject of the revolution."[14]

Marcuse's project was stillborn for at that point in time his colleagues wanted nothing whatsoever to do with this kind of analysis and a program of studies based on it. And after Horkheimer returned to Frankfurt four years later, Marcuse never received from him a firm offer of employment at the Institute and the University of Frankfurt. He was fifty-six years old, still without a permanent job, still hoping in vain for a chance to rejoin his old colleague, when he reluctantly accepted the offer of a faculty position at Brandeis University in 1954.[15] He moved to the University of California, San Diego, in 1965. His whole academic career was spent in the United States.

The Utopian Theme in Marcuse's Later Writings

In a chapter entitled "Fantasy and Utopia" of his famous 1955 book, *Eros and Civilization: A Philosophical Inquiry into Freud,* Marcuse developed most extensively the utopian theme that had once formed the heart of critical theory. The capacity for fantasy, in which the notion and desire for utopia is nurtured, is presented here as a permanent and necessary function of the human mind as such:

As a fundamental, independent mental process, fantasy has a truth value of its own, which corresponds to an experience of its own —namely, the surmounting of the antagonistic human reality. Imagination envisions the reconciliation of the individual with the whole, of desire with realization, of happiness with reason. While this harmony has been removed into utopia by the established reality principle, fantasy insists that it must and can become real, that behind the illusion lies *knowledge*.[16]

And then, for the first time in any of the works of the principal Frankfurt School social theorists, Marcuse goes on to lay out, not the design of a utopian future, but its prehistory and at least some of its specific preconditions and goals.

Marcuse imagines an early stage of human history, a "primitive" utopia, occurring during a time of low economic productivity, where there was a near equal distribution of resources among members of a tribe, little accumulation of wealth across generations, and a quasi-democratic structure of authority. (This "model" may have existed, for example, in the nomadic tribes of indigenous North American peoples who inhabited the Great Plains.[17])

Opposed to this model is the phase of human development that begins with large-scale settled societies and an expanding population that brings political domination by a ruling elite made up of an alliance of priests and kings. Here a large economic surplus—material wealth beyond basic survival needs—is generated which, instead of being retained by the common people who produce it in order to reduce labor time, create leisure, and satisfy higher needs, is appropriated by the rulers as private wealth and for public monuments and warfare. The common people continue to experience life as dictated by necessity, hard labor, scarcity, and repression, compensated, as it were, by the promise that all would be made well in the afterlife of the soul.

Now Marcuse imagines a second version of utopia, occurring in a "fully developed industrial society after the conquest of scarcity." He takes the level of economic activity in the United States prevailing at the time of writing (the early 1950s) as his starting point. If consumption was limited to "basic needs" such as food, housing, clothing, and leisure, the existing industrial technologies would be able to satisfy them for everyone with a drastically reduced workweek.

Marcuse draws the necessary conclusion: choosing this option means "a considerable reduction" in the prevailing standard of living, at least for those in the upper half of the spectrum of material wealth. What would be offered in return? The degree of repression necessary for life in civilized society is relative to the struggle with nature and the level of wealth achieved thereby. Where that struggle is artificially maintained at a level of intensity no longer required by social order, a "surplus repression" results that could be reduced through reforming social and economic institutions. This is the case in advanced industrial societies. Reducing necessary labor to an absolute minimum would offer new possibilities of human fulfillment to everyone. "[T]he reduction of the working day to a point where the mere quantum of labor time no longer arrests human development is the first prerequisite for freedom." The striking fact is that *this "option" already exists*.

Marcuse interpreted this conclusion in terms derived in part from Freud. Extending Freud's theory of the instincts, he argued that labor in the service of survival is the response to necessity, that is, the "reality principle," which is set in opposition to the "pleasure principle," that is, gratification of needs (including aesthetic needs, represented in culture). On this account repression appears to be a necessary feature of the human psyche. But where Freud had treated the instincts as quasi-biological constants, Marcuse reinterpreted them as historically malleable. In a free society "Eros, the life instincts, would be released to an unprecedented degree." These words were published in 1955, during a decade in which American popular culture embraced a repressive, conformist, suburban lifestyle as the pinnacle of human achievement.

But for anyone who lived through the decades of the 1950s and 1960s in the nations of the West, Marcuse's words are eerily prophetic of the social movement that would erupt there a mere ten years later. They are, in fact, such an uncannily accurate forecast of what was to come, such a precise representation of the underlying spirit of the counterculture of the New Left and the "hippies" that exploded onto the scene in the mid-1960s, that rereading them fifty years later one pauses in astonishment. No one who was even slightly touched by the events of that period would doubt the truth of the prophecy made in *Eros and Civilization* a short time earlier: "The utopian claims of imagination have become saturated with historical reality."[18]

Taken at its best, the counterculture celebrated a rejection of endless consumerism, of rigid nuclear-family suburban lifestyles, of sexual repression—especially for women, of the fear of intoxication (except for alcoholic excess, still today the one officially approved recreational drug in American culture), of hypocritical churchgoing, and of the social ideologies that affirmed war, racism, and inequality. Without a doubt, the counterculture had its own darker side, in drug excess, in persistent male domination, in "communes" where the old games of leaders and followers were reproduced, in the failure to bridge the racial divide in America or to take up the cause of the poorest and most exploited social strata.

As a California resident Marcuse had a front-row seat, as it were, witnessing both the triumph and the denouement of this movement. But by 1968 Marcuse was more than a local figure. He had become a household name around the world—when he was already seventy years old!—in the double context of the growing resistance against the war in Vietnam and the "cultural revolution" represented by the student movement on university campuses and the streets of major cities not only in America but also in Europe, Latin America, and Japan.

For those who knew him one of the most remarkable features of his transformation into a leading figure of the new social movements was the contrast between his position and that of his former colleagues in the Frankfurt School. At the very time Marcuse's book *One-Dimensional Man* became the "official text" at training sessions for the antiwar activists of the Students for a Democratic Society, Horkheimer and Adorno were nervously hunkered down inside their office building in Frankfurt, distancing themselves from those in the streets who were rallying in their name.

To understand this strange division, it is necessary to return to themes from Marcuse's early sources as they affected his unique formulation of critical theory.

Technology and Revolution

The Two Dimensions

The critique of technology is the counterpart to the utopian hopes of the nineteenth century. Rousseau and Schiller, writing at the end of the eighteenth century, condemned the division of labor for splitting human beings into narrowly specialized fragments of a whole person.

With the development of manufacturing in England, and eventually of industrial production, doubts about the direction of progress were expressed more and more vocally, especially by writers in the romantic tradition. Nostalgia for earlier, more organic forms of social life was widespread in literary circles. While the art critic John Ruskin condemned capitalism for its ugliness, philosophers such as Kierkegaard and Nietzsche denounced the passionless conformism of a business-oriented society. Critics more sensitive to human suffering attacked capitalism for its inhumanity. Technology appears in these traditions as the villain, restructuring social life around mechanical, inanimate forms with the dire consequences the critics denounce.

The twentieth century is truly the century of technology. It is in this period that utopia is transformed into dystopia, an imaginary society as supreme in its evil as utopia is good. In the most famous of these dystopias, *Brave New World* (1932), human beings have become little more than robots, themselves no different from other mechanical components. Meanwhile, prophets of doom such as Oswald Spengler in Germany foresaw the "decline of the West." Such pessimistic speculations had little influence on mainstream culture until the 1960s and remained the specialty of disillusioned literary intellectuals, with obvious resonances in the work of Heidegger and the Frankfurt School.

Despite a shared skepticism about the blessings of technology, neither Horkheimer nor Adorno was influenced by Heidegger as was Marcuse. Adorno's contempt for Heidegger was notorious. Although Marcuse was critical of Heidegger's betrayal of Enlightenment ideals, indeed, as he put it, of philosophy itself, he remained in some deep sense under Heidegger's influence. This influence showed up interestingly in Marcuse's 1964 book *One-Dimensional Man*.

Themes from both the Frankfurt School and existentialism lie in the background to this book. Toward the end of World War II, Horkheimer and Adorno worked in exile in Los Angeles on their classic *Dialectic of Enlightenment* (1944). This book announced the new and far more pessimistic direction of critical theory in the postwar period. They noted the astonishing success of Enlightenment in banishing myth in the development of modern science and technology, which culminated paradoxically by the twentieth century in the terrifying return of myth in the form of fascism and mass culture.

Dialectic of Enlightenment was an eloquent assault on the modern triumph of pure instrumental rationality and its technology. The old notion of a reason that was more than instrumental, that was wise in its choice of goals, had been defeated. Its last chance, the failed socialist revolution, lay irrevocably in the past. Reason, they argued, had been stripped of any reference to humane ends and reduced to a mere tool of the powerful. The Enlightenment hope for a pacified and prosperous society in which individual happiness was available to all remained valid, but the prospects of its fulfillment were increasingly poor. They conclude, "The fully enlightened earth radiates disaster triumphant."[19] Significantly for the later development of their views, they offered no solution to the dilemma they described, no renewed revolutionary possibility that could again set Enlightenment on a humane path.

Adorno and Horkheimer's book was little read in the postwar period, but in 1949 Heidegger offered a similar diagnosis of the times in a far more famous text called "The Question Concerning Technology." Heidegger argued that the modern world was shaped entirely by the technological spirit, which reduced all of being to a component in a vast system of instrumentalities. More fundamental than any particular goal pursued with the aid of the technological apparatus was this reductive tendency that affected every aspect of life. Even the human beings before whom being was revealed and through whom it took on meaning in experience were becoming mere cogs in the mechanism.

These two texts were the deepest theoretical expressions of the type of culture criticism that came to prominence in the 1960s. It seemed that *Brave New World* had actually arrived and the old idea of individuality was threatened with technological obsolescence. For many intellectuals dystopian fears now began to replace utopian hopes, although faith in science and technology remained the dominant mood at least in the United States. It was in this climate of growing technophobia that Marcuse brought out *One-Dimensional Man*.

In this book Marcuse argued that instrumental reason had triumphed over an earlier form of rationality that embraced ends as well as means. This was not simply an intellectual phenomenon but was rooted in the very structure of experience. It is not knowledge or technical devices that are primary but the technological relation to reality that makes progress in science and technique possible in the first place. Just as Heidegger had argued that the structure of experience is oc-

cluded by the technological "revealing," so Marcuse held that "technological rationality" distorted and reduced experience to an impoverished remnant.

But Marcuse did not treat this transformation as essentially spiritual
as had Heidegger. Like Adorno and Horkheimer he saw it as a social
phenomenon based on the perpetuation of capitalism under the new
conditions of advanced technology that had made the old "reality principle" obsolete. Now mass production, mass consumption, and mass
culture prevail over traditional forms of consciousness and a society
that "delivers the goods" integrates the working class once and for all.

In the course of explaining the historical character of the technological reduction of experience, Marcuse also referenced Husserl. In
his later work, Husserl argued that science was rooted in the "lifeworld"
of everyday practice. The technical operations of scientific reason reflect in refined form more basic nontechnical experiences, which are
obscured by the natural attitude. Husserl had hoped that regrounding
science in experience would open the way to restoring Enlightenment
values.

Marcuse took over the notion of the lifeworld but argued that it is
fundamentally political, as are the scientific concepts derived from it.
When the scientifically purified concepts return to the lifeworld as
technology, they reveal the project of the dominant social groups concealed in their abstract forms. In its very indifference to values, science
already prepares this politically biased outcome. Marcuse's daring position is summed up in the following passage:

> Technology serves to institute new, more effective, and more pleas-
> ant forms of social control and social cohesion. . . . In the face of
> the totalitarian features of this society, the traditional notion of the
> "neutrality" of technology can no longer be maintained. Technol-
> ogy as such cannot be isolated from the use to which it is put;
> the technological society is a system of domination which operates
> already in the concept and construction of techniques. . . . As a
> technological universe, advanced industrial society is a *political*
> universe, the latest stage in the realization of a specific historical
> *project* — namely, the experience, transformation, and organization
> of nature as the mere stuff of domination. . . . As this project unfolds,

it shapes the entire universe of discourse and action, intellectual and material culture. In the medium of technology, culture, politics, and the economy merge into an omnipresent system which swallows up or repulses all alternatives. The productivity and growth potential of this system stabilize the society and contain technical progress within the framework of domination. Technological rationality has become political rationality.[20]

Marcuse pursued this analysis in terms of the notion of the two dimensions of being he had introduced in his early thesis on Hegel. These two dimensions correspond to existence and essence, the bare empirical facts and the ideal toward which the facts tend in their process of development. Ancient Greek philosophy held the two dimensions in tension: essences are teleological goals toward which beings strive. If Aristotle defined man as a "rational animal" it was not because he believed all men achieve rationality but because this is the ultimate form toward which their nature tends.

The history of art testifies to the fidelity of human beings to this two-dimensional ontology by depicting an imagined better world in which the potential for peace, harmony, and fulfillment is finally realized. But in advanced industrial society the tension between the two dimensions is systematically reduced. New modes of experience and thought confine consciousness to the immediate facts. And insofar as those facts are governed by those who hold power, reason becomes conformist and compliant.

This pessimistic message resonated with the dystopian spirit of Adorno, Horkheimer, and Heidegger, and yet something surprising happens in the final chapter of this book. This chapter, entitled "The Chances of the Alternatives," sketches a new concept of reason capable of uniting value and fact and guiding the recovery of a two-dimensional universe. A new science and technology are possible that would again incorporate humane ends in the very structure of rationality. Marcuse concluded, "The rationality of art, its ability to 'project' existence, to define yet unrealized possibilities could then be envisaged as *validated by and functioning in the scientific-technological transformation of the world.*"[21]

Marcuse refused to give up hope and suggested that we have the technical power and the imaginative capacity to finally realize essence in existence, to create a good society. This explicit appeal to alternatives marked a significant departure unnoticed by many of Marcuse's contemporary readers and recalled by few today. But with the rise of the New Left and the counterculture, it became the main theme of his later writings.

The Agent of Revolution

Marcuse memorialized the counterculture's brighter side in his short book *An Essay on Liberation* (1969). The book's opening sentence referred to "utopian speculation," and in this manner he linked the new developments to the legacy of critical theory. He saw in the New Left movement of the day what he called the "new sensibility" of the counterculture: new popular music, new forms of language, a visceral need for peace and fellowship, all of which incorporated elements from oppressed subcultures. These elements included the explicit rejection of the dominant consumer culture, in addition to the waste and war associated with it, and the celebration of eroticism and "outlawed" forms of enjoyment. This spontaneous cultural movement offered the theory of social revolution a solution for what was otherwise a hopeless paradox:

> By virtue of its basic position in the production process, by virtue of its numerical weight and the weight of exploitation, the working class is still the historical agent of revolution; by virtue of its sharing the stabilizing needs of the system, it has become a conservative, even counterrevolutionary force.

This paradox was, in fact, rooted in a dilemma as old as the Marxian theory of class revolution itself: in order to carry out its historical mission, as the class that will abolish all classes, the proletariat must, in effect, anticipate in its attitudes and acts a kind of future that has never existed in all of previous history.[22] In Marcuse's words, "the awareness of the transcendent possibilities of freedom must become a driving power in the consciousness and the imagination which prepare the soil for this revolution [in the capitalist world]."[23]

How was it possible to imagine that the working class—exploited, brutalized, largely uneducated, and kept in severe deprivation by the capitalist system—could take on such a mission? As far back as the second decade of the twentieth century, Marxist theorists had grappled with this paradox. It was the subject of one of the most famous essays in Western Marxism, published by György Lukács in 1923: "Reification and the Consciousness of the Proletariat."[24]

This essay foreshadows the later dystopian critiques discussed above. The theory of reification, which is built upon Marx's notion of "the fetishism of commodities," argues that the capitalist labor process has a profound impact on the way in which workers experience the world around them. These changes transform the individual worker into a cog in the machine, an insignificant bit-player, spending the working day either on the mechanized assembly line of the factory, or in the immense office system of a business or government bureaucracy.

From the standpoint of the individual, these twin, highly rational-ized systems of production appear to have a life of their own, that is, they appear to exist as powerful agents capable of determining the fate of the living, breathing person. The word "reification" incorporates the Latin root *res* meaning "thing." The vast factory system and the corpo-rate and bureaucratic structures are inanimate things that appear to be alive and that transform human beings into things obedient to their laws. The mechanical workings of the market and the bureaucracy and the actual mechanism of the machinery of capitalism now determine the individual's fate.

At the same time as Lukács was working out the theory of reification within the context of Marxist theory, the great writer Franz Kafka, in his novels of the 1920s, *The Trial* and *The Castle*, gave the most telling and poignant representation ever conceived of a world of fully reified social relations. Novelists do not provide "solutions" to problems, of course. The solution adopted in theory by Lukács reflected the practi-cal achievement of Lenin and his Bolsheviks in the Soviet Union: the notion that the Communist Party would be the agent capable of guid-ing the working class to its predestined future. But by the 1960s there was almost no one in the West—including Marcuse—who did not re-gard this proposition as either unlikely or, worse yet, intellectually and morally bankrupt. In rejecting this solution, Adorno and Hork-heimer were stuck with a vision of unrelieved reification that left no room for hope.

What is most interesting about Lukács's argument is not his outdated strategy but his explanation of the origins of the revolutionary consciousness that made that strategy plausible at the time. He argued that the reification of the worker was necessarily incomplete because the human life process could never be fully incorporated into the abstract forms of the business and bureaucratic systems. There would always be a residue appearing in misery, hunger, and the sense of injustice capable of inspiring revolutionary aspirations under the right conditions.

This tension between capitalist forms and the content of working-class experience was Lukács's Marxist reinterpretation of the conflict of soul and form he had explored in his earlier literary criticism. But it was no longer a matter of the isolated hero against society. Reinterpreted in terms of Marxist social theory, that conflict was no longer an accident of individual biography but was essential to the nature of the system and the very existence of the worker.

As a seller of labor power the worker was the embodiment of the capitalist category of the commodity, the "self-consciousness of the commodity." But this self-consciousness was fraught with contradiction. "The quantitative differences in exploitation which appear to the capitalist in the form of quantitative determinants of the objects of his calculation, must appear to the worker as the decisive, qualitative categories of his whole physical, mental and moral existence."[25] Simply put, for the capitalist lowering the cost of labor is a matter of business, while for the worker, to be "worth" just so and so much an hour, is to be hungry.

Until then Marxists had emphasized the objective contradiction between the economic interests of workers and capitalists in the hope that workers would eventually understand their suffering in the terms of Marx's economic science. What was original about Lukács's solution to the dilemma of the revolution was the identification of the very contradictions of capitalism in the structure of the lived experience of the working class. This was the "lifeworldly" source of the abstractions of Marxist science and of the practical efficacy of the strategies based on that science.

This approach no doubt influenced Marcuse's early revision of Heidegger's phenomenology. It is thus not surprising that when Marcuse confronted the old paradox of revolution in the 1960s, he arrived, perhaps unconsciously, at a solution that resembled that of Lukács in important respects.

Marcuse's concept of a new sensibility was in fact an original version of the idea of an experiential revolt against the confining forms of a mechanical civilization. What makes this possible is the immense contrast between the possibilities for a better life sustained by modern technology and the perpetuation of competition, poverty, and war by a class system that cannot realize that potential without itself going under. The tension between the two dimensions has been recorded in art for millennia, but now it is no longer a question of abstract possibilities and idle hopes for a distant future. The second dimension is now *technically* realizable for the first time and the individuals are increasingly aware of this fact.

The utopian impulse confronts empirical reality in the consciousness of specific marginal groups such as students and racial minorities. They experience a literally somatic revulsion toward the system that confines them. These groups bring to the surface the possibilities of change not simply in the form of radical political opinions but in the very structure of their experience and their needs. As Lukács wrote in 1923, "the decisive, qualitative categories of [their] whole physical, mental and moral existence" stand in open conflict with the technological forms of their existence. It is in these marginal groups that one initially finds "the feeling, the awareness, that the joy of freedom and the need to be free must precede liberation."[26]

Just as Marcuse completed this new book, in May of 1968, a student revolt triggered a much larger labor conflict in France where ten million workers went on strike, many of them demanding socialism rather than mere wage increases. For Marcuse these French May Events were a sign that marginal groups could play a catalytic role in a wider social movement. All the elements of a new theory of revolution were now united.

The May revolt was soon defeated and subsequently the New Left faded away. But a marker had been planted for the future so that those who may one day traverse this path again, and who resolve to push farther along it, will know what they must be capable of, namely, "the development of a radically different consciousness (a veritable *counter-consciousness*) capable of breaking through the fetishism of the consumer society. . . ."[27] This was Marcuse's final word on the subject. The endless and ever-expanding sphere of consumer needs, lashed by a perpetual cycle of fashion that drives its devotees back to the shops with no less desperation than the heroin addict's hunger for the needle, is the sphere within which the contest must begin to be fought—if it is to be fought at all.

Marcuse's last essays and speeches retreat from his most optimistic conclusions. In the 1970s he witnessed the "preventive counterrevolution" that suppressed the New Left and breathed new confidence into capitalism. Yet something fundamental had been achieved by the movement: the renewed imagination of revolution.

This achievement is reflected in his final reflections on feminism and the problem of nature. Marcuse saw in the feminist and environmental movements the emergence of a less aggressive stance foreshadowing a more humane world. In these reflections Marcuse returned to ideas he had first expressed in his interpretation of Marx's *Economic and Philosophical Manuscripts*. There he had found a concept of lived nature that resonated with his phenomenological training. Not the nature of natural science, but that of direct experience expressed itself in beauty and called to us for respect and care. This call, like the call for compassion of suffering humanity, was the ground and the reason for hope.

A Summing Up

Simply stated, what chiefly distinguishes Marcuse's career as a thinker and activist from those of his closest colleagues in the Frankfurt School is that unlike them he never gave up. For more than thirty years after their trails turned in different directions, Marcuse never ceased reinterpreting and reconfiguring the critical theory of society with a single aim in mind: to track the obscure path to the socialist utopia through the latest transformations in capitalist societies in an epoch marked by an astonishing rise in material wealth.

Some will ask: What was the point of this quixotic venture? The alternative visions—whether in the form of democratic socialism, or anarchistic dope-fueled hippie communes, or Soviet communism—are gone, they will say, never to return. Even if one granted, for the sake of argument, that some aspects of those visions were worthy of respect and admiration, this would remain a purely academic exercise: their time has passed. Actually, many will contend, the dream of socialist utopia had turned into a nightmare as long ago as the 1920s, and there were very good reasons why, after 1945, people turned to technocratic liberalism rather than socialism as the vehicle of progress.

This may well be history's final judgment on the matter. If so, then in looking ahead, one might conclude that the task awaiting humanity is to expand the paradise of consumer satisfaction, which now makes life so satisfying for the privileged strata around the world. Perhaps. But consider these questions:

1. Is it *really* possible to imagine extending the consumer paradise to everyone on the globe? All six or eight billion? Who will then cut and sew and stitch and label the brand-name goods for these happy consumers? Who will clean and wash and cook and garden, who will man the guard posts at the entrances to their gated communities, who will fight their wars for them? Can one *really* believe that serried ranks of clever automated machines, toiling endlessly without protest in sterile unlit underground factories, caring for themselves without human intervention, will do it all?

2. If not this scenario, then what? Will the great inequalities in the world's distribution of wealth, both within and among nations, continue indefinitely? Will the overwhelming majority of the poor and downtrodden just have to settle for the crumbs from the table, as they do now? Perhaps these inequalities will even widen, rather than narrow, so that should any future redistribution occur, it will proceed *from* the poor *to* the wealthy, as has been happening within the United States, the richest of the rich, for the past quarter-century. But is it likely that, as the numbers of the less privileged grow, they will remain docile, taking the advice of their preachers to wait until the hereafter for a better deal? And is it acceptable to enlarge the proportion of the citizenry who are incarcerated in high-security prisons for most of their natural lives in order to protect the rights of the privileged?

3. If the first scenario is unlikely or improbable, and the second is immoral and deeply disgraceful, then what does the future hold?

And so, on the other hand, there may be a need to keep alive the spark of utopia after all. Its function for us today is primarily negative: to undermine the complacency that makes the intolerable tolerable. Marcuse had the art of inspiring a longer view in the light of past experience and future possibilities. His critique of globalization, war, and the threats to democracy is still relevant. We need his "negative thinking" as much now as when he wrote the texts included in this collection. But that is not all.

Perhaps there will come a time when a demand will arise again for something resembling the old vision that inspired the democratic socialists: a society with fewer private goods than are enjoyed by the wealthy today but also richer in public goods and human sympathy — in parks, schools, and medical care; a society more just, more egalitarian, more helpful to the world's poorest peoples, less warlike, less racist, and less frantic in the pursuit of money; a society more considerate of the needs of other animals, more respectful of wilderness and Earth's remaining solitudes.

If that time comes, those who take part in the movement will want to read the writings of Herbert Marcuse.

The selections from Marcuse's writings collected here are divided into three parts. A first part introduces Marcuse's political thought, a second part develops his relation to the most influential theoretical trends he encountered during his lifetime, and the last part introduces some of his most important philosophical ideas.

Part I: This section begins with an essay on the fate of individuality in advanced society. The essay is notable for its analysis of neo-imperialism, which has been amply confirmed by recent events. The second essay presents Marcuse's critique of science and technology. Part I concludes with his critique of tolerance. This last essay stirred up tremendous controversy and influenced the thinking of many in the New Left.

Part II: In the course of his career, Marcuse was influenced by and responded to three of the main trends in European thought: Marxism, existentialism, and psychoanalysis. The essays in this part exemplify his critical appropriation of Marxism and psychoanalysis and his negative critique of Heidegger and Sartre's existentialism.

Part III: Marcuse's thought was elaborated in dialogue within the tradition of Western philosophy. In the first selection he addresses

Aristotle, Hegel, and Nietzsche, all three major influences on his unique version of Critical Theory. The second and third essays discuss the social function of art and nature as they are experienced in modern times.

Notes

For the most thorough intellectual biography of Marcuse, see Douglas Kellner, *Herbert Marcuse and the Crisis of Marxism* (Berkeley: University of California, 1984).

1. Herbert Marcuse, *"Beiträge zu Einer Phänomenologie des historischen Materialismus," Herbert Marcuse Schriften* (Franfurt, Suhrkamp Verlag, 1978) , vol. I, p. 358. This and other early texts are available in Herbert Marcuse, *Heideggerian Marxism*, eds. R. Wolin and J. Abromeit (Lincoln: University of Nebraska Press, 2005). For an interpretation of Marcuse's relation to Heidegger, see Andrew Feenberg, *Heidegger and Marcuse: The Catastrophe and Redemption of History* (New York: Routledge, 2005).

2. Herbert Marcuse, *Hegel's Ontology and the Theory of Historicity*, tr. Seyla Benhabib (Cambridge, Mass.: MIT Press, 1987).

3. See Hans Sluga, *Heidegger's Crisis: Philosophy and Politics in Nazi Germany* (Cambridge: Cambridge University Press, 1993).

4. See Rolf Wiggershaus, *The Frankfurt School: Its History, Theories, and Political Significance*, tr. Michael Robertson (Cambridge, MA: MIT Press, 1994).

5. "Traditional and Critical Theory," tr. Matthew J. O'Connell, in Max Horkheimer, *Critical Theory* (New York: Herder & Herder, 1972), pp. 198–99, 208, 210.

6. Ibid., pp. 226–27.

7. "Philosophy and Critical Theory," tr. Jeremy J. Shapiro, in Herbert Marcuse, *Negations: Essays in Critical Theory* (Boston: Beacon Press, 1968), pp. 135, 142–43, 145.

8. See, e.g., J.C. Davis, *Utopia and the Ideal Society: A Study of English Utopian Writing, 1516–1700* (Cambridge University Press, 1981).

9. Jacoby, *Picture Imperfect: Utopian Thought for an Anti-Utopian Age* (New York: Columbia University Press, 2005), pp. 31–36.

10. *Critical Theory*, p. 220.

11. This and the following quotation are from *Negations*, pp. 154–55.

12. See Wiggershaus, pp. 386–92.

13. Now translated by John Abromeit and published under the title "33

Theses," in the *Collected Papers of Herbert Marcuse*, ed. Douglas Kellner, vol. I, *Technology, War and Fascism* (London and New York: Routledge, 1998), pp. 215–27.

14. Ibid., Theses 1, 19, 25, 32.

15. Wiggershaus, pp. 390–92, 462–66.

16. *Eros and Civilization* (Boston: Beacon Press, 1955), p. 143; italics in original.

17. This example is suggested by the present authors, not by Marcuse himself.

18. The foregoing discussion is based on pages 150–57 of *Eros and Civilization*.

19. Theodor Adorno and Max Horkheimer, *Dialectic of Enlightenment*, tr. J. Cummings (New York: Herder and Herder, 1972), p. 3.

20. Herbert Marcuse, *One-Dimensional Man* (Boston: Beacon Press, 1964), pp. xv–xvi.

21. Ibid., p. 239. Italics in original.

22. See W. Leiss, "Critical Theory and Its Future," *Political Theory*, vol. 2 (1974), pp. 330–49.

23. This and the preceding quotation are from Herbert Marcuse, *An Essay on Liberation* (Boston: Beacon Press, 1969), pp. 16, 23.

24. The essay is included in Lukács, *History and Class Consciousness*, tr. Rodney Livingstone (Cambridge, MA: MIT Press, 1971). For commentary see W. Leiss, *Under Technology's Thumb* (Montreal: McGill-Queen's University Press, 1990), ch. 5; and A. Feenberg, *Lukács, Marx and the Sources of Critical Theory* (Totowa, NJ: Rowman and Littlefield, 1981).

25. *History and Class Consciousness*, p. 166.

26. *An Essay on Liberation*, p. 89.

27. Marcuse, *Counter-Revolution and Revolt* (Boston: Beacon Press, 1972), p. 32.

PART I
Political Critique

THE INDIVIDUAL IN THE
GREAT SOCIETY (1965)

Nineteen sixty-five, when this essay was written, was the year President Lyndon Johnson began sending hundreds of thousands of troops to Vietnam. At the same time, LBJ was engaged in implementing his "Great Society" programs, which were supposed to end poverty and discrimination in the U.S., Marcuse evaluated the chances of the Great Society and identified a fatal contradiction at its heart. It would be impossible he argued, as it turned out correctly, to supply both guns and butter in sufficient quantity to "pacify" both Vietnamese and American society.

This article contains an analysis of the psychological function of the new imperialism represented by the war in Vietnam. The alienation of the individuals in the labor process of advanced industrial society has become visibly unnecessary given its technical progress and extraordinary wealth. The art of rule under these conditions involves focusing public dissatisfaction on an external Enemy. The choice of Enemy may be determined by various strategic considerations, but its psychic function is entirely internal to the imperialist homeland where it serves to maintain an oppressive social hierarchy.

On a personal note: In 1965, the editors of this book asked Marcuse for an article for their antiwar student journal. This is the article he gave us. It was later published in *Toward a Critical Theory of Society,* edited by Douglas Kellner.

Part I: Rhetoric and Reality

Prior to exploring the presumed function of the "individual" in the "great society," a brief definition (or rather redefinition) of these terms is required. For I propose to proceed by placing the official and semi-official ideas and speeches about the great society in the context of their prospective realization, and in the context of the prevailing conditions (political, economic, intellectual) which determine the possibility of their realization. Unless this factor is brought to bear on the idea, it remains mere speech, publicity or propaganda—at best a statement of intentions. It is the responsibility of the scholar to take them seriously, that is to say, to go beyond the words or rather to stay this side of the words, in the given universe of powers, capabilities, tendencies which defines their content.

I start with the notion of the Great Society as presented by President Johnson. I think its essentials can be summed up as follows: it is a society

- of "unbridled growth," resting on "abundance and liberty for all," demanding an "end to poverty and racial injustice";
- where progress is the "servant of our needs";
- in which leisure is a "welcome chance to build and reflect," serving "not only the needs of the body and demands of commerce, but the desire for beauty and the hunger for community."

This picture is preceded by the statement that our society can be a place where "we will raise our families, free from the dark shadow of war and suspicion among nations." And it is followed by an enumeration of the areas where the construction of the Great Society can begin, namely:

1. The rebuilding of our cities, and of the transportation between them, in accord with the needs of the constantly growing population,
2. The reconstruction of the polluted and destroyed countryside, in order to regain "contact with nature" and to protect "America the beautiful,"
3. The improvement and enlargement of education and educational facilities.

And when all this is done, we will not have reached the end of the struggle, for "most of all, the Great Society is not a safe harbor, a resting place, a final objective, a finished work. It is a challenge constantly renewed, beckoning us toward a destiny where the meaning of our lives matches the marvelous products of our labor."

Let me pause here and register my first dissent. I begin intentionally with the most speculative, most "utopian" aspect because it is here where the basic direction of the program and its innermost limitations are best visible. First a slight matter of style: the meaning of our lives should "match" the "products of our labor" — shouldn't it be the other way around? In a free society, the meaning of life is determined by the free individuals, who determine the products of their labor accordingly. By itself, the phrasing may not preclude this interpretation, but in the context of the whole section it assumes special significance.

Why should the Great and Free Society *not* be a resting place, a safe harbor? Why should it be a challenge constantly renewed? The dynamic of endlessly propelled productivity is not that of a peaceful, humane society in which the individuals have come into their own and develop their own humanity; the challenge they meet may be precisely that of protecting and preserving a "safe harbor," a "resting place" where life is no longer spent in the struggle for existence. And such a society may well reject the notion and practice of "unbridled growth"; it may well restrict its technical capabilities where they threaten to increase the dependence of man on his instruments and products.

Even today, long before the start on the road to a free society, the war on poverty might be waged far more effectively by a redirection rather than increase of production, by the elimination of productivity from the areas of socially necessary waste, planned obsolescence, armament, publicity, manipulation. A society which couples abundance and liberty in the dynamic of unbridled growth and perpetual challenge is the ideal of a system based on the perpetuation of scarcity. It requires more and more artificially created scarcity, namely, the need for ever more and ever new goods of abundance. In such a system, the individuals must spend their life in the competitive struggle for existence in order to satisfy the need for the increasing products of labor, and the products of labor must be increased because they must be sold at a profit, and the rate of profit depends on the growing productivity of labor.

In a less ideological language, this was called the law of the enlarged accumulation of capital. Under this aspect, the Great Society appears as the streamlined and improved continuation of the existing not so great society—after the latter has succeeded in cleansing itself from its sore spots and blemishes. Its ability to do so is assumed. But the scholar cannot grant the assumption without examination: we leave the speculation on the Great Society and return to the program for its construction, or rather for its preparation within the existing society.

Foremost is the war on poverty. The critical literature on it already is so large that I can be brief in my references. This war is supposed to be waged by the "affluent society" against poverty in the "affluent society"; thus it may turn out to be a war of this society against itself. The real conquest of poverty would mean either full employment as the normal, long range condition of the system, or, unemployment and a dole sufficiently large to live the good life—also as the normal, long range condition of the system. Both achievements are within the technical capabilities of advanced industrial civilization.

The concept "advanced industrial society" has to be broken down into its actual main forms: capitalist and socialist. Here, we are concerned with the former only. In it, the real conquest of poverty is counteracted, and "contained" by the prevailing social institutions. Full employment, as constant condition, implies a constantly high (and, with rising productivity, a constantly rising) level of real wages, not cancelled by rising prices. This would be equivalent to a decline in the rate of profit below the limit tolerable to private enterprise. It is perhaps conceivable that something like full employment can be attained by an expanding war or defense economy, plus an expanding production of waste, status symbols, planned obsolescence, and parasitarian services.

But even disregarding the clear and present danger of an international explosion, such a system would produce and reproduce human beings who could by no stretch of the imagination be expected to build a free humane society. For the construction of a Great Society depends on a "human factor" which hardly appears in the program, namely, the existence of individuals who, in their attitudes, goals, and needs, are qualitatively different from those who are educated, trained, and rewarded today: the aggression mobilized and repressed in the maintenance of a society geared to permanent defense militates against progress toward higher forms of freedom and rationality. To be sure, non-destructive full employment remains a real possibility: it requires nothing more, and nothing less than the actual reconstruction outlined in the President's program, that is, the rebuilding of the cities, of the countryside, and of education. But this very program requires elimination of the particular interests which stand in the way of its fulfillment. Today, they include capital and labor, city and countryside politics, Republicans and Democrats, and they are the powerful interests on which this Administration largely relies.

The truism must be repeated: not only the magnitude but the economic basis of the program is incompatible with these interests. The transformation of the cities into a human universe involves far more than slum clearings. It involves the literal dissolution of the cities and rebuilding according to rigidly enforced architectural plans. If undertaken for the population as a whole rather than for those who can pay, the reconstruction would be plainly unprofitable, and its public financing would mean the abrogation of some of the most powerful lobbies in the country. It would, for example, imply the establishment of a wide and efficient network of public transportation, replacing the private automobile as the main vehicle of business and leisure—the end of the motor industry as now organized. The "beautification" of the countryside would imply the rigidly enforced elimination of all billboards, neon signs, the reduction of the innumerable service stations, roadside stands, noise makers, etc., which have rendered impossible the desired "contact with nature." Generally, and perhaps most important, reconstruction would require the elimination of all planned obsolescence, which has become an essential prop for the system inasmuch as it insures the necessary turnover and the competitive rat race.

In all these aspects, the realization of the program seems irreconcilable with the spirit of capitalist enterprise, and this contradiction becomes perhaps most strikingly apparent in the program's insistence on beauty. Here, the words assume a false ring, the language becomes that of commercial poetry, and it comes almost as a relief when Mrs. Johnson, dropping the ideological language, goes out to proclaim beauty as an economic asset: according to the *Los Angeles Times* (September 8, 1965): "Preserving the attractiveness of a city is a primary economic asset, a way to get payrolls. The city that is beautiful brings a high return on the dollar."

I now come to the "human factor" and I shall take up education, the third area of reconstruction. Who are the human beings, the individuals who are supposed to build the Great Society?

They live in a society where they are (for good or bad) subjected to an apparatus which, comprising production, distribution, and consumption, material and intellectual, work and leisure, politics and fun, determines their daily existence, their needs and aspirations. And this life, private, social, rational, is enclosed in a very specific historical universe. The individuals who make up the bulk of the population in the "affluent societies" live in a universe of permanent defense and aggression. It manifests itself in the war against the Vietcong and in the struggle against the Negroes, in the huge network of industries and services which work for the military establishments and its accessories. It also manifests itself in the violence released and made productive by science and technology, in the entertainment of terror and fun inflicted on captive audiences.

Against the age-old argument that violence and aggression have always been a normal factor in all societies, I must insist on qualitative differences. It is not only the magnitude of the destructive potential and the scope of its realization which distinguishes a chariot race from an automobile race, a cannon from a missile, hydraulic from nuclear energy. Similarly, it is not only the speed and range which distinguishes the means of mass communication from their predecessors. The new quality is introduced by the progressive transfer of power from the human individual to the technical or bureaucratic apparatus, from living to dead labor, from personal to remote control, from a machine or group of machines to a whole mechanized system. I should like to reiterate that I do not yet evaluate this development: it may be progressive or regressive, humanizing or dehumanizing. But what actually occurs in this transfer of power is also a transfer of guilt-feeling responsibility. It releases the individual from being an autonomous person in work and in leisure, in his needs and satisfactions, in his thought and emotions.

At the same time, however, the release is not liberation from alienated labor: the individuals must go on spending physical and mental energy in the struggle for existence, status, advantage. They must suffer, service, and enjoy the apparatus which imposes on them this necessity. The new slavery in the work world is not compensated by a new autonomy over the work world. Alienation is intensified as it becomes transparently irrational; it becomes unproductive as it sustains repressive productivity. And where the established society delivers the goods that raise the standard of living, alienation reaches the point at which even the consciousness of alienation is largely repressed: individuals identify themselves with their being-for-others, their image.

Under such circumstances, society calls for an Enemy against whom the aggressive energy can be released which cannot be channeled into the normal, daily struggle for existence. The individuals who are called upon to develop the Great Society live in a society which wages war or is prepared to wage war all over the world. Any discussion which does not place the program of the Great Society into the international framework must remain ideological, propaganda. The Enemy is not one factor among others, not a contingency which the evaluation of the chances of the Great Society can ignore or to which it can refer in passing. The Enemy is a determining factor at home and abroad, in business and education, in science and relaxation.

We are here concerned only with the Enemy in relation to the program of the Great Society, more specifically, with the way in which the Enemy (or rather the presentation of the Enemy and the struggle against him) affects the individuals, the people who are supposed to change the "affluent society" into a Great Society. Thus the question is not to what degree the armament industry and its "multipliers" have become an indispensable part of the "affluent society," nor whether the present dominance and policy of the military establishment are in the "national interest." Rather the question I want to raise is: does the existence of the Enemy prejudge—and prejudge negatively—the capability and capacity to build the Great Society? Before I enter into the brief discussion of the question, I must define "the Enemy." And I shall do so by submitting a precarious hypothesis.

Is the Enemy still Communism *per se?* I think not. First, Communism today exists in many forms, some of which are in conflict with the others. And this country does not combat all of them, and not only for tactical reasons. Secondly, capitalist business and trade with communist countries is constantly increasing, and precisely with those countries where Communism seems to be most stable. Moreover, Communism is most firmly and solidly constituted in the Soviet Union, but for quite some time, the USA and USSR have not really treated each other as Enemies. In fact, one even hears talk of cooperation and collusion, while the Enemy against whom the system is mobilized is presented as precluding cooperation and collusion. Lastly, it is difficult to consider Communism threatening in this country—even on the campuses and among the Negroes. Looking at the facts, geographical and otherwise, I would say that war is actually waged against semi-colonial and formerly colonial peoples, backward peoples, have-nots, whether Communist or not.

This is not the old colonialism and imperialism (although in some aspects, the contrast has been overdrawn: there is little essential difference between a direct government by the metropolitan power, and a native government which functions only by grace of a metropolitan power). The objective rationale for the global struggle is not the need for immediate capital export, resources, surplus exploitation. It is rather the danger of a subversion of the established hierarchy of Master and Servant, Top and Bottom, a hierarchy which has created and sustained the have-nations, Capitalist *and* Communist. This is a very primitive threat of subversion—a slave revolt rather than a revolution, and precisely for this reason more dangerous to societies which are capable of containing or defeating revolutions. For the slaves are everywhere and countless, and they indeed have nothing to lose but their chains.

To be sure, the established societies have faced the subversion of their hierarchy before: from within, by one of their own classes. This time, the threat comes from without—and precisely for this reason it threatens the system as a whole. The threat appears as a total one and those who represent it have not even a potential vested interest in the established societies. They may have no blueprint for positive reconstruction, or they may have one which would not work, but they simply do not want to be slaves any longer, and they are driven by the vital need to change intolerable conditions—and to do it differently from the old powers. This primitive rebellion, this revolt indeed implies a social program, namely, the awareness that their society cannot be constructed along the line of the have-nations which perpetuate servitude and domination. Their struggle for liberation is *objectively* anti-capitalist even if they reject socialism and want the benefits of capitalism and their struggle is *objectively* anti-Communist even if they are Communists, for it aims beyond the established Communist systems. I used the term "objectively" in order to emphasize that I do not imply that the factors or tendencies just outlined are those intentionally pursued by the policy makers. I rather suggest that they are operative "behind the back" of the policy makers, even asserted against their will—as historical tendencies which can be extrapolated from the prevailing social and political conditions.

In this country there is a far more obvious surface rationale for permanent mobilization and defense, that which is expressed in the Domino Theory and the notion of the Communist drive for world revolution. The notion as presented by the makers of policy and information does not correspond to the facts. However, there is a kernel of truth in the Domino Theory. Any spectacular victory of the rebellious have-nots in any one place would activate their consciousness and their rebellion in other places—at home as well. Moreover, for capitalism, such a victory would mean a further dangerous narrowing of the world market—a rather remote danger, which would materialize only if and when the backward countries have reached real independence, but a danger serious enough, for example, with respect to Latin America. For the Soviet Union, the economic danger does not prevail, but the threat to the established regime seems real enough. One can safely say that the attitude of the Soviet leaders toward revolution and rebellion is at best ambivalent if not hostile—as is clear from the conflict with China.

It is the most advanced industrial society which feels most directly threatened by the rebellion, because it is here that the social necessity of repression and alienation, of servitude and heteronomy is most transparently unnecessary, and unproductive in terms of human progress. Therefore the cruelty and violence mobilized in the struggle against the threat, therefore the monotonous regularity with which the people are made familiar with, and accustomed to inhuman attitudes and behavior—to wholesale killing as patriotic act. What the free press achieves in this respect will perhaps once be remembered as one of the most shameful acts of civilization. Hardly a day passes when the headlines do not celebrate a victory by announcing "136 Vietcong Killed," "Marines Kill at least 156 Vietcong," "More than 240 Reds Slain." I have lived through two World Wars, but I cannot recall any such brazen advertisement of slaughter. Nor can I remember—even in the Nazi press—a headline such as that which announces: "U.S. Pleased Over Lack of Protests on Tear Gas" (*L.A. Times*, September 9, 1965). This sort of reporting, consumed daily by millions, appeals to killers and the need for killers. And a New York judge has epitomized the situation when, in paroling two youths "who were arraigned on a charge of murdering an East Side derelict and then rearrested on a charge of killing one of their companions," he remarked, according to the *N.Y. Times* (Sept. 8, 1965): "They should go to Vietnam, where we need soldiers to kill Vietcong."

I have suggested that the international situation of the affluent society is in a very specific sense an expression of its internal contradiction: on the one hand, its social and political need to preserve the established power structure within the nation and abroad, and on the other, the historical obsolescence of this need as dramatized in the rebellion of the backward people. In this conflict, society mobilizes the aggressive energy of individuals to such an extent that they seem hardly capable of becoming the builders of a *peaceful* and free society. It seems that such an undertaking, which would aim at a qualitatively different society, would mean a break, a rupture with the established one, and thus would require the emergence of "new" individuals, with qualitatively different needs and aspirations.

REMARKS ON A REDEFINITION
OF CULTURE (1965)

In 1964 Marcuse published a major book entitled *One-Dimensional Man*. This essay, which came out a year later, summarizes many of the arguments of that book in more accessible language. Marcuse presents the paradox of a society that has become capable of realizing its highest cultural values in the lives of its members but instead employs its powers to silence criticism and maintain the harsh struggle for existence that its own development has made obsolete.

Marcuse distinguishes between "culture," the values toward which society aspires, and "civilization," the material base of life in the society. The difference between the two is reflected in art and literature which present values in purified form, whereas in actual life these values are necessarily realized only partially and imperfectly. This difference is a source of progress where culture contradicts civilization in a permanent and productive tension. However, in advanced industrial society, culture is measured by the standards of empirical research and practical success. By these standards it appears idealistic in the bad sense, romantic or metaphysical. The increased success of the civilization in realizing some cultural values becomes the excuse for dismissing all those aspects of culture that cannot yet be realized.

The role of science in this constellation is ambiguous. On the one hand science has always been dedicated to serving human needs in the struggle with nature. Its ability to achieve success in this struggle has been greatly enhanced in modern times by the abandonment of traditional metaphysical assumptions for empirical methods. However, the very conditions of scientific advance have exposed science to control by the established powers. Modern science is neutral; it tells us how things work not what purpose they should serve. But just for this reason it is unable to resist control by the state and corporations, which use it for their own purposes. Modern science thus becomes the instrument of their hegemony despite its historic commitment to human progress. The delegitimation of nonscientific aspects of culture (by reference to scientific method) strengthens the established powers' domination still further by disarming the traditional resources of social criticism. Reversing this condition will require radical changes in culture and education.

● ● ●

I take as starting point the definition of culture given by Webster, namely, culture as the complex of distinctive beliefs, attainments, traditions, etc., constituting the "background" of a society. In the traditional usage of the term, "attainments" such as destruction and crime, and "traditions" such as cruelty and fanaticism have usually been excluded; I shall follow this usage, although it may prove necessary to re-introduce these qualities into the definition. My discussion will be focused on the relationship between the "background" (culture) and the "ground": culture thus appears as the complex of moral, intellectual, aesthetic goals (values) which a society considers the purpose of the organization, division, and direction of its labor—"the good" that is supposed to be achieved by the way of life it has established. For example, increase in personal and public freedom, reduction of inequalities which prevent the development of the "individual" or "personality," and an efficient and rational administration may be taken as the "cultural values" representative of advanced industrial society (their denial is officially condemned in the East as well as in the West).

We speak of an existing culture (past or present) only if the representative goals and values were (or are) somehow translated into the social reality. There may be considerable variations in the extent and adequacy of the translation, but the prevailing institutions and the relationships among the members of the respective society must show a demonstrable affinity to the proclaimed values: they must provide a basis for their *possible* realization. In other words, culture is more than a mere ideology. Looking at the professed goals of Western civilization and at the claims of their realization, we should define culture as a

process of *humanization,* characterized by the collective effort to protect human life, to pacify the struggle for existence by keeping it within
manageable bounds, to stabilize a productive organization of society, to
develop the intellectual faculties of man, to reduce and sublimate ag-
gressions, violence, and misery.

Two qualifications must be made at the outset: (1) the "validity" of
culture has always been confined to a *specific* universe, constituted by
tribal, national, religious, or other identity. (The exceptions were condemned to remain ideological.) There has always been a "foreign" universe to which the cultural goals were not applied: the Enemy, the
Other, the Alien, the Outcast—terms referring not primarily to individuals but to groups, religions, "ways of life," social systems. In meeting
the Enemy (who has his epiphany also within one's own universe) culture is suspended or even prohibited, and inhumanity can often run its
course. (2) It is only the exclusion of cruelty, fanaticism, and unsublimated violence which allows the definition of culture as the process of
humanization. However, these forces (and their institution) may well
be an integral part of culture, so that the attainment or approximation
of the cultural goals takes place *through* the practice of cruelty and violence. This may explain the paradox that much of the "higher culture"
of the West has been protest, refusal, and indictment of culture—not
only of its miserable translation into reality, but of its very principles
and content.

Under the preceding assumptions, the re-examination of a given
culture involves the relation of values to facts, not as a logical or epistemological problem, but as a problem of social structure: how are the
means of society related to its self-professed ends? The ends are supposedly those defined by the (socially accepted) "higher culture"; thus they
are values to be embodied, more or less adequately, in the social institutions and relations. The question can therefore be formulated more
concretely: *how are the literature, arts, philosophy, science, religion of a
society related to its actual behavior?* The vastness of this problem precludes any discussion here other than in terms of some hypotheses referring to present-day trends.

In traditional discussion, there is widespread agreement that the relation between cultural ends and actual means is not (and cannot be?)

one of coincidence, and that it is rarely, if ever, one of harmony. This opinion has found expression in the distinction between *culture* and *civilization*, according to which "culture" refers to some higher dimension of human autonomy and fulfillment, while "civilization" designates the realm of necessity, of socially necessary work and behavior, where man is not really himself and in his own element but is subject to heteronomy, to external conditions and needs. The realm of necessity can be (and has been) reduced and alleviated. Indeed, the concept of progress is applicable only to this realm (technical progress), to the advance in *civilization*; but such advance has not eliminated the tension between *culture* and civilization. It may even have aggravated the dichotomy to the degree to which the immense potentialities opened by technical progress appear in sharpening contrast with their limited and distorted realization. At the same time, however, this tension itself is being suppressed by the systematic, organized incorporation of culture into daily life and work—and suppressed so effectively that the question arises whether, in view of the tendencies prevalent in advanced industrial society, the distinction between culture and civilization can still be maintained. More exactly, has not the tension between means and ends, cultural values and social facts been resolved in the absorption of the ends by the means—has not a "premature," repressive, and even violent coordination of culture with civilization occurred by virtue of which the latter is freed from some effective brakes on its destructive tendencies? With this integration of culture into society, the society tends to become totalitarian even where it preserves democratic forms and institutions.

Some of the implications in the distinction between culture and civilization may be tabulated as follows:

Civilization	*Culture*
manual work	intellectual work
working day	holiday
labor	leisure
realm of necessity	realm of freedom
nature	spirit *(Geist)*
operational thought	non-operational thought

In the academic tradition, these dichotomies once found their parallel in the distinction between the natural sciences on the one hand, and all others on the other, the social sciences, humanities, etc. This distinction between the sciences has now become entirely obsolete: natural science, the social sciences, and even the humanities are being assimilated into each other in their methods and concepts, as exemplified by the spread of positivist empiricism, the struggle against whatever may be called "metaphysics," the direct application of "pure" theory, the susceptibility of all disciplines to organization in the national or corporate interest. This change within the educational establishment is in accord with the fundamental changes in contemporary society which affect the entire dichotomy tabulated above: technological civilization tends to eliminate the transcendent goals of culture (transcendent with respect to the socially *established* goals), thereby eliminating or reducing those factors and elements of culture which were antagonistic and alien to the given forms of civilization. There is no need here to repeat the familiar proposition that the facile assimilation of work and relaxation, of frustration and fun, of art and the household, of psychology and corporate management alters the traditional function of these elements of culture: they become affirmative, that is to say, they serve to fortify the hold of the Establishment over the mind — that Establishment which has made the goods of culture available to the people — and they help to strengthen the sweep of what *is* over what *can be* and *ought to be*, ought to be if there is truth in the cultural values. This proposition is not condemnation: wide access to the traditional culture, and especially to its authentic oeuvres, is better than the retention of cultural privileges for a limited circle on the basis of wealth and birth. But in order to preserve the cognitive content of these oeuvres, intellectual faculties and an intellectual awareness are required which are not exactly congenial to the modes of thought and behavior required by the prevailing civilization in advanced industrial countries.

In its prevailing form and direction, progress of this civilization calls for operational and behavioral modes of thought, for acceptance of the productive rationality of the given social systems, for their defense and improvement, but not for their negation. And the content (and mostly hidden content) of the higher culture was to a great extent precisely this negation: indictment of the institutionalized destruction of human potentialities, commitment to a hope which the established civilization denounced as "utopian." To be sure, the higher culture always had an affirmative character inasmuch as it was divorced from the toil and misery of those who by their labor reproduced the society whose culture it was—and to that degree it became the ideology of the society. But as ideology, it was also dissociated from the society, and in this dissociation it was free to communicate the contradiction, the indictment, and the refusal. Now the communication is technically multiplied, vastly facilitated, much rewarded, but the content is changed because the mental and even physical space in which effective dissociation can develop is closed.

As to the elimination of the former antagonistic content of culture, I shall try to show that what is involved here is not the fate of some romantic ideal succumbing to technological progress, nor the progressive democratization of culture, nor the equalization of social classes, but rather the closing of a vital space for the development of autonomy and opposition, the destruction of a refuge, of a barrier to totalitarianism. Here I can indicate only some aspects of the problem, starting again with the situation in the academic establishment.

The division into natural sciences, social, or behavioral, sciences, and humanities appears as a highly extraneous division, since the distribution of subject matter, at least between the last two, is more than questionable—the academic quandary reflects the general condition! There is indeed a noticeable divorce of the social sciences from the humanities, at least from what the humanities were supposed to be: experience of the dimension of *humanitas* not yet translated into reality; modes of thought, imagination, expression essentially non-operational and transcendent, transcending the established universe of behavior not toward a realm of ghosts and illusions, but toward historical possibilities. In our present situation, does the analysis of society, of social and even of individual behavior, demand *abstraction from humanitas?* Does our cultural situation, our universe of social behavior repudiate and invalidate the humanities and make them truly *nonbehavioral* and thus "nonscientific" sciences, concerned mainly with personal, emotional, metaphysical, poetic values unless they translate themselves into behavioral terms? But in so doing, the humanities would cease to be what they are. They would surrender their essentially non-operational truths to the rules governing the established society, for the standards of the behavioral sciences are those of the society to whose behavior they are committed.

Now, the expelled non-operational dimension was the core of the traditional culture, the "background" of modern society until the end of its liberalist period; roughly, the era between the two world wars marks the terminal stage of this period. By virtue of its remoteness from the world of socially necessary labor, of socially useful needs and behavior, because of its separation from the daily struggle for existence, culture could create and preserve the mental space in which critical transgression, opposition, and denial could develop—a space of privacy and autonomy in which the mind could find an Archimedean point outside the Establishment from which to view it in a different light, comprehend it in different concepts, discover tabooed images and possibilities. This Archimedean point seems to have disappeared.

To avoid any romantic misinterpretation, let me repeat: culture has always been the privilege of a small minority, a matter of wealth, time, good luck. For the underprivileged populace, the "higher values" of culture have always been mere words or empty exhortations, illusions, deceptions; at best they were hopes and aspirations that remained unfulfilled. However, the privileged position of culture, the gap between the material civilization and the intellectual culture, between necessity and freedom, was also the gap which protected the realm of non-scientific culture as a "reservation." There literature and the arts could attain and communicate truths which were denied and repressed in the established reality, or transformed into socially useful concepts and standards. Similarly, philosophy—and religion—could formulate and communicate moral imperatives of universal human validity— often in radical contradiction to the socially useful morality. In this sense, I dare say that the non-scientific culture was less sublimated than the form in which it became translated into actual social values and behavior—and it was certainly less sublimated than the uninhibited novels of our days—less sublimated because the inhibited, mediated style of the higher culture evoked, as the "negative," the uncompromised needs and hopes of man, which present-day literature presents in their socially prevalent realization, permeated with the prevalent repression.

The higher culture still exists. It is more available than ever before; it is more widely read and seen and heard than ever before; but society has been closing the mental and physical space in which this culture could be understood in its *cognitive* substance, in its exact *truth*.

Operationalism, in thought and behavior, relegates these truths to the personal, subjective, emotional dimension; in this form they can easily be fitted into the Establishment—the critical, qualitative transcendence of culture is being eliminated and the negative is integrated into the positive. The oppositional elements of culture are thus being reduced: civilization takes over, organizes, buys and sells culture; substantially non-operational, non-behavioral ideas are translated into operational, behavioral terms; and this translation is not merely a methodological but a social, even political process. After the preceding remarks, we may now express the main effect of this process in one formula: the integration of cultural values into the established society *cancels the alienation of culture from civilization*, thereby flattening out the tension between the "ought" and the "is" (which is a real, historical tension), between the potential and the actual, future and present, freedom and necessity.

The result: the autonomous, critical contents of culture become educational, elevating, relaxing—a vehicle of adjustment.

Every authentic oeuvre of literature, art, music, philosophy speaks a metalanguage which communicates facts and conditions other than those accessible in behavioral language—this is their irreducible, untranslatable substance. It seems that their untranslatable substance now dissolves in a process of translation which affects not only the suprahuman and supranatural (religion) but also the human and natural contents of culture (literature, the arts, philosophy): the radical, irreconcilable conflicts of love and hate, hope and fear, freedom and necessity, subject and object, good and evil become more manageable, comprehensible, normal—in one word, behavioral. Not only the gods, heroes, kings, and knights have disappeared whose world was that of tragedy, romance, song, and festival, but also many of the riddles they could not solve, many of the struggles with which they were concerned, many of the forces and fears with which they had to cope. An ever increasing dimension of unconquered (and unconquerable) forces is being conquered by technological rationality and by physical and social science. And many archetypal problems become susceptible to diagnosis and treatment by the psychologist, social worker, scientist, politician. The fact that they are badly diagnosed and treated, that their still valid content is distorted, reduced, or repressed should not conceal the radically progressive potentialities of this development. They can be summed up in the proposition that mankind has reached the historical stage where it is *technically* capable of creating a world of peace—a world without exploitation, misery, and toil. This would be a civilization which has become culture.

The technological corrosion of the transcendent substance of higher culture invalidates the medium in which it found adequate expression and communication, bringing about the collapse of the traditional literary and artistic forms, the operational redefinition of philosophy, the transformation of religion into status symbol. Culture is redefined by the existing state of affairs: the words, tones, colors, shapes of the perennial works remain the same, but that which they expressed is losing its truth, its validity; the works which previously stood shockingly apart from and against the established reality have been neutralized as classics; thus they no longer preserve their alienation from the alienated society. In philosophy, psychology, and sociology, a pseudo-empiricism predominates which refers its concepts and methods to the restricted and repressed experience of people in the administered world and devalues non-behavioral concepts as metaphysical confusions. Thus the historical validity of ideas like Freedom, Equality, Justice, Individual was precisely in their yet unfulfilled content—in that they could not be referred to the established reality, which did not and could not validate them because they were denied by the functioning of the very institutions that were supposed to realize these ideas. They were normative ideas—non-operational, not by virtue of their metaphysical, unscientific character, but by virtue of the servitude, inequality, injustice, and domination institutionalized in society. The modes of thought and research which dominate in advanced industrial culture tend to identify the normative concepts with their prevailing social realization, or rather they take as norm the way in which society is translating these concepts into reality, at best trying to improve the translation; the untranslated residue is considered obsolete speculation.

To be sure, the contrast between the original and the translation is obvious and part of the daily experience; moreover, the conflict between the potential and the actual sharpens with technical progress, with society's increasing capacity to conquer scarcity, fear, and toil. However, it is also this progress and this capacity which block compre-

hension of the causes of the conflict and of the chances of its solution —
the chances of a pacification of the struggle for existence, individual
and social, within the nation and on the international scale. In the most
highly developed areas of industrial civilization, which provide the
model of culture in the contemporary period, the overwhelming productivity of the established system augments and satisfies the needs of
the populace through a total administration which sees to it that the
needs of the individual are those which perpetuate and fortify the system. The rationale for qualitative change thus evaporates, and with it
the rationale for the alienation of culture from civilization.

If the changing relation between culture and civilization is the
work of the new technological *society* and if it is constantly sustained by
it, then a theoretical "redefinition," no matter how justified, must remain academic inasmuch as it goes *against* the predominant trend. But
here too the very remoteness and "purity" of the theoretical effort, its
apparent weakness in the face of realities may turn into a position of
strength if it does not sacrifice its abstractness by accommodating to
a fallacious positivism and empiricism, fallacious inasmuch as these
modes of thought are oriented to an experience which, in reality, is only
a mutilated sector of experience, isolated from the factors and forces
which determine experience. The administrative absorption of culture
by civilization is the result of the established direction of scientific and
technical progress, of the expanding conquest of man and nature by
the powers which organize this conquest and which utilize the rising
standard of living for perpetuating their organization of the struggle for
existence.

Today this organization operates through the permanent mobilization of the people for the eventuality of nuclear war, and through the
continued mobilization of socially necessary aggression, hostility, frustration, and resentment generated by the struggle for existence in the
"affluent society." This is the universe which, in the most advanced
areas of industrial civilization, determines and confines experience —
confines it by repressing the real, non-utopian alternatives. They are
qualitative alternatives, for the pacification of the struggle for existence,
the redefinition of work in terms of a free realization of human needs
and faculties presuppose not only essentially different institutions but
also essentially different men — men who no longer have to earn a

living in alienated labor. This difference cannot emerge within the tightening framework of institutions essentially designed to organize alienated labor. Under these circumstances, altering the established direction of progress would mean fundamental social change. But social change presupposes the vital *need* for it, the experience of intolerable conditions and of their alternatives—and it is this need and this experience which are barred from developing in the established culture. Their liberation is preconditioned on the restoration of the lost cultural dimension which was (no matter how precariously) protected from the totalitarian power of society: it was the mental dimension of autonomy.

Education for intellectual and emotional independence—this sounds like setting a goal which is generally recognized. In reality it is an all but subversive program which involves violation of some of the strongest democratic taboos. For the prevailing democratic culture fosters heteronomy in the guise of autonomy, arrests the development of needs in the guise of their promotion, and restricts thought and experience in the guise of extending them everywhere and to all. The people enjoy a considerable range of freedom in buying and selling, in looking for jobs and in choosing jobs, in expressing their opinion, in moving about—but their liberties nowhere transcend the established social system which determines their needs, their choice, and their opinions. Freedom itself operates as the vehicle of adjustment and confinement. These repressive (and regressive) tendencies accompany the transformation of industrial society into technological society under the total administration of men, and the simultaneous changes in the occupation, mentality, and political function of the "people" affect the very foundations of democracy. An enumeration of some of the familiar phenomena must here suffice.

We may note first a growing passivity of the people vis-à-vis the omnipresent political and economic apparatus; submission to its affluent productivity and to its use "from above"; divorce of the individuals from the sources of power and information, which makes the recipients into objects of administration. The needs of the established society are introjected and become individual needs; required behavior and desirable aspirations become spontaneous. At the higher stages of development, this total coordination proceeds without terror and without abrogation of the democratic process.

On the contrary, there is at the same time a growing dependence of the elected leaders on the electorate which is constituted by a public opinion shaped by the predominant political and economic interests. Their dominion appears as that of productive and technological rationality. As such, the dominion is accepted and defended, and the people make it their own. The result is a state of general interdependence which obfuscates the real hierarchy. Behind the veil of technological rationality, universal heteronomy is accepted as liberties and comforts offered by the "affluent society."

Under such conditions, the creation (or re-creation) of a refuge of mental independence (practical, political independence is effectively blocked by the concentrated power and coordination in advanced industrial society) must assume the form of withdrawal, willful isolation, intellectual "elitism." And indeed, a redefinition of culture would run counter to the most powerful trends. It would mean the liberation of thought, research, teaching, and learning from the established universe of application and behavior, and the elaboration of methods and concepts capable of rationally surmounting the limits of the established facts and "values." In terms of the academic disciplines, this would mean shifting the main emphasis to "pure" theory, that is, *theoretical* sociology, political science, and psychology; to speculative philosophy, etc. More important would be the consequences for the *organization* of education: the shift would lead to the establishment of "elite" universities, separated from colleges that would retain and strengthen their character as vocational schools in the largest sense. Complete financial independence would be a prerequisite for the former: today more than ever before, this is a matter of the source of material support. No individual private patron would be capable of financing an education which might prepare the mental ground for a qualitatively different hierarchy of values and powers. Such an education could possibly be imagined as the concern of a government willing and capable of counteracting the prevailing political and popular trend—a condition which has only to be formulated in order to reveal its utopian character.

The very notion of intellectual-elite universities is today denounced as antidemocratic bias—even if the emphasis is on "intellectual," and if the term "elite" designates selection made from the school and college population as a whole, a selection solely according to merit, that is to say, according to the inclination and ability for theoretical thought. The notion is antidemocratic indeed if the established mass democracy and its education are assumed to be the realization of a democracy corresponding exactly to the historically possible forms of freedom and equality. I do not believe that this is the case. The prevailing positivistic and behavioral trend serves all too often to cut the roots of self-determination in the mind of man—a self-determination which today (as in the past) requires critical dissociation from the given universe of experience. Without this *critique of experience*, the student is deprived of the intellectual methods and tools which would enable him to comprehend and evaluate his society and its culture as a whole, in the historical continuum in which this society fulfills, distorts, or denies its own possibilities and promises. Instead, the student is trained for comprehending and evaluating the established conditions and possibilities only *in terms of* the established conditions and possibilities: his thinking, his ideas, his goals are programmatically and scientifically restricted—not by logic, experience, and facts, but by a purged logic, a mutilated experience, incomplete facts.

The protest against this stifling behaviorism finds an irrational outlet in the numerous existentialist, metapsychological, and neotheological philosophies which oppose the positivistic trend. The opposition is faulty—and even illusory. They too contribute to the decline of critical reason inasmuch as they abstract from the real stuff of experience without ever returning to it after the abstraction has attained the conceptual level. The existential experience to which they refer is also a restricted, mutilated experience, but in contrast to positivism, experience is distorted not only by the nexus of the established social universe of experience but also by the insistence that the existential decision or choice can break through this universe and reach the dimension of individual freedom. To be sure, no effort of thought, no mode of thought can do so, but they can help or hinder the development of that consciousness which is a precondition for accomplishing the task.

The concepts of critical reason are philosophical, sociological, and historical in one. In this interrelation, and linked to the growing mastery of nature and society, they are the intellectual catalysts of culture: they open the mental space and faculties for the emergence of new historical projects, new possibilities of existence. This theoretical dimension of thought is today severely reduced. The emphasis here placed on its extension and restoration may appear less irrelevant if we recall that our culture (and not only our intellectual culture) was projected and predefined, even in its most practical aspects, by science, philosophy, and literature before it became a fully developed and organized reality: the new astronomy and physics, the new political theory anticipated (in affirmation and negation) the subsequent historical experience. The liberation of theoretical thought from its commitments to a repressive practice was a precondition of progress.

The reorganization of culture I have suggested above would also violate the taboo placed on the position of *science* today. (I use intentionally the frightful term "organization" in this context because culture has become an object of organization; to "abstract" culture from its prevailing administration means first to reorganize and disorganize it.) The role of science in an established culture must be evaluated not only with respect to the scientific truths (nobody in his right mind would deny them or minimize their "value") but also with respect to their ascertainable impact on the human condition. Science is responsible for this impact—and this is not the moral and personal responsibility of the scientist but the function of the scientific method and concepts themselves. No teleology, no extraneous ends have to be superimposed on science: it has its inherent historical ends from which no scientism and no repression can separate it.

Science as intellectual activity is, prior to all practical application, an instrument in the struggle for existence, in man's struggle with nature and with man: its guiding hypotheses, projections, and abstractions emerge in this struggle and anticipate, preserve, or change the conditions under which this struggle develops. To say that the very rationale of science is to improve these conditions may be a value judgment, but it is a value judgment no more and no less than that which makes science itself a value, which makes truth a value. We have accepted this value, "civilization" has been its gradual and painful realization; it has been a determining factor in the relation between science and society, and even the purest theoretical achievements have entered into this relation, regardless of the scientist's own consciousness and intentions. The very elimination of "ends" from science tightened the relation between science and society and increased immensely the instrumentalist capabilities of science in the struggle for existence. The Galilean projection of Nature without an objective Telos, the shift of the scientific quest from *Why* to *How,* the translation of quality into quantity, and the expulsion from science of the non-quantifiable subjectivity—this method has been the prerequisite of whatever technical and material progress has been made since the Middle Ages. It has guided the rational concepts of man and nature, and it has served to create the preconditions for a rational society—preconditions for *humanity.* It has done so while at the same time increasing the rational means of destruction and domination, that is, the means for *preventing* the realization of humanity. From the beginning, construction was bound up with destruction, productivity with its repressive utilization, pacification with aggression. This dual responsibility of science is not contingent: quantified science, and nature as mathematized quantity, as mathematical universe, are "neutral," susceptible to whatever utilization and transformation, limited only by the limits of scientific knowledge and by the resistance of brute matter. In this neutrality, science becomes susceptible and subject to the objectives which predominate in the society in which science develops. It is still a society in which the conquest of nature takes place through the conquest of man, the exploitation of natural and intellectual resources through the exploitation of man, and the struggle with nature through the struggle for existence in aggressive and repressive forms, on the personal as well as on the national and international levels. But science itself has attained a level of comprehension and productivity which places it in *contradiction* to this state of affairs: "pure" scientific rationality involves the real possibility of abolishing scarcity, toil, and injustice the world over—the possibility of pacifying the struggle for existence. What is at stake is not the undoing or the curtailing of science, but its liberation from the masters whom science itself has helped to set up. And this liberation would not be an external event which would leave the scientific enterprise in its structure intact: it may well affect the scientific method itself, the scientific experience and projection of nature. In a rational and humane society, science would have a new function, and this function might well necessitate a reconstruction of scientific method—not a return to pre-Galilean qualitative science-philosophy, but rather the scientific quantification of new goals, derived from a new experience of man and nature—the goals of pacification.

Today the question must be asked whether, in the "affluent societies," science has not ceased to be a vehicle of liberation, whether it does not (via destruction research and planned obsolescence) perpetuate and intensify the struggle for existence instead of alleviating it. The traditional distinction between science and technology becomes questionable. When the most abstract achievements of mathematics and theoretical physics satisfy so adequately the needs of IBM and of the Atomic Energy Commission, it is time to ask whether such applicability is not inherent in the concepts of science itself.[1] I suggest that the question cannot be pushed aside by separating pure science from its applications and putting the blame on the latter only: the specific "purity" of science facilitated the union of construction and destruction, humanity and inhumanity in the progressive mastery of nature. In any case it is impossible to measure the destructive against the constructive efforts of science; nor is it possible to distinguish, within the whole of scientific research, between life-preserving and life-impairing fields, methods, and concepts—they seem to be internally linked. Science has created its own culture, and this culture is absorbing an ever larger part of civilization. The notion of the "two cultures" is misleading, but even more misleading, under the prevailing conditions, is the plea for their reunion.

The non-scientific culture (I shall confine myself here to literature as its representative) speaks a language of its own, substantially different from that of science. The language of literature is a *meta*language inasmuch as it does not pertain to the established universe of discourse which communicates the existing state of affairs. It communicates "a different world," governed by different standards, values, and principles. This different world appears *in* the established one; it ingresses into the daily business of life, into the experience of one's self and of others, into the social and natural environment. However this difference may be constituted, it makes the world of literature an essentially *other* one—a negation of the given reality. And to the degree to which science has become an integral part, or even a driving power behind the given reality, literature is also the negation of science. There is no such thing as (scientific) realism in the authentic literature of the West, not even in Zola's oeuvre: his society of the Second Empire is the negation of that society in its reality.

The gap between scientific and non-scientific culture *today* may be a very promising circumstance. The neutrality of pure science has made it impure, incapable or unwilling to refuse collaboration with the theoreticians and practitioners of legalized destruction and exploitation. The aloofness of non-scientific culture may preserve the much needed refuge and reservation in which forgotten or suppressed truths and images are sustained. When society tends toward total coordination and administration (through scientific means), the alienation of non-scientific culture becomes a prerequisite of opposition and refusal. Whether or not a poet or writer or classicist knows the Second Law of Thermodynamics or the "overthrow of parity" is his personal business: it certainly would not do him any harm (nor would it be harmful if such knowledge were to become part of the general education). It may also be entirely irrelevant for what he has to say. For the "natural order" which the quantifying sciences define and master is not *the* natural order, and the "scientific edifice of the physical world" is *not*, "in its intellectual depth, complexity and articulation, the most beautiful and wonderful collective work of the mind of man."[2] It seems to me that the edifice of literature, art, and music is infinitely more beautiful, wonderful, deep, complex, and articulate, and I believe that this is not simply a matter of preference. The world of non-scientific culture is a multidimensional world in which "secondary qualities" are irreducible, and in which all objectivity is qualitatively related to the human subject. Scientific modesty often conceals a frightening absolutism, a happy rejection of non-scientific but rational modes of thought into the realm of fiction, poetry, preference.

I have referred to *The Two Cultures* because the message of the book seems to me merely another exhortation to conformity in the guise of scientific rationality. The union or reunion of the scientific and non-scientific culture may be prerequisite to progress beyond the society of total mobilization and permanent defense or deterrent, but such progress cannot be accomplished within the established culture of defense and deterrent which science so efficiently sustains. In order to make this progress, science must liberate itself from the fatal dialectic of Master and Servant which transforms the conquest of nature into the tool of exploitation, and into the technology of their perpetuation in "higher" forms. Prior to this liberation of science, the non-scientific culture preserves the images of the ends which science by itself cannot and does not define, namely, the ends of humanity. Evidently the redirection of science involves social and political changes, that is to say, the emergence of an essentially different society whose continuation can dispense with the institutions of aggressive defense and deterrent. Within the established institutions, preparation for such an eventuality will be primarily a negative one, namely, reduction of the overwhelming pressure on non-conformist, critical-transcendent modes of thought, to counteract the oligopoly of behavioral pseudo-empiricism.

If there is still any meaning in Kant's statement that education should be not for the present but for a better society, education would also (and perhaps foremost) alter the place of science in the universities and in the area of "research and development" as a whole. The overwhelmingly generous financial support which the physical sciences enjoy today is support not only for research and development in the interest of humanity but also in the opposite interest. Since this fusion of opposites cannot be dissolved within the framework of the existing social system, a modicum of progress may perhaps be attained by a policy of discrimination with respect to support and priority. However, such a policy would presuppose the existence of governments, foundations, and corporations which are willing and powerful enough to reduce rigorously the military establishment—a rather unrealistic assumption. One can envisage the establishment of an academic reservation where scientific research is undertaken entirely free of any military connections, where the inauguration, continuation, and publication of research is left entirely to an independent group of scientists committed to a humanist pursuit. Granted that there are many universities and colleges that today refuse to engage in any government-sponsored research which involves military projects: one might still advocate some establishment that would not merely exercise such restraint but would actively further publication of documents on abuses of science for inhumane ends.

Today, even these modest, sensible ideas are scorned as naive and romantic, are heaped with ridicule. The fact that they are condemned before the omnipotent technical and political apparatus of our society does not necessarily demolish the value which they may possibly have. By virtue of the impenetrable union between political and technological rationality today, ideas not bent to this union appear as irrational and detrimental to progress—as reactionary. For example, one hears comparison of the protest against the ever growing programs of outer space with the opposition of medieval Aristotelianism against Copernicus and Galileo. However, there is nothing regressive in the insistence that all energy and money devoted to outer space is wasted so long as it is withdrawn from use for the humanization of the earth. The undeniable technical discoveries and improvements resulting from the conquest of outer space must be evaluated in terms of priority: the possibility of staying (perhaps even living) in outer space should have lower priority than that of abolishing intolerable living conditions on earth. The notion that both projects can be effectively carried out at the same time and by the same society is ideological. The conquest of outer space may accelerate and extend communication and information, but the question must be asked whether they are not already fast and extensive enough, or even too fast and too extensive for much of what is communicated and done. The ancient concept of *hubris* makes good non-metaphysical sense when applied to destruction wrought, not by the gods but by man. The rationality of global military and political competition (or rather conflict) is not necessarily synonymous with human progress. When the latter is bound to the former, protest against this bondage is made to appear as a form of irrational regression; but this perversion is itself the work of politics. Evidently the notion of an education within the existing society for a better future society is a contradiction, but a contradiction that must be solved if progress is to take place.

Notes

1. I have discussed this question in my *One-Dimensional Man* (Boston: Beacon Press, 1964), Chapters 6 and 7.

2. C. P. Snow, *The Two Cultures: And a Second Look* (The New American Library 1964), p. 20.

REPRESSIVE TOLERANCE (1965)

This 1965 essay is undoubtedly the most controversial of Marcuse's political writings. It was read by his critics as an attack on the ideal of free speech and by many in the New Left as a rationale for interrupting or refusing discussion and debate. Yet the essay is more complicated than appeared to either side. In the background of Marcuse's argument lies the memory of the rise of Nazism under the protection of the democratic constitution of the Weimar Republic. The dire results of that all too principled commitment to free speech remind us that the historic struggle for tolerance has always been partisan, and began with repression of regressive forces opposed to progress in freedom. Tolerance cannot mean equal time for Nazis and Jews.

   The ideal of tolerance presupposes social conditions in which contending opinions all have a fair hearing. This is not the case today in advanced societies dominated by one-sided propaganda. What then prevails is not rational debate in the search for truth, but manipulative persuasion in the interests of a hegemony. Regressive social forces control the government and the mass media and falsify the principle of tolerance by privileging conservative voices over all others in the public sphere. Where dissent is completely marginalized, appeals to tolerance, like the so-called objectivity of the news media, block criticism of the very evils tolerance was established to fight. Marcuse's essay attempted to right the balance by arguing for intolerance toward warmongering, racism, and other reactionary tendencies dominating public discourse.

Marcuse's argument is best understood in this context: when radical students on his campus challenged military research in support of the war in Vietnam, university administrations appealed to academic freedom to discredit the protests and defend the right of professors to contribute to the war effort. Tolerance was demanded for research on high-altitude imaging to improve the kill ratios of bombing over North Vietnam. Marcuse's essay gave the students arguments against this abuse of the principle of tolerance.

"Repressive Tolerance" was dedicated to Marcuse's Brandeis University students.

● ● ●

This essay examines the idea of tolerance in our advanced industrial society. The conclusion reached is that the realization of the objective of tolerance would call for intolerance toward prevailing policies, attitudes, opinions, and the extension of tolerance to policies, attitudes, and opinions which are outlawed or suppressed. In other words, today tolerance appears again as what it was in its origins, at the beginning of the modern period—a partisan goal, a subversive liberating notion and practice. Conversely, what is proclaimed and practiced as tolerance today, is in many of its most effective manifestations serving the cause of oppression.

The author is fully aware that, at present, no power, no authority, no government exists which would translate liberating tolerance into practice, but he believes that it is the task and duty of the intellectual to recall and preserve historical possibilities which seem to have become utopian possibilities—that it is his task to break the concreteness of oppression in order to open the mental space in which this society can be recognized as what it is and does.

Tolerance is an end in itself. The elimination of violence, and the reduction of suppression to the extent required for protecting man and animals from cruelty and aggression are preconditions for the creation of a humane society. Such a society does not yet exist; progress toward it is perhaps more than before arrested by violence and suppression on a global scale. As deterrents against nuclear war, as police action against subversion, as technical aid in the fight against imperialism and communism, as methods of pacification in neo-colonial massacres, violence and suppression are promulgated, practiced, and defended by democratic and authoritarian governments alike, and the people subjected to these governments are educated to sustain such practices as necessary for the preservation of the status quo. Tolerance is extended to policies, conditions, and modes of behavior which should not be tolerated because they are impeding, if not destroying, the chances of creating an existence without fear and misery.

This sort of tolerance strengthens the tyranny of the majority against which authentic liberals protested. The political locus of tolerance has changed: while it is more or less quietly and constitutionally withdrawn from the opposition, it is made compulsory behavior with respect to established policies. Tolerance is turned from an active into a passive state, from practice to non-practice: laissez-faire the constituted authorities. It is the people who tolerate the government, which in turn tolerates opposition within the framework determined by the constituted authorities.

Tolerance toward that which is radically evil now appears as good because it serves the cohesion of the whole on the road to affluence or more affluence. The toleration of the systematic moronization of children and adults alike by publicity and propaganda, the release of destructiveness in aggressive driving, the recruitment for and training of special forces, the impotent and benevolent tolerance toward outright deception in merchandising, waste, and planned obsolescence are not distortions and aberrations, they are the essence of a system which fosters tolerance as a means for perpetuating the struggle for existence and suppressing the alternatives. The authorities in education, morals, and psychology are vociferous against the increase in juvenile delinquency; they are less vociferous against the proud presentation, in word and deed and pictures, of ever more powerful missiles, rockets, bombs—the mature delinquency of a whole civilization.

According to a dialectical proposition it is the whole which determines the truth—not in the sense that the whole is prior or superior to its parts, but in the sense that its structure and function determine every particular condition and relation. Thus, within a repressive society, even progressive movements threaten to turn into their opposite to the degree to which they accept the rules of the game. To take a most controversial case: the exercise of political rights (such as voting, letter-writing to the press, to Senators, etc., protest-demonstrations with a priori renunciation of counterviolence) in a society of total administration serves to strengthen this administration by testifying to the existence of democratic liberties which, in reality, have changed their content and lost their effectiveness. In such a case, freedom (of opinion, of assembly, of speech) becomes an instrument for absolving servitude. And yet (and only here the dialectical proposition shows its full intent) the existence and practice of these liberties remain a precondition for the restoration of their original oppositional function, provided that the effort to transcend their (often self-imposed) limitations is intensified. Generally, the function and value of tolerance depend on the equality prevalent in the society in which tolerance is practiced. Tolerance itself stands subject to overriding criteria: its range and its limits cannot be defined in terms of the respective society. In other words, tolerance is an end in itself only when it is truly universal, practiced by the rulers as well as by the ruled, by the lords as well as by the peasants, by the sheriffs as well as by their victims. And such universal tolerance is possible only when no real or alleged enemy requires in the national interest the education and training of people in military violence and destruction. As long as these conditions do not prevail, the conditions of tolerance are "loaded": they are determined and defined by the institutionalized inequality (which is certainly compatible with constitutional equality), i.e., by the class structure of society. In such a society, tolerance is *de facto* limited on the dual ground of legalized violence or suppression (police, armed forces, guards of all sorts) and of the privileged position held by the predominant interests and their "connections."

These background limitations of tolerance are normally prior to the explicit and judicial limitations as defined by the courts, custom, governments, etc. (for example, "clear and present danger," threat to national security, heresy). Within the framework of such a social structure, tolerance can be safely practiced and proclaimed. It is of two kinds: (1) the passive toleration of entrenched and established attitudes and ideas even if their damaging effect on man and nature is evident; and (2) the active, official tolerance granted to the Right as well as to the Left, to movements of aggression as well as to movements of peace, to the party of hate as well as to that of humanity. I call this non-partisan tolerance "abstract" or "pure" inasmuch as it refrains from taking sides —but in doing so it actually protects the already established machinery of discrimination.

The tolerance which enlarged the range and content of freedom was always partisan—intolerant toward the protagonists of the repressive status quo. The issue was only the degree and extent of intolerance. In the firmly established liberal society of England and the United States, freedom of speech and assembly was granted even to the radical enemies of society, provided they did not make the transition from word to deed, from speech to action.

Relying on the effective background limitations imposed by its class structure, the society seemed to practice general tolerance. But liberalist theory had already placed an important condition on tolerance: it was "to apply only to human beings in the maturity of their faculties." John Stuart Mill does not only speak of children and minors; he elaborates: "Liberty, as a principle, has no application to any state of things anterior to the time when mankind have become capable of being improved by free and equal discussion." Anterior to that time, men may still be barbarians, and "despotism is a legitimate mode of government in dealing with barbarians, provided the end be their improvement, and the means justified by actually effecting that end." Mill's often-quoted words have a less familiar implication on which their meaning depends: the internal connection between liberty and truth. There is a sense in which truth is the end of liberty, and liberty must be defined and confined by truth. Now in what sense can liberty be for the sake of truth? Liberty is self-determination, autonomy—this is almost a tautology, but a tautology which results from a whole series of synthetic judgments. It stipulates the ability to determine one's own life: to be able to determine what to do and what not to do, what to suffer and what not. But the subject of this autonomy is never the contingent, private individual as that which he actually is or happens to be; it is rather the individual as a human being who is capable of being free with the others. And the problem of making possible such a harmony between every individual liberty and the other is not that of finding a compromise between competitors, or between freedom and law, between general and individual interest, common and private welfare in an *established* society, but of *creating* the society in which man is no longer enslaved by institutions which vitiate self-determination from the beginning. In other words, freedom is still to be created even for the freest of the existing societies. And the direction in which it must be sought, and the institutional and cultural changes which may help to attain the goal are, at least in developed civilization, *comprehensible*, that is to say, they can be identified and projected, on the basis of experience, by human reason.

In the interplay of theory and practice, true and false solutions become distinguishable—never with the evidence of necessity, never as the positive, only with the certainty of a reasoned and reasonable chance, and with the persuasive force of the negative. For the true positive is the society of the future and therefore beyond definition and determination, while the existing positive is that which must be surmounted. But the experience and understanding of the existent society may well be capable of identifying what is *not* conducive to a free and rational society, what impedes and distorts the possibilities of its creation. Freedom is liberation, a specific historical process in theory and practice, and as such it has its right and wrong, its truth and falsehood.

The uncertainty of chance in this distinction does not cancel the historical objectivity, but it necessitates freedom of thought and expression as preconditions of finding the way to freedom—it necessitates *tolerance*. However, this tolerance cannot be indiscriminate and equal with respect to the contents of expression, neither in word nor in deed; it cannot protect false words and wrong deeds which demonstrate that they contradict and counteract the possibilities of liberation. Such indiscriminate tolerance is justified in harmless debates, in conversation, in academic discussion; it is indispensable in the scientific enterprise, in private religion. But society cannot be indiscriminate where the pacification of existence, where freedom and happiness themselves are at stake: here, certain things cannot be said, certain ideas cannot be expressed, certain policies cannot be proposed, certain behavior cannot be permitted without making tolerance an instrument for the continuation of servitude.

The danger of "destructive tolerance" (Baudelaire), of "benevolent neutrality" toward *art* has been recognized: the market, which absorbs equally well (although with often quite sudden fluctuations) art, anti-art, and non-art, all possible conflicting styles, schools, forms, provides a "complacent receptacle, a friendly abyss" [1] in which the radical impact of art, the protest of art against the established reality is swallowed up. However, censorship of art and literature is regressive under all circumstances. The authentic oeuvre is not and cannot be a prop of oppression, and pseudo-art (which can be such a prop) is not art. Art stands against history, withstands history which has been the history of oppression, for art subjects reality to laws other than the established ones: to the laws of the Form which creates a different reality—negation of the established one even where art depicts the established reality. But in its struggle with history, art subjects itself to history: history enters the definition of art and enters into the distinction between art and pseudo-art. Thus it happens that what was once art becomes pseudo-art. Previous forms, styles, and qualities, previous modes of protest and refusal cannot be recaptured in or against a different society. There are cases where an authentic oeuvre carries a regressive political message—Dostoevski is a case in point. But then, the message is canceled by the oeuvre itself: the regressive political content is absorbed, *aufgehoben* in the artistic form: in the work as literature.

Tolerance of free speech is the way of improvement, of progress in liberation, *not* because there is no objective truth, and improvement must necessarily be a compromise between a variety of opinions, but because there *is* an objective truth which can be discovered, ascertained only in learning and comprehending that which is and that which can be and ought to be done for the sake of improving the lot of mankind. This common and historical "ought" is not immediately evident, at hand: it has to be uncovered by "cutting through," "splitting," "breaking asunder" *(dis-cutio)* the given material—separating right and wrong, good and bad, correct and incorrect. The subject whose "improvement" depends on a progressive historical practice is each man as man, and this universality is reflected in that of the discussion, which a priori does not exclude any group or individual. But even the all-inclusive character of liberalist tolerance was, at least in theory, based on the proposition that men were (potential) *individuals* who could learn to hear and see and feel by themselves, to develop their own thoughts, to grasp their true interests and rights and capabilities, also against established authority and opinion. This was the rationale of free speech and assembly. Universal toleration becomes questionable when its rationale no longer prevails, when tolerance is administered to manipulated and indoctrinated individuals who parrot, as their own, the opinion of their masters, for whom heteronomy has become autonomy.

The telos of tolerance is truth. It is clear from the historical record that the authentic spokesmen of tolerance had more and other truth in mind than that of propositional logic and academic theory. John Stuart Mill speaks of the truth which is persecuted in history and which does *not* triumph over persecution by virtue of its "inherent power," which in fact has no inherent power "against the dungeon and the stake." And he enumerates the "truths" which were cruelly and successfully liquidated in the dungeons and at the stake: that of Arnold of Brescia, of Fra Dolcino, of Savonarola, of the Albigensians, Waldensians, Lollards, and Hussites. Tolerance is first and foremost for the sake of the heretics —the historical road toward *humanitas* appears as heresy: target of persecution by the powers that be. Heresy by itself, however, is no token of truth.

The criterion of progress in freedom according to which Mill judges these movements is the Reformation. The evaluation is *ex post*, and his list includes opposites (Savonarola too would have burned Fra Dolcino). Even the ex post evaluation is contestable as to its truth: history corrects the judgment—too late. The correction does not help the victims and does not absolve their executioners. However, the lesson is clear: intolerance has delayed progress and has prolonged the slaughter and torture of innocents for hundreds of years. Does this clinch the case for indiscriminate, "pure" tolerance? Are there historical conditions in which such toleration impedes liberation and multiplies the victims who are sacrificed to the status quo? Can the indiscriminate guaranty of political rights and liberties be repressive? Can such tolerance serve to contain qualitative social change?

I shall discuss this question only with reference to political movements, attitudes, schools of thought, philosophies which are "political" in the widest sense—affecting the society as a whole, demonstrably transcending the sphere of privacy. Moreover, I propose a shift in the focus of the discussion: it will be concerned not only, and not primarily, with tolerance toward radical extremes, minorities, subversives, etc., but rather with tolerance toward majorities, toward official and public opinion, toward the established protectors of freedom. In this case, the discussion can have as a frame of reference only a democratic society, in which the people, as individuals and as members of political and other organizations, participate in the making, sustaining, and changing of policies. In an authoritarian system, the people do not tolerate— they suffer established policies.

Under a system of constitutionally guaranteed and (generally and without too many and too glaring exceptions) practiced civil rights and liberties, opposition and dissent are tolerated unless they issue in violence and/or in exhortation to and organization of violent subversion. The underlying assumption is that the established society is free, and that any improvement, even a change in the social structure and social values, would come about in the normal course of events, prepared, defined, and tested in free and equal discussion, on the open marketplace of ideas and goods.[2] Now in recalling John Stuart Mill's passage, I drew attention to the premise hidden in this assumption: free and equal discussion can fulfill the function attributed to it only if it is *rational*—expression and development of independent thinking, free from indoctrination, manipulation, extraneous authority. The notion of pluralism and countervailing powers is no substitute for this requirement. One might in theory construct a state in which a multitude of different pressures, interests, and authorities balance each other out and result in a truly general and rational interest. However, such a construct badly fits a society in which powers are and remain unequal and even increase their unequal weight when they run their own course. It fits even worse when the variety of pressures unifies and coagulates into an overwhelming whole, integrating the particular countervailing powers by virtue of an increasing standard of living and an increasing concentration of power. Then, the laborer whose real interest conflicts with that of management, the common consumer whose real interest conflicts with that of the producer, the intellectual whose vocation conflicts with that of his employer find themselves submitting to a system against which they are powerless and appear unreasonable. The ideas of the available alternatives evaporate into an utterly utopian dimension in which it is at home, for a free society is indeed unrealistically and undefinably different from the existing ones. Under these circumstances, whatever improvement may occur "in the normal course of events" and without subversion is likely to be improvement in the direction determined by the particular interests which control the whole.

By the same token, those minorities which strive for a change of the whole itself will, under optimal conditions which rarely prevail, be left free to deliberate and discuss, to speak and to assemble—and will be left harmless and helpless in the face of the overwhelming majority, which militates against qualitative social change. This majority is firmly grounded in the increasing satisfaction of needs, and technological and mental coordination, which testify to the general helplessness of radical groups in a well-functioning social system.

Within the affluent democracy, the affluent discussion prevails, and within the established framework, it is tolerant to a large extent. All points of view can be heard: the Communist and the Fascist, the Left and the Right, the white and the Negro, the crusaders for armament and for disarmament. Moreover, in endlessly dragging debates over the media, the stupid opinion is treated with the same respect as the intelligent one, the misinformed may talk as long as the informed, and propaganda rides along with education, truth with falsehood. This pure toleration of sense and nonsense is justified by the democratic argument that nobody, neither group nor individual, is in possession of the truth and capable of defining what is right and wrong, good and bad. Therefore, all contesting opinions must be submitted to "the people" for its deliberation and choice. But I have already suggested that the democratic argument implies a necessary condition, namely, that the people must be capable of deliberating and choosing on the basis of knowledge, that they must have access to authentic information, and that, on this basis, their evaluation must be the result of autonomous thought.

In the contemporary period, the democratic argument for abstract tolerance tends to be invalidated by the invalidation of the democratic process itself. The liberating force of democracy was the chance it gave to effective dissent, on the individual as well as social scale, its openness to qualitatively different forms of government, of culture, education, work—of the human existence in general. The toleration of free discussion and the equal right of opposites was to define and clarify the different forms of dissent: their direction, content, prospect. But with the concentration of economic and political power and the integration of opposites in a society which uses technology as an instrument of domination, effective dissent is blocked where it could freely emerge: in the formation of opinion, in information and communication, in speech and assembly. Under the rule of monopolistic media—themselves the mere instruments of economic and political power—a mentality is created for which right and wrong, true and false are predefined wherever they affect the vital interests of the society. This is, prior to all expression and communication, a matter of semantics: the blocking of effective dissent, of the recognition of that which is not of the Establishment which begins in the language that is publicized and administered. The meaning of words is rigidly stabilized. Rational persuasion, persuasion to the opposite is all but precluded. The avenues of entrance are closed to the meaning of words and ideas other than the established one—established by the publicity of the powers that be, and verified in their practices. Other words can be spoken and heard, other ideas can be expressed, but, at the massive scale of the conservative majority (outside such enclaves as the intelligentsia), they are immediately "evaluated" (i.e. automatically understood) in terms of the public language—a language which determines "a priori" the direction in which the thought process moves. Thus the process of reflection ends where it started: in the given conditions and relations. Self-validating, the argument of the discussion repels the contradiction because the antithesis is redefined in terms of the thesis. For example, thesis: we work for peace; antithesis: we prepare for war (or even: we wage war); unification of opposites: preparing for war *is* working for peace. Peace is redefined as necessarily, in the prevailing situation, including preparation for war (or even war) and in this Orwellian form, the meaning of the word "peace" is stabilized. Thus, the basic vocabulary of the Orwellian language operates as a priori categories of understanding: preforming all content. These conditions invalidate the logic of tolerance which involves the rational development of meaning and precludes the closing of meaning. Consequently, persuasion through discussion and the equal presentation of opposites (even where it is really equal) easily lose their liberating force as factors of understanding and learning; they are far more likely to strengthen the established thesis and to repel the alternatives.

Impartiality to the utmost, equal treatment of competing and conflicting issues is indeed a basic requirement for decision-making in the democratic process—it is an equally basic requirement for defining the limits of tolerance. But in a democracy with totalitarian organization, objectivity may fulfill a very different function, namely, to foster a mental attitude which tends to obliterate the difference between true and false, information and indoctrination, right and wrong. In fact, the decision between opposed opinions has been made before the presentation and discussion get under way—made, not by a conspiracy or a sponsor or a publisher, not by any dictatorship, but rather by the "normal course of events," which is the course of administered events, and by the mentality shaped in this course. Here, too, it is the whole which determines the truth. Then the decision asserts itself, without any open violation of objectivity, in such things as the make-up of a newspaper (with the breaking up of vital information into bits interspersed between extraneous material, irrelevant items, relegating of some radically negative news to an obscure place), in the juxtaposition of gorgeous ads with unmitigated horrors, in the introduction and interruption of the broadcasting of facts by overwhelming commercials. The result is a *neutralization* of opposites, a neutralization, however, which takes place on the firm grounds of the structural limitation of tolerance and within a preformed mentality. When a magazine prints side by side a negative and a positive report on the FBI, it fulfills honestly the requirements of objectivity: however, the chances are that the positive wins because the image of the institution is deeply engraved in the mind of the people. Or, if a newscaster reports the torture and murder of civil rights workers in the same unemotional tone he uses to describe the stock market or the weather, or with the same great emotion with which he says his commercials, then such objectivity is spurious— more, it offends against humanity and truth by being calm where one should be enraged, by refraining from accusation where accusation is in the facts themselves. The tolerance expressed in such impartiality serves to minimize or even absolve prevailing intolerance and suppression. If objectivity has anything to do with truth, and if truth is more than a matter of logic and science, then this kind of objectivity is false, and this kind of tolerance inhuman. And if it is necessary to break the established universe of meaning (and the practice enclosed in this universe) in order to enable man to find out what is true and false, this deceptive impartiality would have to be abandoned. The people exposed to this impartiality are no *tabulae rasae*, they are indoctrinated by the conditions under which they live and think and which they do not transcend. To enable them to become autonomous, to find by themselves what is true and what is false for man in the existing society, they would have to be freed from the prevailing indoctrination (which is no longer recognized as indoctrination). But this means that the trend would have to be reversed: they would have to get information slanted in the opposite direction. For the facts are never given immediately and never accessible immediately; they are established, "mediated" by those who made them; the truth, "the whole truth" surpasses these facts and requires the rupture with their appearance. This rupture—prerequisite and token of all freedom of thought and of speech—cannot be accomplished within the established framework of abstract tolerance and spurious objectivity because these are precisely the factors which precondition the mind *against* the rupture.

The factual barriers which totalitarian democracy erects against the efficacy of qualitative dissent are weak and pleasant enough compared with the practices of a dictatorship which claims to educate the people in the truth. With all its limitations and distortions, democratic tolerance is under all circumstances more humane than an institutionalized intolerance which sacrifices the rights and liberties of the living generations for the sake of future generations. The question is whether this is the only alternative. I shall presently try to suggest the direction in which an answer may be sought. In any case, the contrast is not between democracy in the abstract and dictatorship in the abstract.

Democracy is a form of government which fits very different types of society (this holds true even for a democracy with universal suffrage and equality before the law), and the human costs of a democracy are always and everywhere those exacted by the society whose government it is. Their range extends all the way from normal exploitation, poverty, and insecurity to the victims of wars, police actions, military aid, etc., in which the society is engaged—and not only to the victims within its own frontiers. These considerations can never justify the exacting of different sacrifices and different victims on behalf of a future better society, but they do allow weighing the costs involved in the perpetuation of an existing society against the risk of promoting alternatives which offer a reasonable chance of pacification and liberation. Surely, no government can be expected to foster its own subversion, but in a democracy such a right is vested in the people (i.e. in the majority of the people). This means that the ways should not be blocked on which a subversive majority could develop, and if they are blocked by organized repression and indoctrination, their reopening may require apparently undemocratic means. They would include the withdrawal of toleration of speech and assembly from groups and movements which promote aggressive policies, armament, chauvinism, discrimination on the grounds of race and religion, or which oppose the extension of public services, social security, medical care, etc. Moreover, the restoration of freedom of thought may necessitate new and rigid restrictions on teachings and practices in the educational institutions which, by their very methods and concepts, serve to enclose the mind within the established universe of discourse and behavior—thereby precluding a priori a rational evaluation of the alternatives. And to the degree to which freedom of thought involves the struggle against inhumanity, restoration of such freedom would also imply intolerance toward scientific research in the interest of deadly "deterrents," of abnormal human endurance under inhuman conditions, etc. I shall presently discuss the question as to who is to decide on the distinction between liberating and repressive, human and inhuman teachings and practices; I have already suggested that this distinction is not a matter of value-preference but of rational criteria.

While the reversal of the trend in the educational enterprise at least could conceivably be enforced by the students and teachers themselves, and thus be self-imposed, the systematic withdrawal of tolerance toward regressive and repressive opinions and movements could only be envisaged as results of large-scale pressure which would amount to an upheaval. In other words, it would presuppose that which is still to be accomplished: the reversal of the trend. However, resistance at particular occasions, boycott, non-participation at the local and small-group level may perhaps prepare the ground. The subversive character of the restoration of freedom appears most clearly in that dimension of society where false tolerance and free enterprise do perhaps the most serious and lasting damage, namely, in business and publicity. Against the emphatic insistence on the part of spokesmen for labor, I maintain that practices such as planned obsolescence, collusion between union leadership and management, slanted publicity are not simply imposed from above on a powerless rank and file, but are *tolerated* by them—and by the consumer at large. However, it would be ridiculous to speak of a possible withdrawal of tolerance with respect to these practices and to the ideologies promoted by them. For they pertain to the basis on which the repressive affluent society rests and reproduces itself and its vital defenses—their removal would be that total revolution which this society so effectively repels.

To discuss tolerance in such a society means to re-examine the issue of violence and the traditional distinction between violent and non-violent action. The discussion should not, from the beginning, be clouded by ideologies which serve the perpetuation of violence. Even in the advanced centers of civilization, violence actually prevails: it is practiced by the police, in the prisons and mental institutions, in the fight against racial minorities; it is carried, by the defenders of metropolitan freedom, into the backward countries. This violence indeed breeds violence. But to refrain from violence in the face of vastly superior violence is one thing, to renounce a priori violence against violence, on ethical or psychological grounds (because it may antagonize sympathizers) is another. Non-violence is normally not only preached to but exacted from the weak—it is a necessity rather than a virtue, and normally it does not seriously harm the case of the strong. (Is the case of India an exception? There, passive resistance was carried through on a massive scale, which disrupted, or threatened to disrupt, the economic life of the country. Quantity turns into quality: on such a scale, passive resistance is no longer passive—it ceases to be non-violent. The same holds true for the General Strike.) Robespierre's distinction between the terror of liberty and the terror of despotism, and his moral glorification of the former belongs to the most convincingly condemned aberrations, even if the white terror was more bloody than the red terror. The comparative evaluation in terms of the number of victims is the quantifying approach which reveals the man-made horror throughout history that made violence a necessity. In terms of historical function, there is a difference between revolutionary and reactionary

violence, between violence practiced by the oppressed and by the oppressors. In terms of ethics, both forms of violence are inhuman and
evil—but since when is history made in accordance with ethical standards? To start applying them at the point where the oppressed rebel
against the oppressors, the have-nots against the haves is serving the
cause of actual violence by weakening the protest against it.

> Comprenez enfin ceci: si la violence a commencé ce soir, si l'ex-
> ploitation ni l'oppression n'ont jamais existé sur terre, peut-être la
> non-violence affichée peut apaiser la querelle. Mais si le régime
> tout entier et jusqu'à vos non-violentes pensées sont conditionnées
> par une oppression millénaire, votre passivité ne sert qu'à vous
> ranger du côté des oppresseurs.[3]

The very notion of false tolerance, and the distinction between
right and wrong limitations on tolerance, between progressive and regressive indoctrination, revolutionary and reactionary violence demand the statement of criteria for its validity. These standards must be
prior to whatever constitutional and legal criteria are set up and applied
in an existing society (such as "clear and present danger," and other established definitions of civil rights and liberties), for such definitions
themselves presuppose standards of freedom and repression as applicable or not applicable in the respective society: they are specifications of
more general concepts. By whom, and according to what standards, can
the political distinction between true and false, progressive and regressive (for in this sphere, these pairs are equivalent) be made and its validity be justified? At the outset, I propose that the question cannot be
answered in terms of the alternative between democracy and dictatorship, according to which, in the latter, one individual or group, without
any effective control from below, arrogate to themselves the decision.
Historically, even in the most democratic democracies, the vital and
final decisions affecting the society as a whole have been made, constitutionally or in fact, by one or several groups without effective control
by the people themselves. The ironical question: who educates the ed-
ucators (i.e. the political leaders) also applies to democracy. The only
authentic alternative and negation of dictatorship (with respect to this
question) would be a society in which "the people" have become autonomous individuals, freed from the repressive requirements of a

struggle for existence in the interest of domination, and as such human beings choosing their government and determining their life. Such a society does not yet exist anywhere. In the meantime, the question must be treated *in abstracto* — abstraction, not from the historical possibilities, but from the realities of the prevailing societies.

I suggested that the distinction between true and false tolerance, between progress and regression can be made rationally on empirical grounds. The real possibilities of human freedom are relative to the attained stage of civilization. They depend on the material and intellectual resources available at the respective stage, and they are quantifiable and calculable to a high degree. So are, at the stage of advanced industrial society, the most rational ways of using these resources and distributing the social product with priority on the satisfaction of vital needs and with a minimum of toil and injustice. In other words, it is possible to define the direction in which prevailing institutions, policies, opinions would have to be changed in order to improve the chance of a peace which is not identical with cold war and a little hot war, and a satisfaction of needs which does not feed on poverty, oppression, and exploitation. Consequently, it is also possible to identify policies, opinions, movements which would promote this chance, and those which would do the opposite. Suppression of the regressive ones is a prerequisite for the strengthening of the progressive ones.

The question, who is qualified to make all these distinctions, definitions, identifications for the society as a whole, has now one logical answer, namely, everyone "in the maturity of his faculties" as a human being, everyone who has learned to think rationally and autonomously. The answer to Plato's educational dictatorship is the democratic educational dictatorship of free men. John Stuart Mill's conception of the *res publica* is not the opposite of Plato's: the liberal too demands the authority of Reason not only as an intellectual but also as a political power. In Plato, rationality is confined to the small number of philosopher-kings; in Mill, every rational human being participates in the discussion and decision — but only as a rational being. Where society has entered the phase of total administration and indoctrination, this would be a small number indeed, and not necessarily that of the elected representatives of the people. The problem is not that of an educational dictatorship, but that of breaking the tyranny of public opinion and its makers in the closed society.

However, granted the empirical rationality of the distinction between progress and regression, and granted that it may be applicable to
tolerance, and may justify strongly discriminatory tolerance on political
grounds (cancellation of the liberal creed of free and equal discussion),
another impossible consequence would follow. I said that, by virtue of
its inner logic, withdrawal of tolerance from regressive movements, and
discriminatory tolerance in favor of progressive tendencies would be
tantamount to the "official" promotion of subversion. The historical
calculus of progress (which is actually the calculus of the prospective
reduction of cruelty, misery, suppression) seems to involve the calcu-
lated choice between two forms of political violence: that on the part of
the legally constituted powers (by their legitimate action, or by their
tacit consent, or by their inability to prevent violence), and that on the
part of potentially subversive movements. Moreover, with respect to
the latter, a policy of unequal treatment would protect radicalism on
the Left against that on the Right. Can the historical calculus be reasonably extended to the justification of one form of violence as against
another? Or better (since "justification" carries a moral connotation), is
there historical evidence to the effect that the social origin and impetus
of violence (from among the ruled or the ruling classes, the have or
the have-nots, the Left or the Right) is in a demonstrable relation to
progress (as defined above)?

With all the qualifications of a hypothesis based on an "open" historical record, it seems that the violence emanating from the rebellion
of the oppressed classes broke the historical continuum of injustice,
cruelty, and silence for a brief moment, brief but explosive enough to
achieve an increase in the scope of freedom and justice, and a better and more equitable distribution of misery and oppression in a new
social system—in one word: progress in civilization. The English civil
wars, the French Revolution, the Chinese and the Cuban Revolutions
may illustrate the hypothesis. In contrast, the one historical change
from one social system to another, marking the beginning of a new period in civilization, which was *not* sparked and driven by an effective
movement "from below," namely, the collapse of the Roman Empire in
the West, brought about a long period of regression for long centuries,
until a new, higher period of civilization was painfully born in the violence of the heretic revolts of the thirteenth century and in the peasant
and laborer revolts of the fourteenth century.[4]

With respect to historical violence emanating from among ruling classes, no such relation to progress seems to obtain. The long series of dynastic and imperialist wars, the liquidation of Spartacus in Germany in 1919, Fascism and Nazism did not break but rather tightened and streamlined the continuum of suppression. I said emanating "from among ruling classes": to be sure, there is hardly any organized violence from above that does not mobilize and activate mass support from below; the decisive question is, on behalf of and in the interest of which groups and institutions is such violence released? And the answer is not necessarily ex post: in the historical examples just mentioned, it could be and was anticipated whether the movement would serve the revamping of the old order or the emergence of the new.

Liberating tolerance, then, would mean intolerance against movements from the Right, and toleration of movements from the Left. As to the scope of this tolerance and intolerance: . . . it would extend to the stage of actions as well as of discussion and propaganda, of deed as well as of word. The traditional criterion of clear and present danger seems no longer adequate to a stage where the whole society is in the situation of the theater audience when somebody cries: "fire." It is a situation in which the total catastrophe could be triggered off any moment, not only by a technical error, but also by a rational miscalculation of risks, or by a rash speech of one of the leaders. In past and different circumstances, the speeches of the Fascist and Nazi leaders were the immediate prologue to the massacre. The distance between the propaganda and the action, between the organization and its release on the people had become too short. But the spreading of the word could have been stopped before it was too late: if democratic tolerance had been withdrawn when the future leaders started their campaign, mankind would have had a chance of avoiding Auschwitz and a World War.

The whole post-fascist period is one of clear and present danger. Consequently, true pacification requires the withdrawal of tolerance before the deed, at the stage of communication in word, print, and picture. Such extreme suspension of the right of free speech and free assembly is indeed justified only if the whole of society is in extreme danger. I maintain that our society is in such an emergency situation, and that it has become the normal state of affairs. Different opinions and "philosophies" can no longer compete peacefully for adherence and persuasion on rational grounds: the "marketplace of ideas" is organized and delimited by those who determine the national and the individual interest. In this society, for which the ideologists have proclaimed the "end of ideology," the false consciousness has become the general consciousness—from the government down to its last objects. The small and powerless minorities which struggle against the false consciousness and its beneficiaries must be helped: their continued existence is more important than the preservation of abused rights and liberties which grant constitutional powers to those who oppress these minorities. It should be evident by now that the exercise of civil rights by those who don't have them presupposes the withdrawal of civil rights from those who prevent their exercise, and that liberation of the Damned of the Earth presupposes suppression not only of their old but also of their new masters.

Withdrawal of tolerance from regressive movements *before* they can become active; intolerance even toward thought, opinion, and word, and finally, intolerance in the opposite direction, that is, toward the self-styled conservatives, to the political Right—these anti-democratic notions respond to the actual development of the democratic society which has destroyed the basis for universal tolerance. The conditions under which tolerance can again become a liberating and humanizing force have still to be created. When tolerance mainly serves the protection and preservation of a repressive society, when it serves to neutralize opposition and to render men immune against other and better forms of life, then tolerance has been perverted. And when this perversion starts in the mind of the individual, in his consciousness, his needs, when heteronomous interests occupy him before he can experience his servitude, then the efforts to counteract his dehumanization must begin at the place of entrance, there where the false consciousness takes form (or rather: is systematically formed)—it must begin with stopping the words and images which feed this consciousness. To be sure, this is censorship, even precensorship, but openly directed against the more or less hidden censorship that permeates the free media. Where the false consciousness has become prevalent in national and popular behavior, it translates itself almost immediately into practice: the safe distance between ideology and reality, repressive thought and repressive action, between the word of destruction and the deed of destruction is

dangerously shortened. Thus, the break through the false consciousness may provide the Archimedean point for a larger emancipation—at
an infinitesimally small spot, to be sure, but it is on the enlargement of
such small spots that the chance of change depends.

The forces of emancipation cannot be identified with any social
class which, by virtue of its material condition, is free from false consciousness. Today, they are hopelessly dispersed throughout the society,
and the fighting minorities and isolated groups are often in opposition
to their own leadership. In the society at large, the mental space for denial and reflection must first be re-created. Repulsed by the concreteness of the administered society, the effort of emancipation becomes
"abstract"; it is reduced to facilitating the recognition of what is going
on, to freeing language from the tyranny of the Orwellian syntax and
logic, to developing the concepts that comprehend reality. More than
ever, the proposition holds true that progress in freedom demands
progress in the *consciousness* of freedom. Where the mind has been
made into a subject-object of politics and policies, intellectual autonomy, the realm of "pure" thought has become a matter of *political education* (or rather: counter-education).

This means that previously neutral, value-free, formal aspects of
learning and teaching now become, on their own grounds and in their
own right, political: learning to know the facts, the whole truth, and to
comprehend it is radical criticism throughout, intellectual subversion.
In a world in which the human faculties and needs are arrested or perverted, autonomous thinking leads into a "perverted world": contradiction and counter-image of the established world of repression. And this
contradiction is not simply stipulated, is not simply the product of con-
fused thinking or fantasy, but is the logical development of the given,
the existing world. To the degree to which this development is actually
impeded by the sheer weight of a repressive society and the necessity of
making a living in it, repression invades the academic enterprise itself,
even prior to all restrictions on academic freedom. The pre-empting of
the mind vitiates impartiality and objectivity: unless the student learns
to think in the opposite direction, he will be inclined to place the facts
into the predominant framework of values. Scholarship, i.e. the acquisition and communication of knowledge, prohibits the purification and
isolation of facts from the context of the whole truth. An essential part

of the latter is recognition of the frightening extent to which history was made and recorded by and for the victors, that is, the extent to which history was the development of oppression. And this oppression is in the facts themselves which it establishes; thus they themselves carry a negative value as part and aspect of their facticity. To treat the great crusades *against* humanity (like that against the Albigensians) with the same impartiality as the desperate struggles *for* humanity means neutralizing their opposite historical function, reconciling the executioners with their victims, distorting the record. Such spurious neutrality serves to reproduce acceptance of the dominion of the victors in the consciousness of man. Here, too, in the education of those who are not yet maturely integrated, in the mind of the young, the ground for liberating tolerance is still to be created.

Education offers still another example of spurious, abstract tolerance in the guise of concreteness and truth: it is epitomized in the concept of self-actualization. From the permissiveness of all sorts of license to the child, to the constant psychological concern with the personal problems of the student, a large-scale movement is under way against the evils of repression and the need for being oneself. Frequently brushed aside is the question as to what has to be repressed before one can be a self, oneself. The individual potential is first a negative one, a portion of the potential of his society: of aggression, guilt feeling, ignorance, resentment, cruelty which vitiate his life instincts. If the identity of the self is to be more than the immediate realization of this potential (undesirable for the individual as human being), then it requires repression and sublimation, conscious transformation. This process involves at each stage (to use the ridiculed terms which here reveal their succinct concreteness) the negation of the negation, mediation of the immediate, and identity is no more and no less than this process. "Alienation" is the constant and essential element of identity, the objective side of the subject—and not, as it is made to appear today, a disease, a psychological condition. Freud well knew the difference between progressive and regressive, liberating and destructive repression. The publicity of self-actualization promotes the removal of the one and the other, it promotes existence in that immediacy which, in a repressive society, is (to use another Hegelian term) bad immediacy (*schlechte Unmittelbarkeit*). It isolates the individual from the one dimension where he could "find himself": from his political existence, which is at the core of his entire existence. Instead, it encourages non-conformity and letting go in ways which leave the real engines of repression in the society entirely intact, which even strengthen these engines by substituting the satisfactions of private and personal rebellion for a more than private and personal, and therefore more authentic, opposition. The desublimation involved in this sort of self-actualization is itself repressive inasmuch as it weakens the necessity and the power of the intellect, the catalytic force of that unhappy consciousness which does not revel in the archetypal personal release of frustration—hopeless resurgence of the Id which will sooner or later succumb to the omnipresent rationality of the administered world—but which recognizes the horror of the whole in the most private frustration and actualizes itself in this recognition.

I have tried to show how the changes in advanced democratic societies, which have undermined the basis of economic and political liberalism, have also altered the liberal function of tolerance. The tolerance which was the great achievement of the liberal era is still professed and (with strong qualifications) practiced, while the economic and political process is subjected to an ubiquitous and effective administration in accordance with the predominant interests. The result is an objective contradiction between the economic and political structure on the one side, and the theory and practice of toleration on the other. The altered social structure tends to weaken the effectiveness of tolerance toward dissenting and oppositional movements and to strengthen conservative and reactionary forces. Equality of tolerance becomes abstract, spurious. With the actual decline of dissenting forces in the society, the opposition is insulated in small and frequently antagonistic groups who, even where tolerated within the narrow limits set by the hierarchical structure of society, are powerless while they keep within these limits. But the tolerance shown to them is deceptive and promotes coordination. And on the firm foundations of a coordinated society all but closed against qualitative change, tolerance itself serves to contain such change rather than to promote it.

These same conditions render the critique of such tolerance abstract and academic, and the proposition that the balance between tolerance toward the Right and toward the Left would have to be radically redressed in order to restore the liberating function of tolerance becomes only an unrealistic speculation. Indeed, such a redressing seems to be tantamount to the establishment of a "right of resistance" to the point of subversion. There is not, there cannot be any such right for any group or individual against a constitutional government sustained by a majority of the population. But I believe that there is a "natural right" of resistance for oppressed and overpowered minorities to use extralegal means if the legal ones have proved to be inadequate. Law and order are always and everywhere the law and order which protect the established hierarchy; it is nonsensical to invoke the absolute authority of this law and this order against those who suffer from it and struggle against it—not for personal advantages and revenge, but for their share of humanity. There is no other judge over them than the constituted authorities, the police, and their own conscience. If they use violence, they do not start a new chain of violence but try to break an established one. Since they will be punished, they know the risk, and when they are willing to take it, no third person, and least of all the educator and intellectual, has the right to preach them abstention.

Postscript 1968

Under the conditions prevailing in this country, tolerance does not, and cannot, fulfill the civilizing function attributed to it by the liberal protagonists of democracy, namely, protection of dissent. The progressive historical force of tolerance lies in its extension to those modes and forms of dissent which are not committed to the status quo of society, and not confined to the institutional framework of the established society. Consequently, the idea of tolerance implies the necessity, for the dissenting group or individuals, to become illegitimate if and when the established legitimacy prevents and counteracts the development of dissent. This would be the case not only in a totalitarian society, under a dictatorship, in one-party states, but also in a democracy (representative, parliamentary, or "direct") where the majority does not result from the development of independent thought and opinion but rather from the monopolistic or oligopolistic administration of public opinion, without terror and (normally) without censorship. In such cases, the majority is self-perpetuating while perpetuating the vested interests which *made* it a majority. In its very structure this majority is "closed," petrified; it repels "a priori" any change other than changes within the system. But this means that the majority is no longer justified in claiming the democratic title of the best guardian of the common interest. And such a majority is all but the opposite of Rousseau's "general will": it is composed, not of individuals who, in their political functions, have made effective "abstraction" from their private interests, but, on the contrary, of individuals who have effectively identified their private interests with their political functions. And the representatives of this majority, in ascertaining and executing its will, ascertain and execute the will of the vested interests which have formed the majority. The ideology of democracy hides its lack of substance.

In the United States, this tendency goes hand in hand with the monopolistic or oligopolistic concentration of capital in the formation of public opinion, i.e., of the majority. The chance of influencing, in any effective way, this majority is at a price, in dollars, totally out of reach of the radical opposition. Here too, free competition and exchange of ideas have become a farce. The Left has no equal voice, no equal access to the mass media and their public facilities — not because a conspiracy excludes it, but because, in good old capitalist fashion, it does not have the required purchasing power. And the Left does not have the purchasing power because it is the Left. These conditions impose upon the radical minorities a strategy which is in essence a refusal to allow the continuous functioning of allegedly indiscriminate but in fact discriminate tolerance, for example, a strategy of protesting against the alternate matching of a spokesman for the Right (or Center) with one for the Left. Not "equal" but *more* representation of the Left would be equalization of the prevailing inequality.

Within the solid framework of pre-established inequality and power, tolerance is practiced indeed. Even outrageous opinions are expressed, outrageous incidents are televised; and the critics of established policies are interrupted by the same number of commercials as the conservative advocates. Are these interludes supposed to counteract the sheer weight, magnitude, and continuity of system publicity, indoctrination which operates playfully through the endless commercials as well as through the entertainment?

Given this situation, I suggested in "Repressive Tolerance" the practice of discriminating tolerance in an inverse direction, as a means of shifting the balance between Right and Left by restraining the liberty of the Right, thus counteracting the pervasive inequality of freedom (unequal opportunity of access to the means of democratic persuasion) and strengthening the oppressed against the oppressors. Tolerance would be restricted with respect to movements of a demonstrably aggressive or destructive character (destructive of the prospects for peace, justice, and freedom for all). Such discrimination would also be applied to movements opposing the extension of social legislation to the poor, weak, disabled. As against the virulent denunciations that such a policy would do away with the sacred liberalistic principle of equality for "the other side," I maintain that there are issues where either there is no "other side" in any more than a formalistic sense, or where "the other side" is demonstrably "regressive" and impedes possible improvement of the human condition. To tolerate propaganda for inhumanity vitiates the goals not only of liberalism but of every progressive political philosophy.

I presupposed the existence of demonstrable criteria for aggressive, regressive, destructive forces. If the final democratic criterion of the declared opinion of the majority no longer (or rather not yet) prevails, if vital ideas, values, and ends of human progress no longer (or rather not yet) enter, as competing equals, the formation of public opinion, if the people are no longer (or rather not yet) sovereign but "made" by the real sovereign powers—is there any alternative other than the dictatorship of an "elite" over the people? For the opinion of people (usually designated as The People) who are unfree in the very faculties in which liberalism saw the roots of freedom: independent thought and independent speech, can carry no overriding validity and authority—even if The People constitute the overwhelming majority.

If the choice were between genuine democracy and dictatorship, democracy would certainly be preferable. But democracy does not prevail. The radical critics of the existing political process are thus readily denounced as advocating an "elitism," a dictatorship of intellectuals as an alternative. What we have in fact is government, representative government by a non-intellectual minority of politicians, generals, and businessmen. The record of this "elite" is not very promising, and political prerogatives for the intelligentsia may not necessarily be worse for the society as a whole.

In any case, John Stuart Mill, not exactly an enemy of liberal and representative government, was not so allergic to the political leadership of the intelligentsia as the contemporary guardians of semi-democracy are. Mill believed that "individual mental superiority" justifies "reckoning one person's opinion as equivalent to more than one":

> Until there shall have been devised, and until opinion is willing to accept, some mode of plural voting which may assign to education as such the degree of superior influence due to it, and sufficient as a counterpoise to the numerical weight of the least educated class, for so long the benefits of completely universal suffrage cannot be obtained without bringing with them, as it appears to me, more than equivalent evils.[5]

"Distinction in favor of education, right in itself," was also supposed to preserve "the educated from the class legislation of the uneducated," without enabling the former to practice a class legislation of their own.[6]

Today, these words have understandably an anti-democratic, "elitist" sound — understandably because of their dangerously radical implications. For if "education" is more and other than training, learning, preparing for the existing society, it means not only enabling man to know and understand the facts which make up reality but also to know and understand the factors that establish the facts so that he can change their inhuman reality. And such humanistic education would involve the "hard" sciences ("hard" as in the "hardware" bought by the Pentagon?), would free them from their destructive direction. In other words, such education would indeed badly serve the Establishment, and to give political prerogatives to the men and women thus educated would indeed be anti-democratic in the terms of the Establishment. But these are not the only terms.

However, the alternative to the established semi-democratic process is *not* a dictatorship or elite, no matter how intellectual and intelligent, but the struggle for a real democracy. Part of this struggle is the fight against an ideology of tolerance which, in reality, favors and fortifies the conservation of the status quo of inequality and discrimination. For this struggle, I proposed the practice of discriminating tolerance. To be sure, this practice already presupposes the radical goal which it seeks to achieve. I committed this *petitio principii* in order to combat the pernicious ideology that tolerance is already institutionalized in this society. The tolerance which is the life element, the token of a free society, will never be the gift of the powers that be; it can, under the prevailing conditions of tyranny by the majority, only be won in the sustained effort of radical minorities, willing to break this tyranny and to work for the emergence of a free and sovereign majority—minorities intolerant, militantly intolerant and disobedient to the rules of behavior which tolerate destruction and suppression.

Notes

1. Edgar Wind, *Art and Anarchy* (New York: Knopf, 1964), p. 101.

2. I wish to reiterate for the following discussion that, *de facto*, tolerance is *not* indiscriminate and "pure" even in the most democratic society. The "background limitations" stated on page 35 restrict tolerance before it begins to operate. The antagonistic structure of society rigs the rules of the game. Those who stand against the established system are a priori at a disadvantage, which is not removed by the toleration of their ideas, speeches, and newspapers.

3. Sartre, Preface to Frantz Fanon, *Les Damnés de la Terre,* (Paris: Maspéro, 1961), p. 22.

4. In modern times, fascism has been a consequence of the transition to industrial society *without* a revolution. See Barrington Moore's *Social Origins of Dictatorship and Democracy* (Boston: Beacon Press, 1966).

5. *Considerations on Representative Government* (Chicago: Gateway Edition, 1962), p. 183.

6. Ibid., p. 181.

PART II

Marxism, Existentialism, and Psychoanalysis

A NOTE ON DIALECTIC (1960)

Reason and Revolution: Hegel and the Rise of Social Theory, published in 1941, was Marcuse's first book in English. He wrote a new preface, "A Note on Dialectic," in 1960, and in the introductory paragraph he calls dialectic "the power of negative thinking"—among other things, an oblique reference to a well-known book called *The Power of Positive Thinking* by populist American preacher Norman Vincent Peale. The "negative" in this context refers to the potentialities of human beings and their society. It is negative because it contradicts the given organization of society and is in fact excluded by the "positive," i.e. that which has been achieved so far. Progress requires recognition of the negative as a force and a reality.

   This short essay is a *tour de force,* a clear exposition of the underlying basis of Hegel's philosophical method. It will help the reader to better follow Marcuse's account of Marx's thoroughgoing engagement with Hegel's thought, in the essay "Foundations of Historical Materialism," as well as many of the other essays by Marcuse collected in this volume. It will also aid the reader in understanding one of Marcuse's key ideas throughout his life: his blending of Marx and Hegel in his account of human freedom.

This book was written in the hope that it would make a small contribution to the revival, not of Hegel, but of a mental faculty which is in danger of being obliterated: the power of negative thinking. As Hegel defines it: "Thinking is, indeed, essentially the negation of that which is immediately before us." What does he mean by "negation," the central category of dialectic?

Even Hegel's most abstract and metaphysical concepts are saturated with experience—experience of a world in which the unreasonable becomes reasonable and, as such, determines the facts; in which unfreedom is the condition of freedom, and war the guarantor of peace. This world contradicts itself. Common sense and science purge themselves from this contradiction; but philosophical thought begins with the recognition that the facts do not correspond to the concepts imposed by common sense and scientific reason—in short, with the refusal to accept them. To the extent that these concepts disregard the fatal contradictions which make up reality, they abstract from the very process of reality. The negation which dialectic applies to them is not only a critique of a conformistic logic, which denies the reality of contradictions; it is also a critique of the given state of affairs on its own grounds—of the established system of life, which denies its own promises and potentialities.

Today, this dialectical mode of thought is alien to the whole established universe of discourse and action. It seems to belong to the past and to be rebutted by the achievements of technological civilization. The established reality seems promising and productive enough to repel or absorb all alternatives. Thus acceptance—and even affirmation —of this reality appears to be the only reasonable methodological principle. Moreover, it precludes neither criticism nor change; on the contrary, insistence on the dynamic character of the status quo, on its constant "revolutions," is one of the strongest props for this attitude. Yet this dynamic seems to operate endlessly within the same framework of life: streamlining rather than abolishing the domination of man, both by man and by the products of his labor. Progress becomes quantitative and tends to delay indefinitely the turn from quantity to quality—that is, the emergence of new modes of existence with new forms of reason and freedom.

The power of negative thinking is the driving power of dialectical thought, used as a tool for analyzing the world of facts in terms of its internal inadequacy. I choose this vague and unscientific formulation in order to sharpen the contrast between dialectical and undialectical thinking. "Inadequacy" implies a value judgment. Dialectical thought invalidates the a priori opposition of value and fact by understanding all facts as stages of a single process—a process in which subject and object are so joined that truth can be determined only within the subject-object totality. All facts embody the knower as well as the doer; they continuously translate the past into the present. The objects thus "contain" subjectivity in their very structure.

Now what (or who) is this subjectivity that, in a literal sense, constitutes the objective world? Hegel answers with a series of terms denoting the subject in its various manifestations: Thought, Reason, Spirit, Idea. Since we no longer have that fluent access to these concepts which the eighteenth and nineteenth centuries still had, I shall try to sketch Hegel's conception in more familiar terms:

Nothing is "real" which does not sustain itself in existence, in a life-and-death struggle with the situations and conditions of its existence. The struggle may be blind or even unconscious, as in inorganic matter; it may be conscious and concerted, such as the struggle of mankind with its own conditions and with those of nature. *Reality* is the constantly renewed result of the process of existence—the process, conscious or unconscious in which "that which is" becomes "other than itself"; and *identity* is only the continuous negation of inadequate existence, the subject maintaining itself in being other than itself. Each reality, therefore, is a *realization*—a development of "subjectivity." The latter "comes to itself" in history, where the development has a rational content; Hegel defines it as "progress in the consciousness of freedom."

Again a value judgment—and this time a value judgment imposed upon the world as a whole. But freedom is for Hegel an ontological category: it means being not a mere object, but the subject of one's existence, not succumbing to external conditions, but transforming factuality into realization. This transformation is, according to Hegel, the energy of nature and history, the inner structure of all being! One may be tempted to scoff at this idea, but one should be aware of its implications.

Dialectical thought starts with the experience that the world is un-free; that is to say, man and nature exist in conditions of alienation, ex-ist as "other than they are." Any mode of thought which excludes this contradiction from its logic is a faulty logic. Thought "corresponds" to reality only as it transforms reality by comprehending its contradictory structure. Here the principle of dialectic drives thought beyond the limits of philosophy. For to comprehend reality means to comprehend what things really are, and this in turn means rejecting their mere fac-tuality. Rejection is the process of thought as well as of action. While the scientific method leads from the immediate experience of *things* to their mathematical-logical structure, philosophical thought leads from the immediate experience of *existence* to its historical structure: the principle of freedom.

Freedom is the innermost dynamic of existence, and the very process of existence in an unfree world is "the continuous negation of that which threatens to deny *(aufheben)* freedom." Thus freedom is es-sentially negative: existence is both alienation and the process by which the subject comes to itself in comprehending and mastering alienation. For the history of mankind, this means attainment of a "state of the world" in which the individual persists in inseparable harmony with the whole, and in which the conditions and relations of his world "pos-sess no essential objectivity independent of the individual." As to the prospect of attaining such a state, Hegel was pessimistic: the element of reconciliation with the established state of affairs, so strong in his work, seems to a great extent due to this pessimism—or, if one prefers, this realism. Freedom is relegated to the realm of pure thought, to the Absolute Idea. Idealism by default: Hegel shares this fate with the main philosophical tradition.

Dialectical thought thus becomes negative in itself. Its function is to break down the self-assurance and self-contentment of common sense, to undermine the sinister confidence in the power and language of facts, to demonstrate that unfreedom is so much at the core of things that the development of their internal contradictions leads necessarily to qualitative change: the explosion and catastrophe of the established state of affairs. Hegel sees the task of knowledge as that of recognizing the world as Reason by understanding all objects of thought as ele-ments and aspects of a totality which becomes a conscious world in the history of mankind. Dialectical analysis ultimately tends to become historical analysis, in which nature itself appears as part and stage in its own history and in the history of man. The progress of cognition from common sense to knowledge arrives at a world which is negative in its very structure because that which is real opposes and denies the potentialities inherent in itself—potentialities which themselves strive for realization. Reason is the negation of the negative.

Interpretation of that-which-is in terms of that-which-is-not, confrontation of the given facts with that which they exclude—this has been the concern of philosophy wherever philosophy was more than a matter of ideological justification or mental exercise. The liberating function of negation in philosophical thought depends upon the recognition that the negation is a positive act: that-which-is *repels* that-which-is-not and, in doing so, repels its own real possibilities. Consequently, to express and define that-which-is on its own terms is to distort and falsify reality. Reality is other and more than that codified in the logic and language of facts. Here is the inner link between dialectical thought and the effort of avant-garde literature: the effort to break the power of facts over the word, and to speak a language which is not the language of those who establish, enforce, and benefit from the facts. As the power of the given facts tends to become totalitarian, to absorb all opposition, and to define the entire universe of discourse, the effort to speak the language of contradiction appears increasingly irrational, obscure, artificial. The question is not that of a direct or indirect influence of Hegel on the genuine avant-garde, though this is evident in Mallarmé and Villiers de l'Isle-Adam, in surrealism, in Brecht. Dialectic and poetic language meet, rather, on common ground.

The common element is the search for an "authentic language"— the language of negation as the Great Refusal to accept the rules of a game in which the dice are loaded. The absent must be made present because the greater part of the truth is in that which is absent. This is Mallarmé's classical statement:

Je dis: une fleur! et, hors de l'oubli où ma voix relègue aucun contour, en tant que quelque chose d'autre que les calices sus, musicalement se lève, idée même et suave, l'absente de tous bouquets.

I say: a flower! and, out of the oblivion where my voice banishes all contours, musically rises, different from every known blossom, the one absent from all bouquets—Idea itself and delicate.

In the authentic language, the word

n'est pas l'expression d'une chose, mais l'absence de cette chose. . . .
Le mot fait disparaître les choses et nous impose le sentiment d'un
manque universel et même de son propre manque.[1]

is not the expression of a thing, but rather the absence of this thing. . . .
The word makes the things disappear and imposes upon us the feeling of
a universal want and even of its own want.

Poetry is thus the power "de nier les choses" *(to deny the things)* —
the power which Hegel claims, paradoxically, for all authentic thought.
Valéry asserts:

La pensée est, en somme, le travail qui fait vivre en nous ce qui n'existe pas.[2]

In short, thought is the labor which brings to life in us that which does not
exist.

He asks the rhetorical question: "que sommes-nous donc sans le
secours de ce qui n'existe pas?"[3] *(What are we without the help of that*
which does not exist?)

This is not "existentialism." It is something more vital and more
desperate: the effort to contradict a reality in which all logic and all
speech are false to the extent that they are part of a mutilated whole.
The vocabulary and grammar of the language of contradiction are still
those of the game (there are no others), but the concepts codified in the
language of the game are redefined by relating them to their "determinate negation." This term, which denotes the governing principle of
dialectical thought, can be explained only in a textual interpretation
of Hegel's *Logic*. Here it must suffice to emphasize that, by virtue of
this principle, the dialectical contradiction is distinguished from all
pseudo- and crackpot opposition, beatnik and hipsterism. The negation
is determinate if it refers the established state of affairs to the basic factors and forces which make for its destructiveness, as well as for the possible alternatives beyond the status quo. In the human reality, they are
historical factors and forces, and the determinate negation is ultimately
a *political* negation. As such, it may well find authentic expression in
nonpolitical language, and the more so as the entire dimension of politics becomes an integral part of the status quo.

Dialectical logic is critical logic: it reveals modes and contents of thought which transcend the codified pattern of use and validation. Dialectical thought does not invent these contents; they have accrued to the notions in the long tradition of thought and action. Dialectical analysis merely assembles and reactivates them; it recovers tabooed meanings and thus appears almost as a return, or rather a conscious liberation, of the repressed! Since the established universe of discourse is that of an unfree world, dialectical thought is necessarily destructive, and whatever liberation it may bring is a liberation in thought, in theory. However, the divorce of thought from action, of theory from practice, is itself part of the unfree world. No thought and no theory can undo it; but theory may help to prepare the ground for their possible reunion, and the ability of thought to develop a logic and language of contradiction is a prerequisite for this task.

In what, then, lies the power of negative thinking? Dialectical thought has not hindered Hegel from developing his philosophy into a neat and comprehensive system which, in the end, accentuates the positive emphatically. I believe it is the idea of Reason itself which is the undialectical element in Hegel's philosophy. This idea of Reason comprehends everything and ultimately absolves everything, because it has its place and function in the whole, and the whole is beyond good and evil, truth and falsehood. It may even be justifiable, logically as well as historically, to define Reason in terms which include slavery, the Inquisition, child labor, concentration camps, gas chambers, and nuclear preparedness. These may well have been integral parts of that rationality which has governed the recorded history of mankind. If so, the idea of Reason itself is at stake; it reveals itself as a part rather than as the whole. This does not mean that reason abdicates its claim to confront reality with the truth about reality. On the contrary, when Marxian theory takes shape as a critique of Hegel's philosophy, it does so in the name of Reason. It is consonant with the innermost effort of Hegel's thought if his own philosophy is "cancelled," not by substituting for Reason some extrarational standards, but by driving Reason itself to recognize the extent to which it is still unreasonable, blind, the victim of unmastered forces. Reason, as the developing and applied knowledge of man — as "free thought" — was instrumental in creating the world we live in. It was also instrumental in sustaining injustice, toil, and suffering. But Reason, and Reason alone, contains its own corrective.

In the *Logic*, which forms the first part of his *System of Philosophy*, Hegel anticipates almost literally Wagner's Parsifal message: "the hand that inflicts the wound is also the hand that heals it." [4] The context is the biblical story of the Fall of Man. Knowledge may have caused the wound in the existence of man, the crime and the guilt; but the second innocence, the "second harmony," can be gained only from knowledge. Redemption can never be the work of a "guileless fool." Against the various obscurantists who insist on the right of the irrational versus reason, on the truth of the natural versus the intellect, Hegel inseparably links progress in freedom to progress in thought, action to theory. Since he accepted the specific historical form of Reason reached at his time as *the* reality of Reason, the advance beyond this form of Reason must be an advance of Reason itself; and since the adjustment of Reason to oppressive social institutions perpetuated unfreedom, progress in freedom depends on thought becoming political, in the shape of a theory which demonstrates negation as a political alternative implicit in the historical situation. Marx's materialistic "subversion" of Hegel, therefore, was not a shift from one philosophical position to another, nor from philosophy to social theory, but rather a recognition that the established forms of life were reaching the stage of their historical negation.

This historical stage has changed the situation of philosophy and of all cognitive thought. From this stage on, all thinking that does not testify to an awareness of the radical falsity of the established forms of life is faulty thinking. Abstraction from this all-pervasive condition is not merely immoral; it is false. For reality has become technological reality, and the subject is now joined with the object so closely that the notion of object necessarily includes the subject. Abstraction from their interrelation no longer leads to a more genuine reality but to deception, because even in this sphere the subject itself is apparently a constitutive part of the object as scientifically determined. The observing, measuring, calculating subject of scientific method, and the subject of the daily business of life—both are expressions of the same subjectivity: man. One did not have to wait for Hiroshima in order to have one's eyes opened to this identity. And as always before, the subject that has conquered matter suffers under the dead weight of his conquest. Those who enforce and direct this conquest have used it to create a world in which the increasing comforts of life and the ubiquitous power of the productive apparatus keep man enslaved to the prevailing state of affairs. Those social groups which dialectical theory identified as the forces of negation are either defeated or reconciled with the established system. Before the power of the given facts, the power of negative thinking stands condemned.

This power of facts is an oppressive power; it is the power of man over man, appearing as objective and rational condition. Against this appearance, thought continues to protest in the name of truth. And in the name of fact: for it is the supreme and universal fact that the status quo perpetuates itself through the constant threat of atomic destruction, through the unprecedented waste of resources, through mental impoverishment, and—last but not least—through brute force. These are the unresolved contradictions. They define every single fact and every single event; they permeate the entire universe of discourse and action. Thus they define also the logic of things: that is, the mode of thought capable of piercing the ideology and of comprehending reality whole. No method can claim a monopoly of cognition, but no method seems authentic which does not recognize that these two propositions are meaningful descriptions of our situation: "The whole is the truth," and the whole is false.

Notes

1. Maurice Blanchot, "Le Paradoxe d'Aytre," *Les Temps Modernes* (June 1946), p. 1580ff.

2. *Oeuvres*, Bibliothèque de la Pleiade, vol. I, p. 1333.

3. Ibid., p. 966.

4. *The Logic of Hegel*, trans. W. Wallace, (Oxford: Clarendon Press, 1895), p. 55.

THE FOUNDATIONS OF HISTORICAL
MATERIALISM (1932)

"Historical Materialism" is one of the synonyms used for the writings of Karl Marx (1818–1883). What befell Marx is similar to many other cases where an individual thinker's works were converted by his followers into an overly simplistic "doctrine." One reason that the doctrine was simplistic is that two of Marx's key writings remained unknown and unpublished until long after his death: one, the *Economic and Philosophical Manuscripts of 1844,* first published in 1932, and the other, the *Grundrisse,* resurrected in 1939–41 but not widely known until 1953, a full seventy years after the author's death.

This early text of Marcuse, written in 1932, was one of the first reviews of the newly discovered *Economic and Philosophical Manuscripts,* and it still shows the influence of Heidegger on his thinking. It is here that Marx introduces the concept of "alienation" that became a controversial basis for humanistic Marxism in Western Europe. In 1844 Marx was still following Feuerbach in arguing for a naturalism based not on science but on the immediate relation to nature. Marx's innovation was to analyze this relation as labor and to thus open the way to the economic analysis of his later works. His Heideggerian background helped Marcuse to see beyond the economic implications of the text to Marx's ontological interpretation of labor.

For the early Marx labor is not simply one among many human activities but is the very essence of what it is to be human. Following Hegel, Marx argues that labor is the process of "objectification," wherein human activity first "loses itself" in engaging the world of nature to satisfy needs,

72

becoming entrapped and mystified by its own activity, and inadvertently reinforcing the structures of political oppression. Human fulfillment requires the creative expression of the individual at work, the free objectification of human faculties and needs in the natural world. Where creative labor characterizes human life generally, and not just the lives of a privileged few, it brings forth a world rich in meaning and beauty. Under capitalism, however, labor is alienated and reduced to a struggle for survival. Not only is the individual laborer impoverished, but also the human senses are blunted and experience impoverished as well.

Translator's note: This essay first appeared as "Neue Quellen zur Grundlegung des Historischen Materialismus" in *Die Gesellschaft* (Berlin) in 1932, as a review of Marx's newly published *Economic and Philosophical Manuscripts of 1844.* Marcuse quotes a great deal from the *Manuscripts,* and in order to make the source of these quotations available to the English-speaking reader I have given page references to the translation by Martin Milligan (Karl Marx, *Economic and Philosophical Manuscripts of 1844,* Lawrence and Wishart, London, 1970).

• • •

The publication of the *Economic and Philosophical Manuscripts* written by Marx in 1844[1] must become a crucial event in the history of Marxist studies. These manuscripts could put the discussion about the origins and original meaning of historical materialism, and the entire theory of "scientific socialism," on a new footing. They also make it possible to pose the question of the actual connections between Marx and Hegel in a more fruitful and promising way.

Not only does the fragmentary nature of the *Manuscripts* (substantial sections seem to have been lost and the analysis often breaks off at the crucial points; there are no final drafts ready for publication) necessitate a detailed interpretation constantly relating individual passages to the overall context, but the text also demands an exceptionally high level of technical knowledge on the part of the reader. For, if I may anticipate, we are dealing with a philosophical critique of political economy and its philosophical foundation as a theory of revolution.

It is necessary to place such strong emphasis on the difficulties involved right at the outset, in order to avert the danger that these manuscripts will once again be *taken too lightly* and hastily put into the usual compartments and schemata of Marx scholarship. This danger is all the greater because all the familiar categories of the subsequent critique of political economy are already found together in this work. But in the *Economic and Philosophical Manuscripts* the original meaning of the basic categories is clearer than ever before, and it could become necessary to revise the current interpretation of the later and more elaborate critique in the light of its origins. Perhaps this provisional review of the *Manuscripts* will suffice to show the inadequacy of the familiar thesis that Marx developed from providing a philosophical to providing an economic basis for his theory.

We are dealing with a *philosophical* critique of political economy, for the basic categories of Marx's theory here arise out of his emphatic confrontation with the philosophy of Hegel (e.g. labour, objectification, alienation, supersession, property). This does not mean that Hegel's "method" is transformed and taken over, put into a new context and brought to life. Rather, Marx goes back to the problems at the root of Hegel's philosophy (which originally determined his method), independently appropriates their real content and thinks it through to a further stage. The great importance of the new manuscripts further lies in the fact that they contain the first documentary evidence that Marx concerned himself explicitly with Hegel's *Phenomenology of Mind,* "the true point of origin and the secret of the Hegelian philosophy" (p. 173).

If Marx's discussion of the basic problems of Hegel's philosophy informed the foundation of his theory it can no longer be said that this foundation simply underwent a transformation from a philosophical to an economic basis and that in its subsequent (economic) form philosophy had been overcome and "finished" once and for all. Perhaps the foundation includes the philosophical basis in *all* its stages. This is not invalidated by the fact that its sense and purpose are not at all philosophical but practical and revolutionary: the overthrow of the capitalist system through the economic and political struggle of the proletariat. What must be seen and understood is that economics and politics have become the economic-political *basis* of the theory of revolution through a quite particular, philosophical interpretation of human existence and its historical realization. The very complicated relationship between philosophical and economic theory and between this theory and revolutionary praxis, which can only be clarified by an analysis of the whole situation in which historical materialism developed, may become clear after a full interpretation of the *Economic and Philosophical Manuscripts*. I only want to introduce this process in my paper. A rough formula which could be used as a starting point would be that the revolutionary critique of political economy itself has a philosophical foundation, just as, conversely, the philosophy underlying it already contains revolutionary praxis. The theory is in itself a practical one; praxis does not only come at the end but is already present in the beginning of the theory. To engage in praxis is not to tread on alien ground, external to the theory.

With these introductory remarks we can proceed to describe the overall content of the *Manuscripts*. Marx himself describes their purpose as the *critique of political economy*—a "positive" critique, and thus one which, by revealing the mistakes of political economy and its inadequacy for the subject, also provides it with a basis to make it adequate for its task. The positive critique of political economy is thus a critical *foundation* of political economy. Within this critique the idea of political economy is completely transformed: it becomes the science of the necessary conditions for the communist revolution. This revolution itself signifies—quite apart from economic upheavals—a revolution in the whole history of man and the definition of his being: "This communism . . . is the *genuine* resolution of the conflict between man and nature and between man and man—the true resolution of the strife between existence and essence, between objectification and self-confirmation, between freedom and necessity, between the individual and the species. Communism is the riddle of history solved, and it knows itself to be this solution" (p. 135).

If political economy can gain such central importance it is clear that, from a critical point of view, it must be treated from the outset as more than just another science or specialized scientific field. Instead it must be seen as the scientific expression of a problematic which involves the whole being of man. Thus we must begin by considering more closely *what sort of* political economy is here subject to criticism.

Political economy is criticized as the scientific justification or concealment of the total "estrangement" and "devaluation" of human reality represented in capitalist society—as a science which treats man as "something unessential" (p. 130) whose whole existence is determined by the "separation of labour, capital and land," and by an inhuman division of labour, by competition, by private property, etc. (p. 106). This kind of political economy scientifically sanctions the perversion of the historical-social world of man into an alien world of money and commodities; a world which confronts him as a hostile power and in which the greater part of humanity ceases to be anything more than "abstract" workers (torn away from the reality of human existence), separated from the object of their work and forced to sell themselves as a commodity.

As a result of this "alienation" of the worker and of labour, the realization of all man's "essential powers" becomes the loss of their reality; the objective world is no longer "truly human property" appropriated in "free activity" as the sphere of the free operation and self-confirmation of the whole of human nature. It is instead a world of objects in private possession which can be owned, used or exchanged and whose seemingly unalterable laws even man must obey—in short, the universal "domination of dead matter over mankind" (p. 102).

This whole situation has often been described under the headings of "alienation," "estrangement" and "reification" and is a widely known element of Marxist theory. The important point is, however, to see how and from what angle Marx interprets it here at the starting-point of his theory.

At the beginning of his positive critique of political economy, at the point where he takes up the matter of alienation and estrangement, Marx states: "We proceed from an economic fact *of the present*" (p. 107). But are alienation and estrangement "economic facts" like, for example, ground rent or the price of commodities in its dependence on supply and demand or any other "law" of the process of production, consumption and circulation?

Bourgeois political economy, as criticized here, does not regard alienation and estrangement as such as a fact (the circumstances to which these words refer are covered in the bourgeois theory under quite different headings); for socialist political economy this fact will only "exist" if and in so far as the theory is placed on the foundation which Marx worked out in the context of the studies we are discussing. We must therefore ask what sort of fact this is (since it is essentially different from all other facts in political economy), and on what basis it becomes visible and can be described as such.

The description of the circumstance of alienation and estrangement seems initially to proceed completely on the ground of traditional political economy and its theorems. Marx significantly starts by dividing his investigation into the three traditional concepts of political economy: "The Wages of Labour," "The Profit of Capital" and "The Rent of Land." But more important, and a sign pointing in a completely new direction, is the fact that this division into three is soon exploded and abandoned: "From page xxii to the end of the manuscript Marx wrote across the three columns, disregarding the headings. The text of these six pages (xxii–xxvii) is given in the present book under the title, 'Estranged Labour'" (publisher's note, p. 6).

The development of the concept of labour thus breaks through the traditional framework for dealing with problems; the discussion continues with this concept and discovers the new "fact" which then becomes the basis for the science of the communist revolution. Our interpretation must therefore set out from Marx's concept of labour.

When Marx depicts the manner of labour and the form of existence of the worker in capitalist society—complete separation from the means of production and from the product of his labour which has become a commodity, the balancing of wages around the minimum for mere physical survival, the severance of the worker's labour (performed as "forced labour" in the capitalist's service) from his "human reality" —all these features can in themselves still denote simple economic facts. This impression seems to be confirmed by the fact that Marx, "by analysis from the concept of alienated labour," reaches the concept of "private property" (p. 117) and thus the basic concept of traditional political economy.

But if we look more closely at the description of alienated labour we make a remarkable discovery: what is here described is not merely an economic matter. It is the alienation of man, the devaluation of life, the perversion and loss of human reality. In the relevant passage Marx identifies it as follows: "the concept of alienated labour, i.e. of alienated man, of estranged labour, of estranged life, of estranged man" (p. 117).

It is thus a matter of man as man (and not just as worker, economic subject and the like), and of a process not only in economic history but in the history of man and his reality. In the same sense he writes about private property: "Just as *private property* is only the sensuous expression of the fact that man becomes *objective* for himself and at the same time becomes to himself a strange and inhuman object, ... so the positive abolition of private property [is] the sensuous appropriation for and by man of the human essence and of human life" (pp. 138ff.).

It is not because Marx is limited by a particular kind of philosophical terminology that he so often speaks here of "human essential powers" and "man's essential being," or, for example, that he calls "the established objective existence of industry ... the open book of man's essential powers" or wants to grasp its "connection with man's essential being" (p. 142) and, in the places quoted above, uses a *philosophical* framework to describe labour and private property. His interpretation rather attempts to make it clear that the whole critique and foundation of political economy grew explicitly on a philosophical basis and out of a philosophical dispute, and that the philosophical concepts used cannot be regarded as remnants which were later discarded or as a disguise which we can strip off. As the result of an idea about the essence of man and its realization, evolved by Marx in his dispute with Hegel, a simple economic fact appears as the perversion of the human essence and the loss of human reality. *It is only on this foundation* that an economic fact is capable of becoming the real basis of a revolution which will genuinely transform the essence of man and his world.

What we are trying to show is this: from the outset the basic concepts of the critique—alienated labour and private property—are not simply taken up and criticized as economic concepts, but as concepts for a crucial process in human history; consequently the "positive abolition" of private property by the true appropriation of human reality will revolutionize the entire history of mankind. Bourgeois political economy has to be basically transformed in the critique for this very reason: it never gets to see man who is its real subject. It disregards the essence of man and his history and is thus in the profoundest sense not a "science of people" but of non-people and of an inhuman world of objects and commodities. "Crude and thoughtless communism" (p. 133) is just as sharply criticized for the same reason: it too does not centre on the reality of the human essence but operates in the world of things and objects and thus itself remains in a state of "estrangement." This type of communism only replaces individual private property by "universal private property" (p. 132); "it wants to destroy everything which is not capable of being possessed by all as private property. It wants to do away by force with talent, etc. For it, the sole purpose of life and existence is direct, physical possession. The task of the labourer is not done away with, but extended to all men" (pp. 133ff.).

The objections to the absolute economism of Marxist theory, which have been thoughtlessly raised time and again right up to the present day, were already raised here by Marx himself against the crude communism which he opposed: for him the latter is merely the simple "negation" of capitalism and as such exists on the same level as capitalism—but it is precisely that level which Marx wants to abolish.

Before starting our interpretation we need to avert another possible misunderstanding. If Marx's critique of political economy and his foundation of revolutionary theory are here dealt with as *philosophy* this does not mean that thereby "only theoretical" philosophical matters will be included, which minimize the concrete historical situation (of the proletariat in capitalism) and its praxis. The starting point, the basis and the goal of this investigation is precisely the particular historical situation and the praxis which is revolutionizing it. Regarding the situation and praxis from the aspect of the history of man's essence makes the acutely practical nature of the critique even more trenchant and sharp: the fact that capitalist society calls into question not only economic facts and objects but the entire "existence" of man and "human reality" is for Marx the decisive justification for the proletarian revolution as a *total and radical* revolution, unconditionally excluding any partial upheaval or "evolution." The justification does not lie outside or behind the concepts of alienation and estrangement—it is precisely this alienation and estrangement itself. All attempts to dismiss the philosophical content of Marx's theory or to gloss over it in embarrassment reveal a complete failure to recognize the historical origin of the theory: they set out from an essential separation of philosophy, economics and revolutionary praxis, which is a product of the reification against which Marx fought and which he had already overcome at the beginning of his critique.

I

In capitalist society labour not only produces commodities (i.e. goods which can be freely sold on the market), but also produces "itself and the worker as a commodity," the worker becoming "an ever cheaper commodity the more commodities he creates" (pp. 107ff.). The worker not only loses the product of his own labour and creates alien objects for alien people; he is not only "depressed spiritually and physically to the condition of a machine" through the increasing division and mechanization of labour, so that "from being a man [he] becomes an abstract activity and a belly" (p. 68)—but he even has to "sell himself and his human identity" (p. 70), i.e. he must himself become a commodity in order to exist as a physical subject. So instead of being an expression of the whole man, labour is his alienation; instead of being the full and free realization of man it has become a "loss of realization." "So much does labour's realization appear as loss of realization that the worker loses realization to the point of starving to death" (p. 108).

It should be noted that even in this depiction of the "economic fact" of alienated labour the simple economic description is constantly broken through: the economic "condition" of labour is cast back onto the "existence" of the working man (p. 67); beyond the sphere of economic relations the alienation and estrangement of labour concern the essence and reality of man as "man" and only for this reason can the loss of the object of labour acquire such central significance. Marx makes this quite clear when he states that the "fact" he has just described is the "expression" of a more general state of affairs: "This fact expresses merely that the object which labour produces—labour's product—confronts it as something alien, as a power independent of the producer. The product of labour is labour which has been embodied in an object, which has become material: it is the objectification of labour" (p. 108), and when he says: "All these consequences" (of the capitalist economic system) "result from the fact that the worker is related to the product of his labour as to an alien object" (ibid.). The economic fact of estrangement and reification[2] is thus grounded in a particular attitude by man (as a worker) towards the object (of his labour). "Alienated labour" must now be understood in the sense of this kind of relation of man to the object, and no longer as a purely economic condition. "The alienation of the worker in his product means not only that his labour becomes an object, an external existence, but that it exists outside him, independently, as something alien to him, and that it becomes a power on its own confronting him. It means that the life which he has conferred on the object confronts him as something hostile and alien" (pp. 108ff.). And it will further be shown that the economic fact of "private property" too is *grounded* in the situation of alienated labour, understood as the activity of man: "Private property is thus the product, the result, the necessary consequence, of alienated labour, of the external relation of the worker to nature and to himself" (p. 117).

An amazing, idealistic distortion of the actual facts seems to have taken place here: an economic fact is supposed to have its roots in a general concept and in the relation of man to the object. "Private property thus results by analysis from the concept of alienated labour" (ibid.)—this is Marx, not Hegel, writing! The apparent distortion expresses one of the crucial discoveries of Marx's theory: the breakthrough from economic fact to human factors, from fact *(Tat'sache')* to act *(Tat'handlung')*, and the comprehension of fixed "situations" and their laws (which in their reified form are out of man's power) *in motion, in the course of their historical development* (out of which they have fallen and become fixed). (Cf. the programmatic introduction of the new approach to the problem on pp. 118–19). We cannot go into the revolutionary significance of this method here; we shall continue to pursue the line of approach outlined at the beginning.

If the concept of alienated labour includes the relation of man to the object (and, as we shall see, himself) then the concept of labour as such must also cover a human activity (and not an economic condition). And if the alienation of labour signifies the total loss of realization and the estrangement of the human essence then labour itself must be grasped as the real expression and realization of the human essence. But that means once again that it is used as a *philosophical* category. Despite the above development of the subject we would be loath to use the often misused term ontology in connection with Marx's theory, if Marx himself had not expressly used it here: thus he says that only "through the medium of private property does the *ontological* essence of human passion come into being, in its totality as in its humanity,"[3] and he suggests that "man's feelings, passions, etc., are not merely an-

thropological phenomena . . . but truly ontological affirmations of being
(of nature)" (ibid.).[4]

Marx's positive definitions of labour are almost all given as counter-
concepts to the definition of *alienated* labour, and yet the ontological
nature of this concept is clearly expressed in them. We shall extract
three of the most important formulations: "Labour is man's coming-
to-be for himself within alienation, or as alienated man" (p. 177), it is
"man's act of self-creation or self-objectification" (p. 188), "life-activity,
productive life itself" (p. 113). All three of these formulations, even if
they did not occur within the context of Marx's explicit examination of
Hegel, would still point to Hegel's ontological concept of labour.[5] The
basic concept of Marx's critique, the concept of alienated labour, does
in fact arise from his examination of Hegel's category of objectification,
a category developed for the first time in the *Phenomenology of Mind*
around the concept of labour.[6] The *Economic and Philosophical Manuscripts* are direct evidence of the fact that Marx's theory has its roots in
the centre of Hegel's philosophical problematic.

We can deduce the following from these definitions of labour:
labour is "man's act of self-creation," i.e. the activity through and in
which man really first becomes what he is by his nature as man. He
does this in such a way that this becoming and being are there *for
himself*, so that he can know and "regard" himself as what he is (man's
"becoming-for-himself"). Labour is a knowing and conscious activity:
in his labour man relates to himself and to the object of his labour; he
is not directly one with his labour but can, as it were, confront it and
oppose it (through which, as we shall see, human labour fundamentally
distinguishes itself as "universal" and "free" production from the "un-
mediated" production of, for example, the nest-building animal). The
fact that man in his labour is there "for himself" in objective form
is closely related to the second point: man is an "objective" or, more
exactly, an "objectifying" being. Man can only realize his essence if he
realizes it as something *objective*, by using his "essential powers" to produce an "external," "material," objective world. It is in his work in this
world (in the broadest sense) that he is real and effective. "In creating a
world of objects by his practical activity, in his work upon inorganic nature, man proves himself a conscious species being . . . " (p. 113). In this
activity man shows himself as the human being he is according to his

"species" as distinct from animal, vegetable and inorganic being (we will examine the central concept of objectification at a later stage below). Labour, understood in this way, is the specifically human "affirmation of being" in which human existence is realized and confirmed.

Thus even the most provisional and general characterization of Marx's concept of labour has led far beyond the economic sphere into a dimension in which the subject of the investigation is human existence in its totality. The interpretation cannot progress any further before this dimension has been described. We must first answer the question of how and from what starting point Marx defines man's existence and essence. The answer to this question is a prerequisite for understanding what is really meant by the concept of estranged labour and for understanding the whole foundation of revolutionary theory.

II

There are two passages in the *Economic and Philosophical Manuscripts* in which Marx gives an explicit definition of man, encompassing the totality of human existence: on pages 112–14 and 179–83. Even if they are only a sketchy outline, these passages give a clear enough indication of the real basis of Marx's critique. On several occasions (pp. 135, 137, 181) Marx describes "positive communism," which will achieve the abolition of estrangement and reification, as "humanism"—a terminological hint that for him the basis is a particular kind of realization of the human essence. The development of this humanism, as far as it is a positive definition of the human essence, is here primarily influenced by Feuerbach: as early as in the preface we read: "positive criticism as a whole—and therefore also German positive criticism of political economy—owes its true foundation to the discoveries of Feuerbach" (p. 236, note 3), and "it is only with Feuerbach that positive, humanistic and naturalistic criticism begins" (p. 64). Later the "establishment of true materialism and of real science" is described as Feuerbach's "great achievement" (p. 172). In our interpretation, however, we shall not follow the road of philosophical history and trace the development of "humanism" from Hegel through Feuerbach to Marx, but attempt to unfold the problem from Marx's text itself.

"Man is a species being, not only because in practice and in theory he adopts the species as his object (his own as well as those of other things), but—and this is only another way of expressing it—also because he treats himself as the actual, living species; because he treats himself as a *universal* and therefore a free being" (p. 112). The definition of man as a "species being" has done a lot of damage in Marx-scholarship; our passage is so valuable because it exposes the real origins of Marx's concept of "species." Man is a "species being," i.e. a being which has the "species" (his own and that of the rest of existence) as its object. The species of a being is that which this being is according to its "stock" and "origin"; it is the "principle" of its being that is common to all the particular features of what it is: the general essence of this being. If man can make the species of every being into his object, the general essence of every being can become objective for him: he can possess every being as that which it is in its essence. It is for this reason (and this is expressed in the second half of the sentence quoted) that he can *relate* freely to every being: he is not limited to the particular actual state of the being and his immediate relationship to it, but he can take the being as it is in its essence beyond its immediate, particular, actual state; he can recognize and grasp the *possibilities* contained in every being; he can exploit, alter, mould, treat and take further ("produce") any being according to its "inherent standard" (p. 114). Labour, as the specifically human "life activity," has its roots in man's nature as a "species being"; it presupposes man's ability to relate to the "general" aspect of objects and to the possibilities contained in it. Specifically human *freedom* has its roots in man's ability to relate to his *own* species: the self-realization and "self-creation" of man. The relationship of man as a species being to his objects is then more closely defined by means of the concept of free labour (free productions).

Man as a species being is a "universal" being: *every* being can for him become objective in its "species character"; his existence is a universal relationship to objectivity. He has to include these "theoretically" objective things in his praxis; he must make them the object of his "life activity" and work on them. The whole of "nature" is the medium of his human life; it is man's means of life; it is his prerequisite, which he must take up and reintroduce into his praxis. Man cannot simply accept the objective world or merely come to terms with it; he must appropriate it; he has to transform the objects of this world into organs of his life, which becomes effective in and through them. "The universality of man appears in practice precisely in the universality which makes all nature his inorganic body—both inasmuch as nature is (1) his direct means of life and (2) the material, the object, and the instrument of his life activity. Nature is man's inorganic body—nature, that is, in so far as it is not itself the human body" (p. 112).

The thesis of nature as a means for man implies more than merely that man is dependent simply for his physical survival on objective, organic and inorganic nature as a means of life, or that under the direct pressure of his "needs" he "produces" (appropriates, treats, prepares, etc.) the objective world as objects for food, clothing, accommodation, etc. Marx here explicitly speaks of "spiritual, inorganic nature," "spiritual nourishment" and "man's physical and spiritual life" (p. 112). This is why the universality of man—as distinct from the essentially limited nature of animals—is *freedom*, for an animal "produces only under the dominion of immediate physical need" while man "only truly produces in freedom therefrom" (p. 113). An animal thus only produces itself and "what it immediately needs for itself or its young. It produces one-sidedly, whilst man produces universally" (ibid.). Man does not have objects merely as the environment of his immediate life activity and does not treat them merely as objects of his immediate needs. He can "confront" any object and exhaust and realize its inner possibilities in his labour. He can produce "in accordance with the laws of beauty" and not merely in accordance with the standard of his own needs (p. 114). In this freedom man reproduces "the whole of nature," and through transformation and appropriation furthers it, along with his own life, even when this production does not satisfy an immediate need. Thus the history of human life is at the same time essentially the history of man's objective world and of "the whole of nature" ("nature" in the wider sense given to this concept by Marx, as also by Hegel).[7] Man is not *in* nature; nature is not the *external* world into which he first has to come out of his own inwardness. Man *is* nature. Nature is his "expression," "his work and his reality" (p. 114). Wherever we come across nature in human history it is "*human* nature" while man for his part is always "human *nature*" too. We can thus see provisionally to what extent consistent "humanism" is immediately "naturalism" (pp. 135, 181).

On the basis of the unity thus achieved between man and nature

Marx moves towards the crucial definition of *objectification*, through which the specifically human relationship to objectivity, the human way of producing, is more concretely determined as universality and freedom. Objectification—the definition of man as an "objective being"—is not simply a further point appended to the definition of the unity of man and nature, but is the closer and deeper foundation of this unity. (Objectification as such belongs—like his participation in nature—to the essence of man, and can thus not be "superseded"; according to revolutionary theory only a particular form of objectification —reification, "estrangement"—can and must be superseded.)

As a natural being man is an "objective being," which for Marx is a "being equipped and endowed with objective (i.e. material) essential powers" (p. 180), a being who relates to real objects, "acts objectively," and "can only *express* his life in real, sensuous objects" (pp. 181ff.). Because the power of his being thus consists in living out (i.e. through and in external objects) everything he is, his "self-realization" at the same time means "the establishment of a real, objective world, which is overpowering because it has a form external to him and is thus not part of his being" (p. 180). The objective world, as the necessary objectivity of man, through the appropriation and supersession of which his human essence is first "produced" and "confirmed," is part of man himself. It *is* real objectivity only for self-realizing man, it is the "self-objectification" of man, or human objectification. But this same objective world, since it is real objectivity, can appear as a precondition of his being which does *not* belong to his being, is beyond his control, and is "overpowering." This conflict in the human essence—that it is in itself objective—is the root of the fact that objectification can become reification and that externalization can become alienation. It makes it possible for man completely to "lose" the object as part of his essence and let it become independent and overpowering. This possibility becomes a reality in estranged labour and private property.

Marx then attempts to implant objectification and the conflict appearing within it even more deeply into the definition of man. "An objective being...would not act objectively if the quality of objectivity did not reside in the very nature of his being. He creates, posits objects alone, *because* he is posited by objects—because at bottom he is nature" (p. 180). The quality of being posited by objects is, however, the fundamental determinant of "sensuousness" (to have senses, which are affected by objects) and thus Marx can identify objective being with sensuous being, and the quality of having objects outside oneself with the quality of being sensuous: "To be sensuous, i.e. real, is to be an object of the senses, a sensuous object, and therefore to have objects outside oneself which are subject to the operations of one's senses," and this passage: "*To be* objective, natural and sensuous, and at the same time to have object, nature and sense outside oneself, or oneself to be object, nature and sense for a third party, is one and the same thing" (p. 181). (The second identification also included here will be discussed below.) Thereby "sensuousness" for Marx moves into the centre of his philosophical foundation: "Sensuousness (see Feuerbach) must be the basis of all science" (p. 143).

It is already clear from the above deduction that "sensuousness" is here an ontological concept within the definition of man's essence and that it comes before any materialism or sensualism. The concept of sensuousness here taken up by Marx (via Feuerbach and Hegel) goes back to Kant's *Critique of Pure Reason*. There it is said that sensuousness is the human perception through which alone objects are *given* to us. Objects can only be given to man in so far as they "affect" to him. Human sensuousness is affectibility.[8] Human perception as sensuousness is receptive and passive. It receives what it is given, and it is dependent on and needs this quality of being given. To the extent to which man is characterized by sensuousness he is "posited" by objects, and he accepts these prerequisites through cognition. As a sensuous being he is an affixed, passive and suffering being.

In Feuerbach, to whom Marx explicitly refers in the passage quoted, the concept of sensuousness originally tends in the same direction as in Kant. In fact when Feuerbach, in opposition to Hegel, wants to put the receptivity of the senses back at the starting point of philosophy, he initially almost appears as the preserver and defender of Kantian criticism against "absolute idealism." "Existence is something in which not only I, but also the others, and especially the *object*, participate."[9] "Only through the *senses* does an object in the true sense become given — not through thinking for itself"; "an object is given not to my Ego but to my non-Ego, for only where I am passive does the conception of an activity existing outside me, i.e. objectivity, come into being" (ibid., pp. 321ff.).

This accepting, passive being with needs, dependent on given things, which finds its expression in man's sensuousness, is developed by Feuerbach into the "passive principle" (ibid., pp. 257ff.) and placed at the apex of his philosophy—although he goes in a direction quite different from that of Kant. The definition of man as purely a passive being "with needs" is the original basis for Feuerbach's attack on Hegel and his idea of man as a purely free, creative consciousness: "only a passive being is a necessary being. Existence without needs is superfluous existence...A being without distress is a being without ground...A non-passive being is a being without being. A being without suffering is nothing other than a being without sensuousness and matter" (ibid., pp. 256–57).

The same tendency to go back to sensuousness is now also discernible in Marx—a tendency to comprehend man's being defined by needs and his dependence on pre-established objectivity by means of the sensuousness in his own being. This tendency in turn is subject to the aim of achieving a real, concrete picture of man as an objective and natural being, united with the world, as opposed to Hegel's abstract "being," freed from pre-established "naturalness," which posits both itself and all objectivity. In line with Feuerbach, Marx says: "as a natural, corporeal, sensuous, objective being [man] is a *passive*, conditioned and limited creature" (p. 181) and: "To be sensuous is to *be passive*. Man as an objective, sensuous being is therefore a *passive* being—and because he feels what he suffers, a passionate being" (p. 182). Man's passion, his real activity and spontaneity is ascribed to his passivity and neediness, in so far as it is an aspiration to a pre-established object existing outside him: "Passion is the essential force of man energetically bent on its object" (p. 182).[10] And: "The rich man is simultaneously the man *in need of* a totality of human manifestations of life—the man in whom his own realization exists as an inner necessity, as *need*" (p. 144).

We can now understand why Marx emphasizes that "man's feelings, passions, etc....are truly ontological affirmations of being of [nature]" (p. 165). The distress and neediness which appear in man's sensuousness are no more purely matters of cognition than his distress and neediness, as expressed in estranged labour, are purely economic. Distress and neediness here do not describe individual modes of man's behaviour at all; they are features of his whole *existence*. They are ontological categories (we shall therefore return to them in connection with a large number of different themes in these *Manuscripts*).

It was necessary to give such an extensive interpretation of the concept of sensuousness in order to point once again to its real meaning in opposition to its many misinterpretations as the basis of materialism. In developing this concept Marx and Feuerbach were in fact coming to grips with one of the crucial problems of "classical German philosophy." But in Marx it is this concept of sensuousness (as objectification) which leads to the decisive turn from classical German philosophy to the theory of revolution, for he inserts the basic traits of *practical* and *social* existence into his definition of man's essential being. As objectivity, man's sensuousness is essentially practical objectification, and because it is practical it is essentially a social objectification.

III

We know from Marx's *Theses on Feuerbach* that it is precisely the concept of human *praxis* that draws the line of demarcation between himself and Feuerbach. On the other hand, it is through this (or more exactly, through the concept of labour) that he reaches back beyond Feuerbach to Hegel: "The outstanding achievement of Hegel's *Phenomenology* and of its final outcome...is thus...that Hegel...grasps the essence of labour and comprehends objective man—true, because real man—as the outcome of man's own labour" (p. 177). Things are thus not as simple as we would expect; the road from Feuerbach to Marx is not characterized by a straight rejection of Hegel. Instead of this, Marx, at the origins of revolutionary theory, once again appropriates the decisive achievements of Hegel on a transformed basis.

We saw that man's sensuousness signified that he is posited by pre-established objects and therefore also that he *has* a given, objective world, to which he *relates* "universally" and "freely." We must now describe more closely the way in which he possesses and relates to the world.

In Feuerbach man's possession of, and relation to, the world remains essentially theoretical, and this is expressed in the fact that the way of relating, which really permits "possession" of reality, is "perception."[11] In Marx, to put it briefly, labour replaces this perception, although the central importance of the theoretical relation does not disappear: it is combined with labour in a relationship of dialectical interpenetration. We have already suggested above that Marx grasps labour, beyond all its economic significance, as *the* human "life-activity" and the genuine realization of man. We must now present the concept of labour in its inner connection to the definition of man as a "natural" and "sensuous" (objective) being. We shall see how it is in labour that the distress and neediness, but also the universality and freedom of man, become real.

"Man is directly a natural being. As a natural being and as a living natural being he is on the one hand endowed with natural powers of life—he is an *active* natural being. These forces exist in him as tendencies and abilities—as instincts. On the other hand, as a natural, corporeal, sensuous, objective being he is a suffering, conditioned and limited creature.... That is to say, the objects of his instincts exist outside him, as *objects* independent of him; yet these objects are objects that he *needs*—essential objects, indispensable to the manifestation and confirmation of his essential powers" (p. 181). Objects are thus not primarily objects of perception, but of needs, and as such objects of the powers, abilities and instincts of man. It has already been pointed out that "need" is not to be understood only in the sense of physical neediness: man needs "a totality of human manifestations of life" (p. 144). To be able to realize himself he needs to express himself through the preestablished objects with which he is confronted. His activity and his self-affirmation consist in the appropriation of the "externality" which confronts him, and in the transference of himself into that externality. In his labour man supersedes the mere objectivity of objects and makes them into "the means of life." He impresses upon them the form of his being, and makes them into "his work and his reality." The objective piece of finished work *is* the reality of man; man *is* as he has realized himself in the object of his labour. For this reason Marx can say that in the object of his labour man sees himself in objective form, he becomes "for himself," he perceives himself as an object. "The object of labour is, therefore, the objectification of man's species life: for he duplicates himself not only, as in consciousness, intellectually, but also actively, in reality, and therefore he contemplates himself in a world that he has created" (p. 114).

Objectification of the "species life": for it is not the isolated individual who is active in labour, and the objectivity of labour is not objectivity for the isolated individual or a mere plurality of individuals—rather it is precisely in labour that the specifically human *universality* is realized.

Thus we can already discern the second basic characteristic of objectification: it is essentially a "social" activity, and objectifying man is basically "social" man. The sphere of objects in which labour is performed is precisely the sphere of common life-activity: in and through the objects of labour, men are shown *one another* in their reality. The original forms of communication, the essential relationship of men to one another, were expressed in the common use, possession, desire, need and enjoyment, etc. of the objective world. All labour is labour with and for and against others, so that in it men first mutually reveal themselves for what they really are.[12] Thus every object on which a man works in his individuality is "simultaneously his own existence for the other man, the existence of the other man, and that existence for him" (p. 136).

If the objective world is thus understood in its totality as a "social" world, as the objective reality of human society and thus as human objectification, then through this it is also already defined as a *historical* reality. The objective world which is in any given situation preestablished for man is the reality of a past human life, which, although it belongs to the past, is still present in the form it has given to the objective world. A new form of the objective world can thus only come into being on the basis, and through the supersession of an earlier form already in existence. The real human and his world arise first in this movement, which inserts the relevant aspect of the past into the present: "History is the true natural history of man," his "act of origin" (p. 182), "the creation of man through human labour" (p. 145). Not only man emerges in history, but also nature, in so far as it is not something external to and separated from the human essence but belongs to the transcended and appropriated objectivity of man: "world history" is "the emergence of nature for man" (ibid.).

It is only now, after the totality of the human essence as the unity of man and nature has been made concrete by the practical-social-historical process of objectification, that we can understand the defini-

tion of man as a "universal" and "free" species being. The history of
man is at the same time the process of "the whole of nature"; his history
is the "production and reproduction" of the whole of nature, further-
ance of what exists objectively through once again transcending its
current form. In his "universal" relationship[13] to the whole of nature,
therefore, nature is ultimately not a limitation on or something alien
outside him to which he, as something other, is subjected. It is his expression, confirmation, activity: "externality is . . . the *self-externalizing
world of sense* open to the light, open to the man endowed with senses"
(p. 192).

We now want to summarize briefly the definitions brought together
in the concept of man as a universal and free being. Man "relates" to
himself and whatever exists, he can transcend what is given and pre-
established, appropriate it and thus give it his own reality and realize
himself in everything. This freedom does not contradict the distress
and neediness of man, of which we spoke at the beginning, but is
based upon it in so far as it is freedom only as the transcendence of what
is given and pre-established. Man's "life-activity" is "not a determination with which he directly merges" like an animal (p. 113), it is
"free activity," since man can "distinguish" himself from the immediate determination of his existence, "make it into an object" and transcend it. He can turn his existence into a "means" (ibid.), can himself
give himself reality and himself "produce" himself and his "objectivity." It is in this deeper sense (and not only biologically) that we must
understand the sentence that "man produces man" (pp. 136, 137) and
that human life is genuinely "productive" and "life-engendering life"
(p. 113).

Thereby Marx's definition returns to its starting point: the basic
concept of "labour." It is now clear to what extent it was right to deal
with labour as an ontological category. As far as man, through the creation, treatment and appropriation of the objective world, gives himself
his own reality, and as far as his "relationship to the object" is the "manifestation of human reality" (p. 139), labour is the real expression of
human freedom. Man becomes free in his labour. He freely realizes
himself in the object of his labour: "when, for man in society, the objective world everywhere becomes the world of man's essential powers—human reality, and for that reason the reality of his *own* essential

powers—...all objects become for him the objectification of himself, become objects which confirm and realize his individuality, become *his* objects: that is, *man himself* becomes the object" (p. 140).

IV

In the preceding sections we have attempted to present in its context the definition of man underlying the *Economic and Philosophical Manuscripts* and to reveal it as the basis of the critique of political economy. It almost appears, despite all protestations to the contrary, as if we are moving in the field of philosophical investigations, forgetting that these *Manuscripts* are concerned with the foundation of a theory of revolution and hence ultimately with revolutionary *praxis*. But we only need to put the result of our interpretation next to its starting point to find that we have reached the point where the philosophical critique in itself directly becomes a practical revolutionary critique.

The fact from which the critique and the interpretation set out was the alienation and estrangement of the human essence as expressed in the alienation and estrangement of labour, and hence the situation of man in the historical facticity of capitalism. This fact appears as the total *perversion* and *concealment* of what the critique had defined as the essence of man and human labour. Labour is not "free activity" or the universal and free self-realization of man, but his enslavement and loss of reality. The worker is not man in the totality of his life-expression, but a non-person, the purely physical subject of "abstract" activity. The objects of labour are not expressions and confirmations of the human reality of the worker, but alien things, belonging to someone other than the worker—"commodities." Through all this the existence of man does not become, in estranged labour, the "means" for his self-realization. The reverse happens: man's self becomes a means for his mere existence. The pure physical existence of the worker is the goal which his entire life-activity serves. "As a result, therefore, man [the worker] only feels himself freely active in his animal functions—eating, drinking, procreating, or at most in his dwelling and in dressing-up, etc., and in his human functions he no longer feels himself to be anything but an animal. What is animal becomes human and what is human becomes animal" (p. 111).

We have seen that Marx describes this estrangement and loss of reality as the "expression" of a total perversion of the behaviour of man as man: in his relationship to the product of his labour as an "alien object exercising power over him" and simultaneously in the relationship of the worker to his own activity as "an alien activity not belonging to him" (ibid.). This reification is by no means limited to the worker (even though it affects him in a unique way); it also affects the non-worker—the capitalist. The "dominion of dead matter over man" reveals itself for the capitalist in the state of private property and the manner in which he has and possesses it. It is really a state of being possessed, of being had, slavery in the service of property. He possesses his property not as a field of free self-realization and activity but purely as capital: "Private property has made us so stupid and one-sided that an object is only *ours* when we have it—when it exists for us as capital, or when it is directly possessed, eaten, drunk, worn, inhabited, etc.,—in short, when it is *used* by us...the life which they [realizations of possession] serve as means is the life of private property, labour, and conversion into capital" (p. 139). (We shall return to the definition of "true possession" underlying this description of "false property" below.)

If historical facticity thus reveals the total perversion of all the conditions given in the definition of the human essence, does it not prove that this definition lacks content and sense, and that it is only an idealistic abstraction, which does violence to historical reality? We know the cruel derision with which, in his *German Ideology*, which appeared only a year after these *Manuscripts*, Marx destroyed the idle talk of the Hegelians, such people as Stirner and the "true socialists," about *the* essence, *the* man, etc. Did Marx himself, in his definition of the human essence, give in to this idle chatter? Or does a radical change take place in Marx's fundamental views between our *Manuscripts* and the *German Ideology*?

There is indeed a change, even if it is not in his fundamental views. It must be emphasized again and again that in laying the foundations of revolutionary theory Marx is fighting *on various fronts*: on the one hand against the pseudo-idealism of the Hegelian school, on the other against reification in bourgeois political economy, and then again against Feuerbach and pseudo-materialism. The meaning and the purpose of his fight thus varies according to the direction of his attack and defence. Here, where he is principally fighting reification in political economy, which turns a particular kind of historical facticity into rigid "eternal" laws and so-called "essential relationships," Marx presents this facticity in contrast to the real essence of man. But in doing this he brings out its truth, because he grasps it within the context of the real history of man and reveals the necessity of its being overcome.

These changes, then, result from shifts in the terrain of the conflict. But the following point is still more decisive. To play off essence (the determinants of "the" man) and facticity (his given concrete historical situation) against each other is to miss completely the new standpoint which Marx had already assumed at the outset of his investigations. For Marx essence and facticity, the situation of essential history and the situation of factual history, are no longer separate regions or levels independent of each other: the historical experience of man is *taken up into the definition of his essence*. We are no longer dealing with an abstract human essence, which remains equally valid at every stage of concrete history, but with an essence which can be defined in *history* and *only* in history. (It is therefore quite a different matter when Marx speaks of the "essence of man," as opposed to Bruno Bauer, Stirner and Feuerbach!)[14] The fact that despite or precisely because of this it is always man himself that matters in all man's historical praxis is so self-evident that it is not worth discussing for Marx, who grew up in a direct relationship with the most lively period of German philosophy (just as the opposite seems to have become self-evident for the epigones of Marxism). Even in Marx's extremely bitter struggle with German philosophy in the period of its decline, a philosophical impetus lives on which only complete naïveté could misconstrue as a desire to destroy philosophy altogether.

The discovery of the historical character of the human essence does not mean that the history of man's essence can be identified with his factual history. We have already heard that man is never directly "one with his life-activity"; he is, rather, "distinct" from it and "relates" to it. Essence and existence *separate* in him: his existence is a "means" to the realization of his essence, or—in estrangement—his essence is a means to his mere physical existence (p. 113). If essence and existence have thus become separated and if the real and free *task* of human praxis is the unification of both as factual realization, then the authentic task, when facticity has progressed so far as totally to *pervert* the human essence, is the *radical abolition* of this facticity. It is precisely the unerring contemplation of the essence of man that becomes the inexorable impulse for the initiation of radical revolution. The factual situation of capitalism is characterized not merely by economic or political crisis but by a catastrophe affecting the human essence; this insight condemns any mere economic or political *reform* to failure from the outset, and unconditionally requires the cataclysmic transcendence of the actual situation through *total revolution*. Only after the basis has been established in this way, so firmly that it cannot be shaken by any merely economic or political arguments, does the question of the *historical conditions and the bearers* of the revolution arise: the question of the theory of class struggle and the dictatorship of the proletariat. Any critique which only pays attention to this theory, without coming to grips with its real foundation, misses the point.

We shall now look at the *Manuscripts* to see what they contribute to the preparation of a positive theory of revolution and how they treat the real supersession of reification, the supersession of alienated labour and of private property. We shall once again limit ourselves to the basic state of affairs expressed in the economic and political facts. What also belongs to this positive theory of revolution is—as we shall show—an investigation of the *origin* of reification: an investigation of the historical conditions and emergence of private property. Two main questions must therefore be answered: (1) How does Marx describe the accomplished supersession of private property, i.e. the state of the human essence after the total revolution? (2) How does Marx handle the problem of the origin of private property or the emergence and development of reification? Marx himself explicitly asked both these questions: the answer is given mainly on pages 115–17 and 135–42.

The total estrangement of man and his loss of reality had been traced back to the alienation of labour. In the analysis, *private property* had been revealed as the manner in which alienated labour "must express and present itself in real life" (p. 115) and as the "realization of alienation" (p. 117) (we shall return to the close connection between alienated labour and private property below). The supersession of alienation, if it is to be a genuine supersession (and not merely "abstract" or theoretical), must supersede the real form of alienation (its "realization"); and so "the entire revolutionary movement necessarily finds both its empirical and its theoretical basis in the movement of private property—more precisely, in that of the economy" (p. 136).

Through this connection with alienated labour private property is already *more* than a specific economic category: this extra element in the concept of private property is sharply emphasized by Marx: "Material, immediately sensuous private property is the material, sensuous expression of *estranged human* life. Its movement—production and consumption—is the sensuous revelation of the movement of all production until now, i.e. the realization of the reality of man" (pp. 136ff.). Through the explanatory "i.e. the realization ... of man" which he adds Marx expressly emphasizes the fact that "production," of which the movement of private property is the "revelation," is not economic production but the self-producing process of the whole of human life (as interpreted above). The extent to which private property expresses the movement of estranged human life is more closely described in the following passage: "Just as private property is only the sensuous expression of the fact that man becomes objective for himself and at the same time becomes to himself a strange and inhuman object: just as it expresses the fact that the assertion of his life is the alienation of his life, that his realization is his loss of reality ... so the positive transcendence of private property ..." is more than economic transcendence: namely the positive "appropriation" of the whole of human reality (pp. 138ff.). Private property is the real expression of the way in which estranged man objectifies himself, "produces" himself and his objective world and realizes himself in it. Private property therefore constitutes the realization of an entire form of human *behaviour* and not just a given physical *"state"* external to man,[15] or "a *merely objective* being" (p. 128).

But if an estranged form of behaviour which has lost reality is thus realized in private property, then private property itself can only represent an estranged and unreal form of true and essential human behaviour. There must therefore be *two real "forms"* of property: an estranged and a true form, a property which is merely private and a property which is "truly human" (p. 119).[16] There must be a form of "property" belonging to the essence of man, and positive communism, far from meaning the abolition of all property, will be precisely the *restoration* of this truly human form of property.

How can one "define the general nature of private property, as it has arisen as a result of estranged labour, in its relation to *truly human* and *social property*" (p. 118)? The answer to this question must at the same time make clear the meaning and goal of the positive supersession of private property. "The meaning of private property—apart from its estrangement—is the *existence of essential objects* for man, both as objects of gratification and as objects of activity" (p. 165).

This is the most general positive definition of true property: the availability and usability of all the objects which man needs for the free realization of his essence. This availability and usability is realized as *property*—which is by no means self-evident, but is based on the idea that man never simply and directly has what he needs, but only really possesses objects when he has appropriated them. Thus the purpose of labour is to give to man as his own possessions objects which he has transformed and to make them into a world through which he can freely engage in activity and realize his potentialities. The essence of property consists in "appropriation"; a particular manner of appropriation and realization through appropriation is the basis of the state of property, and not mere having and possessing. We must now more closely define this new concept of appropriation and property which underlies Marx's analysis.

We have seen how private property consists in an untrue mode of having and possessing objects. In conditions of private property an object is "property" when it can be "used"; and this use consists either in immediate consumption or in its capacity to be turned into capital. "Life-activity" stands in the service of property instead of property standing in the service of free life-activity; it is not the "reality" of man which is appropriated but objects as things (goods and commodities) and even this kind of appropriation is "one-sided": it is limited to the physical behaviour of man and to objects which can immediately "gratify" or be turned into capital. In contrast to this, "true human property" is now described in its true appropriation: "the sensuous appropriation for and by man of the human essence and of human life, of objective man, of human achievements—should not be conceived merely in the sense of *immediate*, one-sided *gratification*—merely in the sense of *possession*, of *having*. Man appropriates his total essence in a total manner, that is to say, as a whole man." This total appropriation is then more closely described: "Each of his human relations to the world—seeing, hearing, smelling, tasting, feeling, thinking, observing, experiencing, wanting, acting, loving—in short, all the organs of his individual being . . . are in their objective orientation or in their orientation to the object, the appropriation of that object" (pp. 138–39).

Beyond all economic and legal relations, appropriation as the basis of property thus becomes a category which comprehends the universal and free relationship of man to the objective world: the relationship to the object which is becoming one's own is "total"—it "emancipates" *all* the human senses. The *whole* man is at home in the *whole* objective world which is "his work and his reality." The *economic and legal* supersession of private property is not the *end*, but only the *beginning* of the communist revolution. This universal and free appropriation is *labour*, for as we saw, the specifically human relationship to the object is one of creating, positing, forming. But in this case labour would no longer be an alienated and reified activity, but all-round self-realization and self-expression.

The inhumanity represented by reification is thus abolished at the point where it was most deeply rooted and dangerous: in the concept of property. Man no longer "loses" himself in the objective world, and his objectification is no longer reification, if objects are withdrawn from "one-sided" ownership and possession and remain the work and reality of the one who "produced" or realized them and himself in them. It is not, however, the isolated individual or an abstract plurality of individuals which has been realized in them, but *social* man, man *as* a social being. Man's return to his true property is a return into his social essence; it is the liberation of society.

V

"Man is not lost in his object only when the object becomes for him a *human* object or objective man. This is possible only when the object becomes for him a *social* object, he himself for himself a social being, just as society becomes a being for him in this object" (p. 140). There are thus two conditions for breaking through reification as outlined above: the objective relations must become human—i.e. social—relations and they must be recognized and consciously preserved as such.

These two conditions are fundamentally interrelated, for the objective relations can only become human and social if man himself is conscious of them *as such*, i.e. in his *knowledge* of both himself and the object. Thus we again encounter the central role which a particular kind of insight (man's "coming-to-be for himself") plays in the foundation of Marx's theory. To what extent can cognition, the recognition of objectification as something social, become the real impulse for the abolition of all reification?

We know that objectification is essentially a social activity and that it is precisely in his objects and in his labour on them that man recognizes himself as a social being. The insight into objectification, which breaks through reification, is the insight into society as the subject of objectification. For there is no such thing as "society" as a subject outside the individual; Marx expressly warns against playing society as an independent entity off against the individual: "Above all we must avoid postulating "Society" again as an abstraction *vis-à-vis* the individual. The individual *is the social being*. His life, even if it may not appear in the direct form of a communal life in association with others, *is* therefore an expression and confirmation of social life" (pp. 137–38).

Insight into objectification thus means insight into how and through what man and his objective world *as social relations* have become what they are. It means insight into the historical-social situation of man. This insight is no mere theoretical cognition or arbitrary, passive intuition, but *praxis*: the supersession of what exists, making it a "means" for free self-realization.

This also means that the insight which defines this task is by no means available to everyone: it can only be known by those who are actually *entrusted with this task* by their historical-social situation (we cannot pursue the way in which the proletariat becomes the bearer of this insight in the situation analysed by Marx: its content is presented at the close of Marx's *Introduction to the Critique of Hegel's Philosophy of Right*). It is not a matter of *the* task for man *as such* but of a particular historical task in a particular historical situation. It is therefore necessary that "the transcendence of the estrangement always proceeds from that form of the estrangement which is the dominant power" (p. 154). Because it is dependent on the conditions pre-established by history, the praxis of transcendence must, in order to be genuine transcendence, reveal these conditions and appropriate them. Insight into objectification as insight into the historical and social situation of man reveals the historical conditions of this situation and so achieves the *practical force and concrete form* through which it can become the lever of the revolution. We can now also understand how far questions concerning the *origin* of estrangement and insight into the *origin* of private property must be an integrating element in a positive theory of revolution.

Marx's handling of the question of the origins of private property shows the pioneering new "method" of his theory. Marx is fundamentally convinced that when man is conscious of his history he cannot fall into a situation which he has not himself created, and that only he himself can liberate himself from any situation. This basic conviction already finds its expression in the concept of freedom in the *Manuscripts*. The phrase that the liberation of the working class can only be the work of the working class itself resonates clearly through all the economic explanations; it only enters into "contradiction" with historical materialism if the latter is falsified into a vulgar materialism. If the relations of production have become a "fetter" and an alien force determining man, then this is only because man has at some stage himself alienated himself from his power over the relations of production. This is also true if one sees the relations of production as being determined primarily by the given "natural" forces of production (e.g. climatic or geographical conditions, the condition of the land, the distribution of raw materials) and ignores the fact that all these physical data have always existed in a form historically handed down and have formed a part of particular human and social "forms of intercourse." For the situation of man which exists through such pre-existing forces of production only becomes a historical and social situation through the fact that man "reacts" to what he finds pre-existing, i.e. through the manner in which he appropriates it. In truth these relations of production which have been reified into alien, determining forces are always objectifications of particular social relations, and the abolition of the estrangement expressed in these relations of production can only be total and real if it can account for economic revolution in terms of these human relations. Thus the question of the origin of private property becomes a question of the activity through which man *alienated* property from himself: "How, we now ask, does *man* come to *alienate*, to estrange, his *labour*? How is this estrangement rooted in the nature of human development?" And being aware of the crucial importance of this new way of formulating the question, Marx adds: "We have already gone a long way to the solution of this problem by *transforming* the question of the *origin of private property* into the question of the relation of *alienated labour* to the course of humanity's development. For when one speaks of private property, one thinks of dealing with something external to man. When one speaks of labour, one is directly dealing with man himself. This new formulation of the question already contains its solution" (pp. 118–19).

The answer to this question is not contained in the *Economic and Philosophical Manuscripts*; it is worked out in his later critiques of political economy. The *Economic and Philosophical Manuscripts* do, however, contain a proof within the definition of man's essence that objectification always carries within it a tendency towards reification and labour a tendency towards alienation, so that reification and alienation are not merely chance historical facts. In connection with this it is also shown how the worker even through his alienation "engenders" the non-worker and thus the domination of private property (pp. 116–17), and how he therefore has his fate in his own hands at the origin of estrangement and not just after liberation.

Marx gives his definition of estrangement as self-estrangement in a reference to the real achievement of Hegel's *Phenomenology*: "The real, active orientation of man to himself as a species being...is only possible through the *utilization* of all the powers he has in himself and which he has as belonging to a species..., treating these generic powers as objects and this, to begin with, is again *only possible in the form of estrangement*" (p. 177; my italics).

We fail to find an explanation here as to why this is, to begin with, only possible in the form of estrangement; and it is, strictly speaking, impossible to give one, for we are confronted with a state of affairs that has its roots in man—as an "objective" being—and which can only be revealed as such. It is man's "need"—as already interpreted above—for objects alien to him, "overpowering" and "not part of his being," to which he must relate *as if* they were external objects, although they only become real objects through and for him. Objects first confront him *directly* in an external and alien form and only become *hu-*

man objects, objectifications of man, through conscious historical and social appropriation. The expression of man thus first tends towards alienation and his objectification towards reification, so that he can only attain a universal and free reality through "the negation of negation": through the *supersession* of his alienation and the *return* out of his estrangement.

After the possibility of alienated labour has been shown to have its roots in the essence of man the limits of philosophical description have been reached and the discovery of the real origin of alienation becomes a matter for economic and historical analysis. We know that for Marx the starting point for this analysis is the *division of labour* (cf., for example, p. 159); we cannot go further into this here and shall only look quickly at the way Marx shows that already with the alienation of labour the worker "engenders" the domination of the capitalist and thereby of private property. At the head of this analysis there stands the sentence: "Every self-estrangement of man, from himself and from nature, appears in the relation in which he places himself and nature to *men other than* and differentiated from himself" (p. 116; my italics). We are already acquainted with the context of this sentence: the relation of man to the object on which he works is directly his relation to other men with whom he shares this object and himself as something social. So that although the worker in the self-alienation of his labour "possesses" the object as something alien, overpowering and not belonging to him, this object nowhere confronts him as an isolated thing, belonging to no one and, as it were, outside humanity. The situation is rather this: "If the product of labour does not belong to the worker, if it confronts him as an alien power, then this can only be because it belongs to some *other man than the worker*" (p. 115). With the alienation of labour the worker immediately stands as "servant" in the service of a "master": "Thus, if the product of his labour... is for him an alien... object... then his position towards it is such that someone else is master of this object, someone who is alien... If he is related to his own activity as to an unfree activity, then he is related to it as an activity performed in the service, under the dominion, the coercion, and the yoke of another man" (pp. 116ff.).

It is not a case of a "master" existing first, subordinating someone else to himself, alienating him from his labour, and making him into a mere worker and himself into a non-worker. But nor is it a case of the relationship between domination and servitude being the simple consequence of the alienation of labour. The alienation of labour, as estrangement from its own activity and from its object, already *is* in itself the relationship between worker and non-worker and between domination and servitude.

These distinctions seem to be of only secondary importance, and they do in fact disappear into the background again in the later, purely economic analysis. Nevertheless they must be expressly emphasized in the context of the *Manuscripts*, if only for the fact that they are relevant to Marx's crucial reaction to Hegel. Domination and servitude are here not concepts for particular (pre- or early capitalist) formations, relations of production, etc. They give a general description of the social condition of man in a situation of estranged labour. In this sense they point back to the ontological categories of "domination and servitude" developed by Hegel in his *Phenomenology* (II, pp. 145ff.).[17] We cannot discuss here Marx's further description of the relation between domination and servitude, but we shall select one important point: "everything which appears in the worker as an *activity* of alienation, of estrangement, appears in the non-worker as a *state* of alienation, of estrangement" (p. 119).

We know that the transcendence of estrangement (a state in which both master *and* servant find themselves, although not in the same way) can only be based on the destruction of reification, i.e. on the practical insight into the activity of objectification in its historical and social situation. Since it is only in *labour* and in the objects *of his labour* that man can really come to understand himself, others and the objective world in their historical and social situation, the master, as a *non*-worker, cannot come to this insight. Since what is actually a specific human activity appears to him as a material and objective state of affairs, the worker has an (as it were) irreducible advantage over him. He is the real factor of transformation; the destruction of reification can only be *his* work. The master can only come to this revolutionary insight if he becomes a worker, which, however, would mean transcending his own essence.

From every point of approach and in all directions this theory, arising out of the philosophical critique and foundation of political economy, proves itself to be a *practical theory*, a theory whose immanent meaning (required by the nature of its object) is particular praxis; only particular praxis can solve the problems peculiar to this theory. "We see how the resolution of the *theoretical* antitheses is *only* possible in a *practical* way, by virtue of the practical energy of man. Their resolution is therefore by no means merely a problem of understanding, but a *real* problem of life, which *philosophy* could not solve precisely because it conceived this problem as *merely* a theoretical one" (pp. 141–42). We could add to this sentence: which philosophy can solve, however, if it grasps it as a *practical* problem, i.e. if it transcends itself as "only theoretical" philosophy, which in turn means, if it really "realizes" itself as philosophy for the first time.

Marx calls the practical theory which solves this problem, in so far as it puts man as a historical and social being in the centre, "real humanism" and identifies it with "naturalism" to the extent to which, if it is carried through, it grasps the unity of man and nature: the "naturalness of man" and the "humanity of nature." If the real humanism outlined here by Marx as the basis of his theory does not correspond to what is commonly understood as Marx's "materialism," such a contradiction is entirely in accordance with Marx's intentions: "here we see how consistent naturalism and humanism distinguishes itself both from idealism and materialism, constituting at the same time the unifying truth of both" (p. 181).

VI

Finally we need to examine briefly Marx's critique of Hegel, which was envisaged as the conclusion of the whole *Manuscripts*. We can make the discussion brief because we have already gone into Marx's elaboration of the positive foundations of a critique of Hegel (the definition of man as an "objective," historical and social, practical being) in the context of our interpretation of the critique of political economy.

Marx begins by pointing out the necessity of discussing a question which has still not been adequately answered: "How do we now stand as regards the Hegelian dialectic?" (p. 170). This question, coming at the conclusion of his positive critique of political economy and the foundation of revolutionary theory, shows how much Marx was aware of working in an area opened up by Hegel and how he experienced this fact—in contrast to almost all the Hegelians and almost all his later followers—as a scientific-philosophical obligation towards Hegel. After briefly dispatching Bruno Bauer, Strauss, etc., whose "critical critique" makes the need to come to terms with Hegel anything but superfluous, Marx immediately gives his support to Feuerbach: "the only one who has a serious, critical attitude to the Hegelian dialectic and who has made genuine discoveries in this field" (p. 172). Marx mentions three such discoveries: Feuerbach (1) recognized philosophy (i.e. the purely speculative philosophy of Hegel) as a "form and manner of existence of the estrangement of the essence of man," (2) established "true materialism" by making "the social relationship 'of man to man' the basic principle of his theory" and (3) precisely through this principle opposed Hegel's mere "negation of negation," which does not go beyond negativity, with a "self-supporting positive, positively based in itself" (pp. 172ff.). With this enumeration, Marx simultaneously articulated the three main directions of his own critique of Hegel, and it is to these that we now turn.

"One must begin with Hegel's *Phenomenology*, the true point of origin and the secret of the Hegelian philosophy" (p. 173). From the beginning Marx tackles Hegel's philosophy where its origin is still visible in an unconcealed form: in the *Phenomenology*. If at the beginning of the critique it may still have looked as if it was really only a critique of what one is accustomed to regard as Hegel's "dialectic," we now see that what Marx criticizes as the dialectic is the foundation and actual "content" of Hegel's philosophy—not its (supposed) "method." And while Marx criticizes, he simultaneously extracts the positive aspects, the great discoveries made by Hegel—i.e. only because for Marx there are genuinely positive discoveries in Hegel, on the basis of which he can and must do further work, can and must Hegel's philosophy become for him the subject of a critique. We shall begin with the negative part of his critique—Marx's collation of Hegel's "mistakes"—so that we can then extract the positive aspects from these negative ones and show that the mistakes are really only mistaken interpretations of genuine and true states of affairs.

In the *Phenomenology* Hegel gives "speculative expression" to the movement of the history of the "human essence," but not of its real history, only its "genetic history" (p. 173). That is, he gives the history of the human essence, in which man first becomes what he is and which has, as it were, always already taken place when the real history of man occurs. Even with this general characterization Marx has grasped the sense of the *Phenomenology* more profoundly and accurately than most interpreters of Hegel. He then proceeds to a critique of the core of Hegel's own problematic: Hegel's philosophical description of the history of the human essence fails at the start, because Hegel from the outset grasps it only as abstract "self-consciousness" ("thought," "mind") and thus overlooks its true concrete fullness: "For Hegel the essence of man—man—equals self-consciousness" (p. 178); the history of the human essence runs its course purely as the history of self-consciousness or even as history within self-consciousness. What Marx had shown to be crucial for the definition of man's essence and what he had put at the centre of his conceptual structure—the "objectivity" of man, his "essential objectification"—is precisely what is ominously given a different meaning and perverted by Hegel. The object (i.e. objectivity as such) is in Hegel only an object *for consciousness* in the very strong sense that consciousness is the "truth" of the object and that the latter is only the negative side of consciousness: having been "posited" (created, engendered) by consciousness as its alienation and estrangement, it must also be "transcended" by consciousness again, or "taken back" into consciousness. The object is thus, by the nature of its existence, a purely negative thing, a "nullity" (p. 182); it is merely an object of abstract thought, for Hegel reduces self-consciousness to abstract thought. "The main point is that the object of consciousness is nothing else but self-consciousness, or that the object is only objectified self-consciousness —self-consciousness as an object.... The issue, therefore, is to surmount the object of consciousness. Objectivity as such is regarded as an estranged human relationship which does not correspond to the essence of man" (p. 178). For Marx, however, objectivity was precisely the human relationship in which man could alone come to self-realization and self-activity; it was "real" objectivity, the "work" of human labour and certainly not the object of abstract consciousness. From this standpoint Marx can say that Hegel fixes man as "a non-objective, spiritual being" (p. 178). This being never exists with genuine objects but always only with the self-posited negativity of itself. It is actually always "at home with itself" in its "otherness as such" (p. 183). It is thus ultimately "non-objective," and "a non-objective being is a... non-being" (p. 182).

This also constitutes a critique of the *Phenomenology* in so far as it claims to present the movement of the history of man's essential being. If this being whose history is being presented is a *"non-being,"* then this history must also be "inessential" in the full sense of the word. Marx perceives Hegel's discovery of the movement of human history in the movement of "objectification as loss of the object, as alienation" (p. 177) and in the "transcendence" of this alienation as it recurs in many forms in the whole of the *Phenomenology*. But the objectification is only apparent, "abstract and formal," since the object only has "the semblance of an object" and the self-objectifying consciousness remains "at home with itself" in this seeming alienation (pp. 183ff.). Like estrangement itself, its supersession is only a semblance: alienation remains. The forms of estranged human existence which Hegel cites are not forms of estranged real life but only of consciousness and knowledge: what Hegel deals with and supersedes are not "real religion, the real state, or real nature, but religion as a subject of knowledge, i.e. Dogmatics; the same with Jurisprudence, Political Science and Natural Science" (pp. 186–87). Because alienation is thus only superseded in the mind and not in reality, i.e. because "this supersession of thought leaves its object standing in reality," Marx can say the whole *Phenomenology*, and indeed the whole of Hegel's system in so far as it is based on the *Phenomenology*, remains within estrangement. This comes out in Hegel's system as a whole in the fact, for example, that "nature" is not grasped as man's "self-externalizing world of sense" in its existential unity with man or its "humanity," but is taken as externality "in the sense of alienation, of a mistake, a defect, which ought not to be,"—a "nothing" (p. 192).

We shall not go into the other features of the negative critique here: they are already familiar from the *Critique of Hegel's Philosophy of Right*; e.g. the conversion of mind into an absolute, the hypostatization of an absolute subject as the bearer of the historical process, the inversion of subject and predicate (p. 188), etc. What must be borne in mind is that Marx regards all these "inadequacies" as within a real state of affairs. If Hegel posits the human essence as a "non-being," then it is the non-being of a real being and thus a real non-being; if he has "only found the abstract, logical, speculative expression for the movement of history" (p. 173), then this is still an expression for the movement of real history; if he has described objectification and estrangement in their abstract forms, then he has still seen objectification and estrangement as essential movements of human history. The emphasis of Marx's critique of Hegel is definitely on the *positive* part, to which we now proceed.

"The outstanding achievement of Hegel's *Phenomenology* and of its final outcome, the dialectic of negativity as the moving and generating principle, is thus first that Hegel conceives the self-creation of man as a process, conceives objectification as loss of the object, as alienation and as transcendence of this alienation; that he thus grasps the essence of *labour* and comprehends objective man...as the outcome of man's own labour" (p. 177). The full significance of the interpretation of the *Phenomenology* given here by Marx could only be grasped if we unfolded the central problematic of Hegel's work, which we obviously cannot do here; it would also only then become apparent with what unheard of sureness Marx sees through all the mystifying and misleading interpretations (which begin even within Hegel's work) and gets back to the bedrock of the problems which were raised, for the first time in modern philosophy, in the *Phenomenology*.

In the sentence quoted above Marx has brought together all the discoveries of Hegel which he recognizes as crucial: in what follows we want briefly to explain these, for Marx, "positive moments of the Hegelian dialectic."

The *Phenomenology* presents the "self-creation of man," which means, after what has already been said, the process in which man (as an organic, living being) becomes what he is according to his essence — i.e. human essence. It thus gives the "genetic history" (p. 173) of the human essence or man's essential history. Man's "act of creation" is an "act of self-genesis" (p. 188), i.e. man gives his essence to himself: he must first make himself what he is, "posit" himself, and "produce" himself (we have already gone into the meaning of this concept). This history which is given into man's own hands is grasped by Hegel as a "process" characterized by alienation and its supersession. The process as a whole stands under the title of "objectification." The history of man thus occurs and fulfils itself as objectification: the reality of man consists of creating real objects out of all his "species powers," or "the establishing of a real, objective world" (p. 180). It is this establishing of an objective world which Hegel treats merely as the alienation of "consciousness" or knowledge, or as the relation of abstract thought to "thinghood," while Marx grasps it as the "practical" realization of the whole of man in historical and social labour (ibid.).

Hegel defines the relation of knowledge to the objective world in such a way that this objectification is simultaneously the loss of the object, i.e. the loss of reality or estrangement, so that, "to begin with, [it] is again only possible in the form of estrangement" (p. 177). That is to say: knowledge, in the process of becoming objective, initially *loses* itself in its objects: they confront it as something alien and other, in the form of an external world of things and matters which have lost their inner connection with the consciousness which has expressed itself in them and now continue as a power independent of consciousness. In the *Phenomenology*, for example, morality and right, the power of the state and wealth appear as estranged objective worlds and it is here that Marx accuses Hegel of dealing with these worlds only as "worlds of thought" and not as real worlds (pp. 174ff.), since for Hegel they are externalizations of "Mind" only and not of real, total human existence.

Although objectification consists initially in the loss of the object or estrangement, it is precisely this estrangement which in Hegel becomes the recovery of true being. "Hegel conceives man's self-estrangement, the alienation of man's essence, man's loss of objectivity and his loss of realness as self-discovery, change of his nature, objectification and realization" (pp. 187–88). The human essence—always conceived in Hegel as exclusively knowledge—is such that it must not only express but alienate itself, not only objectify itself but lose its object, to be able to discover itself. Only if it has really lost itself can it come to itself, only in its "otherness" can it become what it is "for itself." This is the "positive meaning" of negation, "the dialectic of negativity as the moving and generating principle" (p. 177). We should have to go into the foundations of Hegel's ontology to justify and clarify this assertion: here we need only show how Marx interprets this discovery by Hegel.

Through the positive concept of negation just referred to, Hegel conceives "labour as man's act of self-genesis" (p. 188); "he grasps labour as the essence of man—as man's essence in the act of proving itself" (p. 177). With reference to this Marx goes so far as to say: "Hegel's standpoint is that of modern political economy" (ibid.)—a seemingly paradoxical statement in which, however, Marx summarizes the colossal, almost revolutionary concreteness of Hegel's *Phenomenology*. If labour is here defined as man's essence in the act of proving itself this obviously refers to labour not purely as an economic, but as an "ontological" category, as Marx defines it in this very passage: "Labour is man's coming-to-be for himself within alienation, or as alienated man" (p. 177). How does it come about that Marx should take precisely the category of labour to interpret Hegel's concept of objectification as self-discovery in estrangement and of realization in alienation?

It is not only because Hegel uses labour to reveal the objectification of the human essence and its estrangement, or because he depicts the relation of the labouring "servant" to his world as the first "supersession" of estranged objectivity (II, pp. 146 ff.). It is not only because of this; although the fact that this is viewed as the real beginning of human history in the *Phenomenology* is neither a coincidence nor the result of a purely arbitrary decision, but expresses the innermost direction of the entire work. Marx has thereby—albeit in an exaggerated form—discovered the original meaning of the history of the human essence as it is elaborated in the *Phenomenology* in the form of the history of self-consciousness. It is praxis, free self-realization, always taking up, superseding and revolutionizing pre-established "immediate" facticity. It has already been pointed out that Marx holds Hegel's real mistake to be the substitution of "Mind" for the subject of this praxis. Hence for Marx, "the only labour which Hegel knows and recognizes is abstract mental labour" (p. 177). But this does not alter the fact that Hegel grasped labour as man's essence in the act of proving itself—a fact which retains its vital importance: despite the "spiritualization" of history in the *Phenomenology*, the actual leading concept through which the history of man is explicated is transforming "activity" (II, pp. 141, 196, 346, 426, etc.).

If the inner meaning of objectification and its supersession is thus praxis, then the various forms of estrangement and their supersession can also be more than mere "examples" taken out of real history and put alongside each other with no necessary connection. They must have their roots in human praxis and be an integral part of man's history. Marx expresses this insight in the sentence that Hegel has found "speculative expression for the movement of history" (p. 173)—a sentence which (as already stated) must be understood positively just as much as negatively and critically. And if the forms of estrangement are rooted as historical forms in human praxis itself, they cannot be regarded simply as abstract theoretical forms of the objectivity of consciousness; under this logical-speculative "disguise" they must have ineluctable practical consequences, they must of necessity be effectively superseded and "revolutionized." A critique must lie hidden already in the *Phenomenology*: critique in the revolutionary sense which Marx gave to this concept. "The *Phenomenology* is, therefore, an occult critique—still to itself obscure and mystifying: but inasmuch as it keeps steadily in view man's estrangement . . . there lie concealed in it all the elements of the critique already *prepared and elaborated* in a manner often rising far above the Hegelian standpoint." In its separate sections it contains "the critical elements of whole spheres such as religion, the state, civil life, etc.—but still in an estranged form" (p. 176).

Thereby Marx has expressed in all clarity the inner connection between revolutionary theory and Hegel's philosophy. What seems amazing, as measured by this critique—which is the result of a *philosophical* discussion—is the decline of later interpretations of Marx (even—*sit venia verbo*—those of Engels!) by people who believed they could reduce Marx's relationship to Hegel to the familiar transformation of Hegel's "dialectic," which they also completely emptied of content.

These suggestions will have to suffice; above all we cannot go into the question if and how the "mistakes" with which Marx charges Hegel can really be attributed to him. It has perhaps become clear through this paper that the discussion really starts at the centre of Hegel's problematic. Marx's critique of Hegel is not an appendage of the preceding critique and foundation of political economy, for his examination of political economy is itself a continuous confrontation with Hegel.

Notes

1. Volume 3 of the first section of the Marx-Engels-Gesamtausgabe (MEGA). They appeared almost simultaneously under the title *Nationalökonomie und*

Philosophie in Kröner's Pocket Editions, Volume 91 (K. Marx, *Der Historische Materialismus. Die Frühschriften I*) pp. 283ff. This edition does not include the piece printed as the *First Manuscript* in MEGA, which is essential for an understanding of the whole. The reading of the text is at variance with MEGA in numerous instances.

2. "Reification" denotes the general condition of "human reality" resulting from the loss of the object of labour and the alienation of the worker which has found its "classical" expression in the capitalist world of money and commodities. There is thus a sharp distinction between reification and objectification. Reification is a specific ("estranged," "untrue") *mode* of objectification.

3. p. 165 (my italics).

4. Cf. the passage in Feuerbach which clearly underlies the sentence quoted: "Human feelings thus do not have an empirical, anthropological significance in the sense of the old transcendental philosophy; they have an ontological, metaphysical significance" (*Grundsätze der Philosophie der Zukunft*, §33; *Sämtliche Werke II*, 1846, p. 324).

5. Cf. for example: Being-for-itself "comes into its own through labour." In labour the consciousness of the worker "is externalized and passes into the condition of permanence," "in working, consciousness, as the form of the thing formed, becomes an object for itself" (*Phenomenology of Mind*, trans. J. B. Baillie, London, 1966, pp. 238–40).

6. For these connections I must refer the reader to the extensive interpretation of Hegel's concept of labour in my book, *Hegels Ontologie und die Grundlegung einer Theorie der Geschichtlichkeit*. Cf. Hegel's definition of labour in the new edition of the *Jenenser Realphilosophie II* (Leipzig, 1931, especially pp. 213ff.).

7. Cf. *Phenomenology of Mind*, p. 220, the concept of "inorganic nature," and pp. 234ff. of my book *Hegels Ontologie, etc.*

8. Second impression, B. 33.

9. Feuerbach, *Sämtliche Werke II*, p. 309.

10. The ontological concept of passion is found similarly in Feuerbach (*Werke II*, p. 323).

11. e.g. *Werke II*, pp. 258, 337. The indications of a more profound definition, which doubtless exist in Feuerbach, are not followed through. Cf., for example, the concept of "resistance" *II*, pp. 321ff.), etc.

12. Cf. the comprehensive formulation in *The Holy Family*: "that the object as being for man or as the objective being of man is at the same time the existence of man for other men, his human relation to other men, the social relation of man to man" (*The Holy Family*, Moscow, 1956, p. 60).

13. Feuerbach: "Man is not a particular being like the animal, but a *univer-*

sal being, thus not a limited and unfree but an unlimited and free being, for universality, absence of limitations, and freedom are inseparable. And this freedom does not for example exist in a particular capacity . . . but extends over his whole being" (*Werke, II*, p. 342).

14. The *German Ideology* says of the critique in the *Deutsch-Französische Jahrbücher:* "Since at that time this was done in philosophical phraseology, the traditionally occurring philosophical expressions such as 'human essence,' 'species' etc., gave the German theoreticians the desired excuse for . . . believing that here again it was a question merely of giving a new turn to their theoretical garments . . ." (*The German Ideology*, Moscow, 1968, p. 259).

15. This turn from a state outside men to a human relation again illustrates the new problematic of Marx's theory: his penetration through the veil of abstract reification towards the comprehension of the objective world as the field of historical-social praxis. Marx emphasizes that this way of posing the question had already entered traditional political economy when Adam Smith recognized labour as the "principle" of economics, but its real sense was immediately completely concealed again since this kind of political economy "merely formulated the laws of *estranged* labour" (p. 117; my italics).

16. Marx directs his heaviest attacks in the *German Ideology* precisely against the concept of "truly human property" (particularly in his polemic against the "true socialists," op. cit., pp. 516ff.); here, within Marx's foundation of the theory of revolution, this concept obviously has a significance quite different from that in Stirner and the "true socialists."

17. I have gone into this in my essay "Zum Problem der Dialektik" (*Die Gesellschaft*, 12, 1931).

HEIDEGGER'S POLITICS (1977)

An Interview with Herbert Marcuse

Frederick Olafson

This interview, published in 1977, is an important, if rather one-sided, source for understanding Marcuse's relations to Heidegger, both biographical and intellectual. As a Heidegger scholar, the interviewer, Frederick Olafson is anxious to discover evidence of Marcuse's lingering interest in Heidegger's thought. He is not very successful and seems to have provoked Marcuse into an extremely negative evaluation of Heidegger's existential analysis, which Marcuse condemns for its false appearance of concreteness and excessive pessimism. Yet occasional indications of interest do appear.

Marcuse concedes some value to Heidegger's critique of technology and aspects of his concept of authenticity. The interview emphasizes, perhaps overemphasizes, the opposition between Marxism and existentialism as can be seen from Marcuse's rather favorable comments on Sartre whose attempted synthesis of these divergent schools of thought impressed him in later years. At one point in the interview Olafson asks whether Heidegger's teaching had a more durable influence than the existential themes Marcuse dismisses here. Marcuse replies that it did as it introduced him to "a certain type and kind of thinking." The reader of Marcuse's writings will find examples of that thinking despite all the disagreements with Heidegger.

OLAFSON Professor Marcuse, you are very widely known as a social philosopher and a Marxist; but I think there are relatively few who know that Martin Heidegger and his philosophy played a considerable role in your intellectual career. Perhaps we could begin by just laying out the basic facts about that contact with Heidegger and with his philosophy.

MARCUSE Here are the basic facts—I read *Sein und Zeit* when it came out in 1927 and after having read it I decided to go back to Freiburg (where I had received my Ph.D. in 1922) in order to work with Heidegger. I stayed in Freiburg and worked with Heidegger until December 1932, when I left Germany a few days before Hitler's ascent to power, and that ended the personal relationship. I saw Heidegger again after the War, I think in 1946–47, in the Black Forest where he has his little house. We had a talk which was not exactly very friendly and very positive, there was an exchange of letters, and since that time there has not been any communication between us.

OLAFSON Would it be fair to say that during the time you were in Freiburg you accepted the principle theses of *Being and Time* and that you were, in some sense, at that time, a Heideggerian? Or were there major qualifications and reservations even then?

MARCUSE I must say frankly that during this time, let's say from 1928 to 1932, there were relatively few reservations and relatively few criticisms on my part. I would rather say on *our* part, because Heidegger at that time was not a personal problem, not even philosophically, but a problem of a large part of the generation that studied in Germany after the first World War. We saw in Heidegger what we had first seen in Husserl, a new beginning, the first radical attempt to put philosophy on really concrete foundations—philosophy concerned with the human existence, the human condition, and not with merely abstract ideas and principles. That certainly I shared with a relatively large number of my generation, and needless to say, the disappointment with this philosophy eventually came—I think it began in the early thirties. But we reexamined Heidegger thoroughly only after his association with Nazism had become known.

OLAFSON What did you make at that stage of the social aspect of Heidegger's philosophy—its implications for political and social life and action? Were you yourself interested in those at that stage, did you perceive them in Heidegger's thought?

MARCUSE I was very much interested in it during that stage, at the same time I wrote articles of Marxist analysis for the then theoretical organ of the German Socialists, *Die Gesellschaft.* So I certainly was interested, and I first, like all the others, believed there could be some combination between existentialism and Marxism, precisely because of their insistence on concrete analysis of the actual human existence, human beings and their world. But I soon realized that Heidegger's concreteness was to a great extent a phony, a false concreteness, and that in fact his philosophy was just as abstract and just as removed from reality, even avoiding reality, as the philosophies which at that time had dominated German universities, namely a rather dry brand of neo-Kantianism, neo-Hegelianism, neo-Idealism, but also positivism.

OLAFSON How did he respond to the hopes that you had for some kind of fruitful integration of his philosophy with, let us say, a Marxist social philosophy?

MARCUSE He didn't respond. You know as far as I can say, it is today still open to question whether Heidegger ever really read Marx, whether Heidegger ever read Lukács, as Lucien Goldman maintains. I tend not to believe it. He may have had a look at Marx after or during the Second World War, but I don't think that he in any way studied Marx.

OLAFSON There are some positive remarks about Marx in Heidegger's writing, indicating that he was not at all . . .

MARCUSE That's interesting. I know of only one: the *Letter on Humanism.*

OLAFSON Yes.

MARCUSE Where he says that Marx's view of history excels all other history. That is the only remark. I know the *Letter* was written under the French occupation after the World War, one didn't know yet how things would go, so I don't give much weight to this remark.

OLAFSON More generally, how do you view the importance of phenomenological and ontological analyses of the kind that Heidegger offered in *Being and Time*, their importance I mean, for purposes of social analysis? You've made it clear that Heidegger himself was not interested in developing them in that direction. Do you think that they might have had uses beyond those that he was interested in?

MARCUSE In my first article ("Contribution to a Phenomenology of Historical Materialism," 1928), I myself tried to combine existentialism and Marxism. Sartre's *Being and Nothingness* is such an attempt on a much larger scale. But to the degree to which Sartre turned to Marxism, he surpassed his existentialist writings and finally dissociated himself from them. Even he did not succeed in reconciling Marx and Heidegger. As to Heidegger himself, he seems to use his existential analysis to get away from the social reality rather than into it.

OLAFSON You see these pretty much dropping out of the work of people who have perhaps begun with ontology and phenomenology, but have gone on to...

MARCUSE Yes.

OLAFSON To Marxism. You don't see a continuing role for that kind of...

MARCUSE I don't think so. You see, I said at the beginning, I spoke about the false concreteness of Heidegger. If you look at his principal concepts (I will use German terms because I am still not familiar with the English translation) *Dasein, das Man, Sein, Seiendes, Existenz,* they are "bad" abstracts in the sense that they are not conceptual vehicles to comprehend the real concreteness in the apparent one. They lead away. For example, *Dasein* is for Heidegger a sociologically and even biologically "neutral" category (sex differences don't exist!); the *Frage nach dem Sein* remains the ever unanswered but ever repeated question; the distinction between fear and anxiety tends to transform very real fear into pervasive and vague anxiety. Even his at first glance most concrete existential category, death, is recognized as the most inexorable brute fact only to be made into an unsurpassable *possibility.* Heidegger's existentialism is indeed a transcendental idealism compared with which Husserl's last writings (and even his *Logical Investigations*) seem saturated with historical concreteness.

OLAFSON Does that leave social theorists then with materialism or behaviorism as some kind of working theory of human nature? I take it that both Heidegger and Sartre have been attempting to resist philosophies of that kind. Does the dropping out of phenomenological and ontological elements in social theory mean an acceptance, de facto, of behaviorism?

MARCUSE No, it does not. It depends entirely on what is meant by ontology. If there is an ontology which, in spite of its stress on historicity, neglects history, throws out history and returns to static transcendental concepts, I would say this philosophy cannot provide a conceptual basis for social and political theory.

OLAFSON Let me take you up on that reference to history. This is one of the things that Heidegger interested himself in quite considerably and there are at least two chapters in *Being and Time* that deal with history. Here of course the treatment is in terms of what Heidegger called historicity, or historicality, which means that the theme is treated in terms of a certain structure of individual (primarily individual) human existence, that is to say the individual's relationship to his own past, the way he places himself in a tradition, the way he modifies that tradition at the same time as he takes it over. Does that work seem to you to have a lasting value, to have an element of concreteness?

MARCUSE I would see in his concept of historicity the same false or fake concreteness because actually none of the concrete material and cultural, none of the concrete social and political conditions which make history, have any place in *Being and Time*. History too is subjected to neutralization. He makes it into an existential category which is rather immune against the specific material and mental conditions which make up the course of history. There may be one exception: Heidegger's late concern (one might say: preoccupation) with technology and technics. The *Frage nach dem Sein* recedes before the *Frage nach der Technik*. I admit that much of these writings I do not understand. More than before, it sounds as if our world can only be comprehended in the German language (though a strange and torturous one).

I have the impression that Heidegger's concepts of technology and technics are the last in the long series of neutralizations: they are treated as "forces in-themselves," removed from the context of power relations in which they are constituted and which determine their use and their function. They are reified, hypostatized as Fate.

OLAFSON Might he not have used the notion of historicity as a structure of personal existence in a different way? Isn't it important for a social theory to show how an individual situates himself in a certain society, in a certain tradition? Isn't it important that there be a characterization of that situation that is not just given at the level of relatively impersonal forces and tendencies, but that shows how the individual ties into those forces and tendencies?

MARCUSE There most certainly is a need for such an analysis, but that is precisely where the concrete conditions of history come in. How does the individual situate himself and see himself in capitalism—at a certain stage of capitalism, under socialism, as a member of this or that class, and so on? This entire dimension is absent. To be sure, Dasein is constituted in historicity, but Heidegger focuses on individuals purged of the hidden and not so hidden injuries of their class, their work, their recreation, purged of the injuries they suffer from their society. There is no trace of the daily rebellion, of the striving for liberation. The Man (the Anonymous Anyone) is no substitute for the social reality.

OLAFSON Heidegger sees individual human beings as concerned above all with the prospect of their individual death, and this supersedes all the kinds of concrete social considerations that you have mentioned. Do you think that that emphasis and that lack of interest in the concrete and the social comes out of his theological training or bent of mind?

MARCUSE It may well be that his very thorough theological training has something to do with it. In any case, it is very good that you bring up the tremendous importance the notion of death has in his philosophy, because I believe that is a very good starting point for at least briefly discussing the famous question of whether Heidegger's Nazism was already noticeable in his philosophy prior to 1933. Now, from personal experience I can tell you that neither in his lectures, nor in his seminars, nor personally, was there any hint of his sympathies for Nazism. In fact, politics were never discussed—and to the very end he spoke very highly of the two Jews to whom he dedicated his books, Edmund Husserl and Max Scheler. So his openly declared Nazism came as a complete surprise to us. From that point on, of course, we asked ourselves the question; did we overlook indications and anticipations in *Being and Time* and the related writings? And we made one interesting observation, *ex-post* (I want to stress that, *ex-post*, it is easy to make this observation): If you look at his view of the human existence, of being-in-the-world, you will find a highly repressive, highly oppressive interpretation. I have just today gone again through the table of contents of *Being and Time*, and had a look at the main categories in which he sees the essential characteristics of existence or *Dasein*. I can just read them to you and you will see what I mean: "idle talk, curiosity, ambiguity, falling and being-thrown-into, concern, being toward death, anxiety, dread, boredom" and so on. Now this gives a picture which plays well on the fears and frustrations of men and women in a repressive society—a joyless existence: overshadowed by death and anxiety; human material for the authoritarian personality. It is for example highly characteristic that love is absent from *Being and Time*—the only place where it appears is in a footnote in a theological context together with faith, sin, and remorse. I see now in this philosophy, ex-post, a very powerful devaluation of life, a derogation of joy, of sensuousness, fulfillment. And we may have had the feeling of it at that time, but it became clear only after Heidegger's association to Nazism became known.

OLAFSON Do you think that Heidegger as a man was simply politically naive? Do you think he understood the implications of his collaboration with the Nazi Party as Rector of the University of Freiburg?

MARCUSE Well, I can speak rather authoritatively because I discussed it with him after the war. In order to prepare my answer, let me first read the statement which he made, I quote literally: "Let not principles and ideas rule your being. Today, and in the future, only the *Führer* himself is German reality and its law." These were Heidegger's own words in November 1933. This is a man who professed that he was the heir of the great tradition of Western philosophy of Kant, Hegel, and so on—all this is now discarded, norms, principles, ideas are obsolete when the

Führer lays down the law and defines reality—the German reality. I talked with him about that several times and he admitted it was an "error"; he misjudged Hitler and Nazism—to which I want to add two things, first, that is one of the errors a philosopher is not allowed to commit. He certainly can and does commit many, many mistakes but this is not an error and this is not a mistake, this is actually the betrayal of philosophy as such, and of everything philosophy stands for. Secondly, he admitted, as I said, it was a mistake—but there he left the matter. He refused (and I think that somehow I find this rather sympathetic), he refused any attempt to deny it or to declare it an aberration, or I don't know what, because he did not want to be in the same category, as he said, with all those of his colleagues who suddenly didn't remember anymore that they taught under the Nazis, that they ever supported the Nazis, and declared that actually they had always been non-Nazi. Now, in the case of Heidegger, as far as I know, he gave up any open identification with Nazism I think in 1935 or 1936. He was not Rector of the University anymore. In other words, from that time on he withdrew, but to me this in no way simply cancels the statement he made. In my view, it is irrelevant when and why he withdrew his enthusiastic support of the Nazi regime—decisive and relevant is the brute fact that he made the statement just quoted, that he idolized Hitler, and that he exhorted his students to do the same. If, "today and in the future," only the *Führer* himself is "German reality and its law," then the only philosophy that remains is the philosophy of abdication, surrender.

OLAFSON In his discussions with you did he give any indication of his reasons for withdrawing, or what he believed the "mistake" of Nazism to be? I'm wondering in particular if it was motivated by anything that one would call a moral consideration, or . . .

MARCUSE In fact, I remember he never did. No, he never did. It certainly wasn't anti-Semitism. That I remember. But he never did, you are quite right. I think I do understand now why he turned against the pre-Hitler democracy of the Weimar Republic—because life under the Weimar Republic certainly in no way conformed to his existential categories: the struggle between capitalism and socialism, waged almost daily on the streets, at the work place, with violence and with the intellect, the outburst of a radically rebellious literature and art—this entire world, "existential" throughout, lies outside his existentialism.

OLAFSON There's one important concept in *Being and Time* which we haven't alluded to, and that is the concept of authenticity or *Eigenlichkeit*, a concept that has known a wide popularity, I guess, both before and after Heidegger, implying a certain false relationship to oneself, and thereby a certain false relationship to one's fellow men and I suppose to one's society. Does this strike you as a concept, in Heidegger's development of it, that has any continuing utility?

MARCUSE It is an interesting concept. Again, if I remember how he actually defines authenticity, the same categories come to my mind, which I would call rather oppressive and repressive categories. What is authenticity? Mainly, if I remember correctly, and please correct me if I don't, the withdrawal from the entire world of the others, *Das Man*, I don't know what the English translation is . . .

OLAFSON The anonymous anyone.

MARCUSE Authenticity would then mean the return to oneself, to one's innermost freedom, and, out of this inwardness, to decide, to determine every phase, every situation, every moment of one's existence. And the very real obstacles to this autonomy? The content, the aim, the What of the decision? Here too, the methodical "neutralization": the social, empirical context of the decision and of its consequences is "bracketed." The main thing is to decide and to act according to your decision. Whether or not the decision is in itself, and in its goals morally and humanly positive or not, is of minor importance.

OLAFSON There is another side to the concept—I agree with what you have been saying about this side of it—but there's another side in which Heidegger treats inauthenticity as a kind of deep attempt that human beings make to present themselves to themselves in a form that suppresses or blocks out the element of decision, the element of responsibility for themselves, that incorporates them into some kind of larger, whether it be physical or social, entity, and thus relieves them of the necessity for decision. Now that bears (it seems to me, perhaps I am wrong) some analogy to things that you have had to say about tendencies in modern technological society.

MARCUSE Yes, I certainly wouldn't deny that authenticity, in a less oppressive sense, is becoming increasingly difficult in the advanced so-

ciety of today, but it seems to me that even in the positive sense, authenticity is overshadowed by death, by the entire interpretation of existence as being toward death, and the incorporation of death into every
hour and every minute of your life. This again I see as a highly oppressive notion, which somehow serves well to justify the emphasis of fascism and Nazism on sacrifice, sacrifice *per se*, as an end-in-itself. I think
there is a famous phrase by Ernst Jünger, the Nazi writer, who speaks
of the necessity of sacrifice *"am Rande des Nichts oder am Rande des
Abgrunds"* — "on the edge of the abyss, or on the edge of nothingness."
In other words a sacrifice that is good because it is a sacrifice, and because it is freely chosen, or allegedly freely chosen, by the individual.
Heidegger's notion recalls the battle cry of the fascist Futurists: *Eviva la
Muerte*.

OLAFSON You mentioned Sartre's name a while ago, and I'd like to
turn now, if I may, to the relationship between Heidegger and Sartre.
As you yourself have pointed out, I think, on occasion — Sartre's *Being
and Nothingness* is very heavily dependent upon Heidegger's *Being and
Time* as, of course, it is upon other works in the German tradition, like
The Phenomenology of Mind. Heidegger, on the other hand, has from
the standpoint of his latter thought, repudiated any suggestion of common ground between these two philosophies, or these two statements.
And that, of course, has been contested by others. How do you see this
problem of the relationship between Heidegger and Sartre, and the relationship of Heidegger to the whole wider phenomenon of existentialism in the post-war period?

MARCUSE Well, it is a large question and I can only answer a small
part of it. I believe there is a common ground between Sartre's early
work and Heidegger, namely the existential analysis, but there the common ground ends. I would do injustice to Sartre if I would prolong it
beyond that point. Even *L'Être et le Néant* is already much more concrete than Heidegger ever was. Erotic relationships, love, hatred, all
this — the body, not simply as abstract phenomenological object but the
body as it is sensuously experienced, plays a considerable role in Sartre
— all this is miles away from Heidegger's own analysis, and, as Sartre developed his philosophy, he surpassed the elements that still linked him
to existentialism and worked out a Marxist philosophy and analysis.

OLAFSON Doesn't the *Critique of Dialectical Reason* still strike you as a very idiosyncratic version of Marxism still marked importantly by the earlier thought?

MARCUSE It is important, and again it contains elements of truth, but I don't know whether you can really incorporate them into his earlier work, and his later work I just haven't followed adequately, so I wouldn't know.

OLAFSON The interesting question that arises of course in connection with that is what Heidegger's place would be in the history of Western philosophy so conceived, because it has seemed, as you were saying, to many that *Being and Time* was a final turn on the transcendental screw, as it were, and that he would stand then in the same tradition as the people that he seems to be criticizing so trenchantly.

MARCUSE In the specific context of the history of philosophy, this may be true. In the larger political context, one may say that German Idealism comes to an end with the construction of the Nazi state. To quote Carl Schmitt: "On January 30, 1933, Hegel died."

OLAFSON And yet Heidegger's philosophy enjoyed enormous prestige in Germany in the post-war period. I think that is beginning to slack off a bit...

MARCUSE True.

OLAFSON ... or has been for the last decade, and I suppose it was more the later philosophy than the philosophy of *Being and Time* that formed the basis for that renaissance of interest in Heidegger. Do you have any impressions of his influence on German intellectual life in the post-war period?

MARCUSE I only know, as you said, that by now it has been reduced considerably. There was a great interest in Heidegger for quite some time after the war, and I think you are right, it was mainly the late work and not the early work.

OLAFSON Theodor Adorno, a former colleague of yours, has characterized that influence in highly critical terms.

MARCUSE Yes.

OLAFSON As a glorification of the principle of heteronomy, which I take to mean essentially the principle of external authority of some kind. If that is true then there is a kind of paradox in the fact that a philosophy of will and self-assertion, of authenticity, has turned around into an ideological basis for an essentially heteronomous and authoritarian social orientation.

MARCUSE Yes, but as we discussed, I think the roots of this authoritarianism you can find (again *ex-post*) in *Being and Time*, and the heteronomy may not only be that of outside authorities and powers, but also, for example, the heteronomy exercised by death over life. I think that Adorno has this too in mind when he speaks of it.

OLAFSON Do you think that Hegel *is* dead, that classical German philosophy is effectively at an end? Can there be continuators, more successful, perhaps, than Heidegger?

MARCUSE You mean the tradition of German Idealism?

OLAFSON I mean, is it still possible for living philosophies to be built on the great classical authors, Hegel and Kant, whether through revision, or however? Are these still living sources of philosophical inspiration?

MARCUSE I would definitely say yes. And I would definitely say that one of the proofs is the continued existence and development of Marxist theory. Because Marx and Engels themselves never failed to emphasize to what extent they considered themselves as the heirs of German Idealism. It is, of course, a greatly modified idealism, but elements of it remain in social and political theory.

OLAFSON I think you've already characterized, in general terms, what permanent effect Heidegger's philosophy, his teaching, had upon your own thought, upon your own philosophical work. Is there anything that you want to add to that? On balance, does the encounter with Heidegger seem to you to have enriched your own philosophical thinking, or is it something that you essentially had to see through and overcome?

MARCUSE I would say more. There was, as I said, the mere fact that at least a certain type and kind of thinking I learned from him, and at least the fact—which again today should be stressed in the age of structuralism—that after all the text has an authority of its own and even if you violate the text, you have to do justice to it. These are elements which I think continue to be valid to this very day.

OLAFSON The analysis of the situation of the individual human being, the conscious human being—is this susceptible, do you think, of continuing treatment?

MARCUSE No. As far as I am concerned, the existential analysis à la Heidegger today, I don't think there is anything in it I could say yes to, except in a very different social and intellectual context.

OLAFSON Could you give us any indication of what the nature of that context might be?

MARCUSE That is very difficult. It would open up a completely new topic. The entire dimension that has been neglected in Marxian theory, for example, how social institutions reproduce themselves in the individuals, and how the individuals, by virtue of their reproducing their own society act on it. There is room for what may be called an existential analysis, but only within this framework.

OLAFSON Well, thank you very much.

MARCUSE You're welcome.

SARTRE'S EXISTENTIALISM (1948)

During and after World War II, French thinkers such as Albert Camus and Jean-Paul Sartre offered a radical version of existentialism that reflected the experience of their generation. This was a philosophy of total disillusionment with official values, such as patriotism, honesty, and justice, all of which were betrayed by the collaborationist government of occupied France. The existentialists did not turn to Marxism to overthrow the hypocritical "bourgeois" regime. Instead, they turned inward to the ideal of the free individual capable of choosing his or her own values and identity.

Camus' notion that life is "absurd" was intended to throw the individual back on him or her self, free from conformist values. If life has no pregiven meaning, the individual must confront it in all its immediacy and indeterminacy. Sartre's much more elaborate ontology made a radical distinction between human consciousness (the "Pour-soi") and things (the "En-soi"). He argued on this basis that no objective condition determines human choices. He dismissed the claim that there are absolute values—or that life's conditions or human nature control individual fate—as mere "bad faith," a particularly odious kind of self-deception. The authentic individual realizes his or her own freedom and creates an independent life.

In 1948, when Marcuse's essay on Sartre came out, existentialism was the principal critical alternative to Marxism. This was familiar territory for him. He had been through a similar theoretical episode with Heidegger whose philosophy he had earlier criticized for its "false concrete-ness." In this essay he developed a similar critique of existentialism's overly abstract ideal of freedom. Freedom, he argued, is a social task to be worked out in society in solidarity with others, and not an abstract choice made by an individual consciousness.

• • •

Introduction

"The following pages deal with the sentiment of absurdity which pre-vails in our world." This opening sentence of Albert Camus's *Le Mythe de Sisyphe* conveys the climate in which Existentialism originates. Camus does not belong to the existentialist school, but the basic expe-rience which permeates his thought is also at the root of Existentialism. The time is that of the totalitarian terror: the Nazi regime is at the height of its power; France is occupied by the German armies. The val-ues and standards of western civilization are co-ordinated and super-seded by the reality of the fascist system. Once again, thought is thrown back upon itself by a reality which contradicts all promises and ideas, which refutes rationalism as well as religion, idealism as well as materi-alism. Once again, thought finds itself in the Cartesian situation and asks for the one certain and evident truth which may make it still pos-sible to live. The question does not aim at any abstract idea but at the individual's concrete existence: what is the certain and evident experi-ence which can provide the foundation for his life here and now, in this world?

Like Descartes, this philosophy finds its foundation in the self-certainty of the Cogito, in the consciousness of the Ego. But whereas for Descartes the self-certainty of the Cogito revealed a rational uni-verse, governed by meaningful laws and mechanisms, the Cogito now is thrown into an "absurd" world in which the brute fact of death and the irretrievable process of Time deny all meaning. The Cartesian sub-ject, conscious of its power, faced an objective world which rewarded calculation, conquest, and domination; now the subject itself has be-come absurd and its world void of purpose and hope. The Cartesian *res cogitans* was opposed by a *res extensa* which responded to the former's knowledge and action; now the subject exists in an iron circle of frustration and failure. The Cartesian world, although held together by its own rationality, made allowance for a God who cannot deceive; now the world is godless in its very essence and leaves no room for any transcendental refuge.

The reconstruction of thought on the ground of absurdity does not lead to irrationalism. This philosophy is no revolt against reason; it does not teach abnegation or the *credo quia absurdum*. In the universal destruction and disillusion, one thing maintains itself: the relentless clarity and lucidity of the mind which refuses all shortcuts and escapes, the constant awareness that life has to be lived "without appeal" and without protection. Man accepts the challenge and seeks his freedom and happiness in a world where there is no hope, sense, progress, and morrow. This life is nothing but "consciousness and revolt," and defiance is its only truth. Camus's *Mythe de Sisyphe* recaptures the climate of Nietzsche's philosophy:

> Absurd man envisages a burning and icy universe, transparent and limited, where nothing is possible but everything is given, beyond which is extinction and the void.[1]

Thought moves in the night, but it is the night

> of desperation which remains lucid, polar night, eve of the mind out of which will perhaps rise that white and integral clarity which designs every object in the light of the intellect.[2]

The experience of the "absurd world" gives rise to a new and extreme rationalism which separates this mode of thought from all fascist ideology. But the new rationalism defies systematization. Thought is held in abeyance between the "sentiment of absurdity" and its comprehension, between art and philosophy. Here, the ways part. Camus rejects existential philosophy: the latter must of necessity "explain" the inexplicable, rationalize the absurdity and thus falsify its reality. To him, the only adequate expression is living the absurd life, and the artistic creation, which refuses to rationalize ("raisonner le concret") and which "covers with images that which makes no sense" ("ce qui n'a pas de raison"). Sartre, on the other hand, attempts to develop the new experience into a philosophy of the concrete human existence: to elaborate the structure of "being in an absurd world" and the ethics of "living without appeal."

The development of Sartre's Existentialism spans the period of the war, the Liberation, and reconstruction. Neither the triumph nor the collapse of fascism produces any fundamental change in the existentialist conception. In the change of the political systems, in war and peace, before and after the totalitarian terror—the structure of the "réalité humaine" remains the same. "Plus ça change, plus c'est la même chose." The historical absurdity which consists in the fact that after the defeat of fascism the world did not collapse, but relapsed into its previous forms, that it did not leap into the realm of freedom but restored with honour the old management—this absurdity lives in the existentialist conception. But it lives in the existentialist conception as a metaphysical, not as a historical fact. The experience of the absurdity of the world, of man's failure and frustration, appears as the experience of his ontological condition. As such, it transcends his historical condition. Sartre defines Existentialism as a doctrine according to which "existence precedes and perpetually creates the essence."[3] But in his philosophy, the existence of man, in creating his essence, is itself determined by the perpetually identical ontological structure of man, and the various concrete forms of man's existence serve only as examples of this structure. Sartre's existential analysis is a strictly philosophical one in the sense that it abstracts from the historical factors which constitute the empirical concreteness: the latter merely illustrates Sartre's metaphysical and meta-historical conceptions. In so far as Existentialism is a philosophical doctrine, it remains an idealistic doctrine: it hypostatizes specific historical conditions of human existence into ontological and metaphysical characteristics. Existentialism thus becomes part of the very ideology which it attacks, and its radicalism is illusory. Sartre's L'Être et le Néant, the philosophical foundation of Existentialism, is an ontological-phenomenological treatise on human freedom and could as such come out under the German occupation (1943). The essential freedom of man, as Sartre sees it, remains the same before, during, and after the totalitarian enslavement of man. For freedom is the very structure of human being and cannot be annihilated even by the most adverse conditions: man is free even in the hands of the executioner. Is this not Luther's comforting message of Christian liberty?

Sartre's book draws heavily on the philosophy of German idealism, in which Luther's Protestantism has found its transcendental stabilization. At the outset, Sartre's concept of the free subject is a reinterpretation of Descartes's Cogito, but its development follows the tradition of German rather than French rationalism. Moreover Sartre's book is in large parts a restatement of Hegel's *Phenomenology of Mind* and Heidegger's *Sein und Zeit*. French Existentialism revives many of the intellectual tendencies which were prevalent in the Germany of the twenties and which came to naught in the Nazi system.

But while these aspects seem to commit Existentialism to the innermost tendencies of bourgeois culture, others seem to point in a different direction. Sartre himself has protested against the interpretation of human freedom in terms of an essentially "internal" liberty—an interpretation which his own analysis so strongly suggests—and he has explicitly linked up his philosophy with the theory of the proletarian revolution.[4]

Existentialism thus offers two apparently contradictory aspects: one the modern reformulation of the perennial ideology, the transcendental stabilization of human freedom in the face of its actual enslavement; the other the revolutionary theory which implies the negation of this entire ideology. The two conflicting aspects reflect the inner movement of existentialist thought[5] which reaches its object, the concrete human existence, only where it ceases to analyse it in terms of the "free subject" and describes it in terms of what it has actually become: a "thing" in a reified world. At the end of the road, the original position is reversed: the realization of human freedom appears, not in the *res cogitans*, the "Pour-soi," but in the *res extensa*, in the body as thing. Here, Existentialism reaches the point where philosophical ideology would turn into revolutionary theory. But at the same point, Existentialism arrests this movement and leads it back into the ideological ontology.

The elucidation of this hidden movement requires a critical restatement of some of the basic conceptions of *L'Être et le Néant*.

I

L'Être et le Néant starts with the distinction of two types of being —Being-for-itself (Pour-soi; consciousness, cogito) and Being-in-itself (En-soi). The latter (roughly identical with the world of things, objectivity) is characterized by having no relation to itself, being what it is, plainly and simply, beyond all becoming, change, and temporality (which emerge only with the Pour-soi), in the mode of utter contingency. In contrast, the Being-for-itself, identical with the human being, is the free subject which continually "creates" its own existence; Sartre's whole book is devoted to its analysis. The analysis proceeds from the question as to the "relationship" *(rapport)* between these two types of being. Following Heidegger, subjectivity and objectivity are understood, not as two separate entities between which a relationship must only be established, but as essential "togetherness," and the question aims at the full and concrete structure of this togetherness.

> The concrete can be only the synthetic totality of which consciousness as well as phenomenon (Being-in-itself) constitute but moments. The concrete — that is man in the world. . . . [6]

The question thus aims at the full and concrete structure of the human being as being-in-the-world *(la réalité humaine).*

In order to elucidate this structure, the analysis orients itself on certain typical "human attitudes" *(conduites exemplaires).* The first of these is the attitude of questioning *(l'attitude interrogative),* the specific human attitude of interrogating, reflecting on himself and his situation at any given moment. The interrogation implies a threefold (potential) negativity: the not-knowing, the permanent possibility of a negative answer, and the limitation expressed in the affirmative answer: "It is thus and not otherwise." The interrogative attitude thus brings to the fore the fact that man is surrounded by and permeated with negativity:

> It is the permanent possibility of not-being, outside of us and in us, which conditions our questions about being (EN, p. 40).

However, the negativity implied in the interrogative attitude serves only as an example and indication of the fundamental fact that negativity surrounds and permeates man's entire existence and all his attitudes:

> The necessary condition which makes it possible to say "no" is that the not-being is perpetually present, in us and outside of us, is that the void haunts being (EN, p. 47).

Negativity originates with and constantly accompanies the human being, manifesting itself in a whole series of negations *(néantisations)* with which the human being experiences, comprehends, and acts upon himself and the world. The totality of these negations constitutes the very being of the subject: man exists "as perpetually detaching himself from what is" (EN, p. 73); he transcends himself as well as his objects toward his and their possibilities, he is always "beyond" his situation, "wanting" his full reality. By the same token, man does not simply exist like a thing *(en soi)* but makes himself and his world exist, "creates" himself and his world at any moment and in any situation.

This characterization of the "réalité humaine" (which is hardly more than a restatement of the idealistic conception of the Cogito or Self-consciousness, especially in the form in which the *Phenomenology of Mind* develops this conception) furnishes the fundamental terms of Sartre's Existentialism—the terms which guide the subsequent development of his philosophy. There is first of all the identification of the human being with liberty. The series of negations by which man constitutes himself and his world at the same time constitutes his essential freedom:

[Liberty] arises with the negation of the appeals of the world, it appears from the moment when I detach myself from the world where I had engaged myself so that I perceive myself as consciousness (EN, p. 77).

Human freedom thus conceived is not one quality of man among others, nor something which man possesses or lacks according to his historical situation, but is the human being itself and as such:

That which we call liberty is therefore indistinguishable from the being of the "human reality." Man does not first exist in order to be free subsequently, but there is no difference between his being and his free-being [being-free] (EN, p. 61).

Secondly, from the identification of the human being with freedom follows the full and unqualified responsibility of man for his being. In order to concretize his idea of freedom and responsibility, Sartre adapts Heidegger's emphasis on the *Geworfenheit* of man into a pre-given "situation." Man always finds himself and his world in a situation which appears as an essentially external one (the situation of his family, class, nation, race, etc.). Likewise, the objects of his environment are not his own: they were manufactured as commodities; their form and their use are pre-given and standardized. However, this essential "contingency" of man's situation is the very condition of life, of his freedom and responsibility. His contingent situation becomes "his" in so far as he "engages" himself in it, accepts or rejects it. No power in heaven or on earth can force him to abdicate his freedom: he himself, and he alone is to decide and choose what he is.

Thirdly, man is by definition (that is to say, by virtue of the fact that he is, as "être-pour-soi," the permanent realization of his possibilities) nothing but self-creation. His Being is identical with his activity (action), or rather with his (free) acts. "L'homme est ce qu'il fait," and, vice versa, everything that is is a "human enterprise."

> Man engages in his life, designs its shape, and outside this shape, there is nothing.... Man is nothing else but a series of enterprises (undertakings), he is the sum total, the organization, the ensemble of the relationships which constitute these enterprises (EH, pp. 57ff.).

Human existence is at any moment a "project" that is being realized, freely designed and freely executed by man himself, or, man's existence is nothing but his own fundamental project. This dynamics is based on the fact that man's actual situation never coincides with his possibilities, that his Being is essentially being-in-want-of *(manque)*. However, the want is not want of something, so that the want would disappear with its satisfaction; it is the manifestation of the basic negativity of the human being:

> Human reality is not something which first exists in order to want for this or that later; it exists as want and in close synthetic union with what it wants.... In its coming into being, (human) reality is cognizant of itself as an incomplete being.... Human reality is a perpetual reaching for a coincidence which is never accomplished (EN, pp. 132ff.).

The existentialist dynamics is thus not an aimless and senseless one: the "projet fondamental" which is man's existence aims at the ever lacking coincidence with himself, at his own completeness and totality. In other words, the *Pour-soi* constantly strives to become *En-soi*, to become the stable and lasting foundation of his own being. But this project, which would make the *Pour-soi* an *En-soi* and vice versa, is eternally condemned to frustration, and this ontological frustration shapes and permeates the entire Being of man:

> Human reality suffers in its being because it emerges into existence as though perpetually haunted by a totality which it is without being able to be it, since in effect it cannot attain Being-in-itself without losing Being-for-itself. It is therefore essentially unhappy consciousness (EN, p. 134).

Sartre's ontological analysis has herewith reached its centre: the determination of the human being as frustration, *Scheitern,* "échec." All fundamental human relationships, the entire "human enterprise" is haunted by this frustration. However, precisely because frustration is permanent and inevitable (since it is the ontological characteristic of the human being), it is also the very foundation and condition of human freedom. The latter is what it is only in so far as it "engages" man within his contingent situation, which in turn, since it is a pre-given situation, prevents him once and for all from ever becoming the founder of his own Being-for-himself. The circle of ontological identifications is thus closed: it combines Being and Nothing, freedom and frustration, self-responsible choice and contingent determination. The *coincidentia oppositorum* is accomplished, not through a dialectical process, but through their simple establishment as ontological characteristics. As such, they are transtemporally simultaneous and structurally identical.

The ontological analysis of the *l'être-pour-soi* furnishes the framework for the interpretation of the *l'existence d'autrui*, of the Other. This transition presents a decisive methodological problem. Sartre has followed so closely the idealistic conception of Self-Consciousness (*Cogito*) as the transcendental origin and "creator" of all Being that he constantly faces the danger of transcendental solipsism. He takes up the challenge in an excellent critique of Husserl and Heidegger (and Hegel), in which he shows that their attempts to establish the Being of the Other as an independent ontological fact fail, that in all of them the existence of the Other is more or less absorbed into the existence of the Ego (EN, pp. 288ff.). Sartre himself renounces all efforts to derive ontologically the existence of the Other:

The existence of the Other has the nature of a contingent and irreducible fact. The Other is encountered; he is not constituted (by the Ego) (EN, p. 307).

However, he continues, the Cogito provides the only point of departure for the understanding of the existence of the Other because all "fait contingent," all "nécessité de fait" is such only for and by virtue of the Cogito:

> The *Cogito* (examined once again) must cast me outside of itself onto the Other. . . . We must ask the Being-for-itself to give us the Being-for-another; absolute immanence must cast us back into absolute transcendence (EN, pp. 308ff.).

The experience of the Cogito which establishes the independent existence of the Other is that of "being-looked-at by another [man]." The relation of being-seen by another (man) constitutes, for the Cogito, "l'existence d'autrui":

> My perception of the Other in the world as probably being (a) man relates to my permanent possibility of being-seen-by-him. . . . On principle, the Other is he who looks at me (EN, p. 315).

"Le regard d'autrui" becomes constitutive of the fundamental interhuman relationships. Sartre illustrates this by the example of a jealous lover who peeps through a keyhole. In this situation, he suddenly feels himself seen by another man. With this glance, he becomes somebody whom another (man) knows in his innermost being, who *is* that which the other sees. His own possibilities are taken away from him (he cannot hide where he intended to hide, he cannot know what he desired to know, etc.); his entire world at once has a new, different focus, structure, and meaning: it emerges as the other's world and as a world-for-the-other. His being thus emerges, in a strict sense, as being "at the liberty" of the other: from now on,

> it is a question of my being as it is inscribed in and through the liberty of the Other. Everything occurs as though I possessed a dimension of being from which I was separated by a profound void, and this void is the liberty of the Other (EN, p. 320).

The other's glance turns me into an object, turns my existence into "nature," alienates my possibilities, "steals" my world.

> By the very emergence of his existence, I have an appearance, a nature; the existence of the Other is my original sin (EN, p. 321).

The appearance of the Other thus transforms the world of the Ego into a world of conflict, competition, alienation, "reification." The Other, that is "la mort cachée de mes possibilités"; the Other, that is he who usurps my world, who makes me an "object of appreciation and appraisal," who gives me my "value."

> Thus, being seen constitutes me as being without any defence against a liberty which is not my liberty. In this sense we may consider ourselves as "slaves" in so far as we appear to the Other. But this bondage is not the historical and surmountable result of the life of an abstract consciousness (EN, pp. 391ff.).

This conception of the Other as the irreconcilable antagonist of the Ego now serves as the basis for Sartre's interpretation of the inter-human relationships. They are primarily corporal relationships (as already indicated by the constitutive role attributed to the "*regard*"). However, the body enters these relationships not merely as a physical-biological "thing" but as the manifestation of the individuality and contingency of the Ego in his "rapport transcendant" with the world (EN, pp. 391ff.). The original experience of the Other as the source of alienation and reification calls for two fundamental reactions which constitute the two fundamental types of inter-human relationships: (1) the attempt, on the part of the Ego, to deny the liberty and mastery of the Other and to make him into an objective thing, totally dependent on the Ego; or, (2) to assimilate his liberty, to accept it as the foundation of the Ego's own liberty and thereby to regain the free Ego (EN, p. 430). The first attitude leads to Sadism, the second to Masochism. But the essential frustration which marks all existential "projects" of the Ego also characterizes these attempts: the complete enslavement of the Other transforms him into a thing, annihilates him *as* the (independent) Other and thus annihilates the very goal which the Ego desired to attain. Similarly, the complete assimilation to the Other transforms the Ego into a thing, annihilates it as a (free) subject and thus annihilates

the very freedom which the Ego desired to regain. The frustration suffered in the sadistic attitude leads to the adoption of the masochistic attitude, and vice versa:

> Each of them implies the death of the other, that is, the failure of
> one motivates the adoption of the other. Therefore, my relations
> with the Other are not dialectical but circular, although each at-
> tempt is enriched by the failure of the other (EN, p. 230).

The two fundamental human relationships produce and destroy themselves "en cercle" (EN, p. 431).

The only remaining possible attitude toward the Other is that
which aims directly at his utter destruction, namely, hate. However,
this attitude too fails to achieve the desired result: the liberation of the
Ego. For even after the death of the Other (or the Others), he (or they)
remain as "having been" and thus continue to haunt the Ego's conscience.

The conclusion: since

> all the complex attitudes of men toward each other are only varia-
> tions of these two attitudes (and of hate) (EN, p. 477).

there is no breaking out of the circle of frustration. On the other hand,
man *must* "engage" in one of these attitudes because his very reality
consists in nothing but such "engagement." Thus, after the failure of
each attempt,

> there is no alternative left for the Being-for-itself but to return into
> the circle and to be tossed about indefinitely from one to the other
> of these two fundamental attitudes (EN, p. 484).

Here, the image of Sisyphus and his absurd task appears most naturally as the very symbol of man's existence. Here, too, Sartre deems it
appropriate to add in a footnote that "these considerations do not exclude the possibility of a morality of liberation and salvation"; however,
such a morality requires a "radical conversion, which we cannot discuss
in this place."

II

The main ontological argument is concluded by this analysis of the fundamental interhuman relationships; the remaining part of the book is taken up by a synopsis of the "réalité humaine" as it has emerged in the preceding interpretation. The synopsis is guided by the concept of freedom. The ontological analysis had started with the identification of Ego (Cogito) and freedom. The subsequent development of the existential characteristics of the Ego had shown how his freedom is inextricably tied up within the contingency of his "situation," and how all attempts to make himself the free foundation of his existence are eternally condemned to frustration. The last part of Sartre's book resumes the discussion at this point in order to justify finally, in the face of these apparent contradictions, the ontological identification of human being and freedom.

For Sartre, the justification cannot be that which is traditionally featured in idealistic philosophy, namely, the distinction between transcendental and empirical freedom. This solution cannot suffice for him because his analysis of the Ego does not remain within the transcendental-ontological dimension. Ever since his Ego, in the Third Part of his book, had to acknowledge the existence of the Other as a plain "nécessité de fait," his philosophy had left the realm of pure ontology and moved within the ontic-empirical world.

Sartre thus cannot claim that his philosophy of freedom is a transcendental-ontological one and therefore neither committed nor equipped to go into the (empirical) actuality of human freedom. Quite in contrast to Heidegger (whose existential analysis claims to remain within the limits of pure ontology), Sartre's philosophy professes to be an "-ism," Existentialism, that is to say, a *Weltanschauung* which involves a definite attitude toward life, a definite morality, "une doctrine d'action" (EH, p. 95). Sartre must therefore show the actuality of the entire "existentialist" conception of man. The last part of *L'Être et le Néant* is chiefly dedicated to this task.

Sartre attempts to demonstrate that the ontological definition actually defines the "réalité humaine," that man is in *reality* the free being-for-himself which the existential ontology posits.

We have seen that, according to Sartre, man, as a Being-for-itself that does not simply exist but exists only in so far as it "realizes" itself, is essentially act, action, activity.

Man is free because he is not merely himself but present to himself. The being which (merely) is what it is cannot be free. Freedom is, actually, the void which is in man's heart and which forces the human reality to *create itself* rather than to *be* (EN, p. 516).

This "se faire" applies to every single moment in man's life: whatever he does or does not do, whatever he is or is not—he himself has "chosen" it, and his choice was absolutely and perfectly free:

Our existence is actually our original choice (EN, p. 539).

As against this proclamation of the absolute freedom of man, the objection arises immediately that man is in reality determined by his specific socio-historical situation, which in turn determines the scope and content of his liberty and the range of his "choice."

"La réalité humaine," that is, for example, a French worker under the German occupation, or a sales clerk in New York. His liberty is limited, and his choice is prescribed to such an extent that their interpretation in the existentialist terms appear like mere mockery. Sartre accepts the challenge and sets out to prove that even in a situation of extreme determinateness, man is and remains absolutely free. True, he says, the worker may live in a state of actual enslavement, oppression, and exploitation, but he has freely "chosen" this state, and he is free to change it at any moment. He has freely chosen it because "enslavement," "oppression," "exploitation" have meaning only for and by the "Pour-soi" which has posited and accepted these "values" and suffers them. And he is free to change his condition at any moment because these values will cease to exist for him as soon as he ceases to posit, accept, and suffer them. Sartre understands this freedom as a strictly individual liberty, the decision to change the situation as a strictly individual project, and the act of changing as a strictly individual enterprise.

The fact that for the individual worker such individual action would mean loss of his job and probably lead to starvation, imprisonment, and even death, does not invalidate his absolute freedom, for it is again a matter of free choice to value life and security higher than starvation, imprisonment, and death. The existentialist proposition thus leads inevitably to the reaffirmation of the old idealistic conception that man is free even in chains, or, as Sartre formulates it: "but the executioner's tools cannot dispense us from being free" (EN, p. 587).

However, Sartre does not want to have this proposition interpreted in the sense of a merely "internal" freedom. The slave is literally and actually free to break his chains, for the very meaning ("sens") of his chains reveals itself only in the light of the goal which he chooses: to remain a slave or to risk the worst in order to liberate himself from enslavement.

> If, for example, he chooses to revolt, slavery, far from being first an obstacle to this revolt, takes its meaning and its coefficient of adversity only from this revolt (EN, p. 635).

All adversities, obstacles, limitations to our liberty, are thus posited by and emerge ("surgir") with ourselves; they are parts of the free "project" which is our existence (EN, pp. 562, 569).

> The coefficient of adversity of things...cannot be an argument against our freedom because it is *through us*, that is, through the preliminary setting of a goal that this coefficient of adversity emerges. The very rock which displays profound resistance if I wish to change its position, will, on the other hand, be a precious help to me if I wish to climb it in order to contemplate the countryside (EN, p. 562).

Sartre does not hesitate to push this conception to its last consequences. Being a Frenchman, a Southerner, a worker, a Jew—is the result of the "Pour soi's" own "making." By the same token, all the restrictions, obstacles, prohibitions which society places upon the Jew "exist" only because and in so far as the Jew "chooses" and accepts them:

> "No Jews allowed here," "Jewish restaurant, Aryans forbidden to enter," etc., can only have meaning on and through the foundation of my free choice (EN, p. 607).

> It is only by recognizing the liberty...of the anti-Semites and by assuming this being-Jewish which I represent to them, that being-

Jewish will appear as the external objective limit of my situation. If, on the other hand, it pleases me to consider them simply as objects, my being-Jewish disappears immediately to give way to the simple consciousness of being a free transcendence (EN, p. 610).

The treatise on human freedom has here reached the point of self-abdication. The persecution of the Jews, and "les tenailles du bour-reau" are the terror which is the world today, they are the brute reality of unfreedom. To the existentialist philosopher, however, they appear as examples of the existence of human freedom. The fact that Sartre's demonstration is ontologically correct and a time-honoured and suc-cessful feature of idealism only proves the remoteness of this demon-stration from the "réalité humaine." If philosophy, by virtue of its existential-ontological concepts of man or freedom, is capable of dem-onstrating that the persecuted Jew and the victim of the executioner are and remain absolutely free and masters of a self-responsible choice, then these philosophical concepts have declined to the level of a mere ideology, an ideology which offers itself as a most handy justification for the persecutors and executioners—themselves an important part of the "réalité humaine." It is true that the "Pour-soi," *qua* "Pour-soi," is and remains free in the hands of the numerous executioners who provide the numerous opportunities for exercising existential freedom, but this freedom has shrunk to a point where it is wholly irrelevant and thus cancels itself. The free choice between death and enslavement is nei-ther freedom nor choice, because both alternatives destroy the "réalité humaine" which is supposed to be freedom. Established as the locus of freedom in the midst of a world of totalitarian oppression, the "Pour-soi," the Cartesian Cogito, is no longer the jumping-off point for the conquest of the intellectual and material world, but the last refuge of the individual in an "absurd world" of prostration and failure. In Sartre's philosophy, this refuge is still equipped with all the parapher-nalia which characterized the heydays of individualistic society. The "Pour-soi" appears with the attributes of absolute autonomy, perpetual ownership, and perpetual appropriation (just as the Other appears as the one who usurps, appropriates, and appraises my world, as the "thief" of my possibilities). Behind the nihilistic language of Existen-tialism lurks the ideology of free competition, free initiative, and equal opportunity. Everybody can "transcend" his situation, carry out his own project: everybody has his absolutely free choice. However adverse the conditions, man must "take it" and make compulsion his self-realization. Everybody is master of his destiny. But in the face of an "absurd world" without meaning and reward, the attributes of the heroic period of bourgeois society assume naturally an absurd and illusory character. Sartre's "Pour-soi" is closer to Stirner's *Einziger und sein Eigentum* than to Descartes's *Cogito*. In spite of Sartre's insistence on the Ego's *Geworfenheit* (being thrown into a pre-given contingent situation), the latter seems to be wholly absorbed by the Ego's ever-transcending power which posits, as its own free project, all the obstacles encountered on its way. True, man is thrown into a "situation" which he himself has not created, and this situation may be such that it "alienates" his freedom, degrades him into a thing. The process of "reification" appears in manifold forms in Sartre's philosophy: as the subordination of the "Pour-soi" to the standardized technics of everyday life (EN, pp. 495ff., 594), and as the interchangeability of the individual (EN, p. 496). But to Sartre reification as well as its negation are only obstacles on which man's freedom thrives and feeds itself: they become parts of the Cogito's existential project, and the whole process once again serves to illustrate the perpetual liberty of the "Pour-soi" which finds only itself in the most alienated situation.

The Self-consciousness that finds itself in its Being-for-Others: Sartre's Existentialism thus revives Hegel's formula for the free and rational condition of man. To Hegel, however, the realization of this condition is only the goal and end of the entire historical process. Sartre takes the ontological shortcut and transforms the process into the metaphysical condition of the "Pour-soi." Sartre accomplishes this transformation by a trick: the term "Pour-soi" covers the We as well as the I; it is the collective as well as the individual self-consciousness.

le Pour-soi "fait qu'il soit daté par ses techniques." (EN, p. 604).

. . . se fait Français, meridional, ouvrier (EN, p. 606).

Thus, the "Pour-soi" creates nation, class, class distinctions, etc., makes them parts of his own free "project," and, consequently, is "responsible" for them. This is the fallacious identification of the ontological and historical subject. While it is a truism to say that the *ideas* "nation," "class," etc., arise with and "exist" only for the "Pour-soi," "nation," "class," etc., are not created by the "Pour-soi," but by the action and reaction of specific social groups under specific historical conditions. To be sure, these groups are composed of individuals who may be ontologically characterized as "Pour-soi," but such characterization is totally irrelevant to the understanding of their concreteness. The ontological concept of the "Pour-soi," which defines equally the wage earner and the entrepreneur, the sales clerk and the intellectual, the serf and the landlord, prejudices the analysis of their concrete existence: in so far as the different existential situations are interpreted in terms of the realization of the "Pour-soi," they are reduced to the abstract denominator of a universal essence. In subsuming the various historical subjects under the ontological idea of the "Pour-soi," and making the latter the guiding principle of the existential philosophy, Sartre relegates the specific differences which constitute the very concreteness of human existence to mere manifestations of the universal essence of man—thus offending against his own thesis that "existence creates the essence." Reduced to the role of examples, the concrete situations cannot bridge the gap between the terms of ontology and those of existence. The ontological foundation of Existentialism frustrates its effort to develop a philosophy of the concrete human existence.

The gap between the terms of ontology and those of existence is concealed by the equivocal use of the term "is." Sartre's "is" functions indiscriminately and without mediation as the copula in the definition of the essence of man, and as the predication of his actual condition. In this twofold sense, the "is" occurs in propositions like "Man is free," "is his own project," etc. The fact that, in the empirical reality, man is not free, not his own project, is obliterated by the inclusion of the negation into the definition of "free," "project," etc. But Sartre's concepts are, in spite of his dialectical style and the pervasive role of the negation, decidedly undialectical. In his philosophy, the negation is no force of its own but is *a priori* absorbed into the affirmation. True, in Sartre's analysis, the development of the subject through its negation into the self-conscious realization of its project appears as a process, but the process-character is illusory: the subject moves in a circle.

Existentialist freedom is safe from the tribulations to which man is subjected in the empirical reality. However, in one respect, the empirical reality does not affect Sartre's concept of human liberty. Although the freedom which is operative as the very being of the "Pour-soi" accompanies man in all situations, the scope and degree of his freedom varies in his different situations: it is smallest and dimmest where man is most thoroughly "reified," where he is least "Pour-soi." For example, in situations where he is reduced to the state of a thing, an instrument, where he exists almost exclusively as body, his "Pour-soi" has all but disappeared. But precisely here, where the ontological idea of freedom seems to evaporate together with the "Pour-soi," where it falls almost entirely into the sphere of things—at this point a new image of human freedom and fulfillment arises. We shall now discuss the brief appearance of this image in Sartre's philosophy.

III

In illustrating the permanent transcendence of the "Pour-soi" beyond every one of its contingent situations (a transcendence which, however free, remains afflicted with the very contingency it transcends), Sartre uses the term "jouer à être." He introduces the term in describing the behaviour of a "garçon de café." The waiter's behaviour exemplifies the manner in which man has to "make himself what he is" (EN, p. 98): every single one of the waiter's motions, attitudes, and gestures shows that he is constantly aware of the obligation to be a waiter and to behave as a waiter, and that he is trying to discharge this obligation. He "is" not a waiter, he rather "makes" himself a waiter. Now "being a waiter" consists of a set of standardized and mechanized motions, attitudes, and gestures which almost amount to being an automaton. Such a set of behaviour patterns is expected from a waiter, and he tries to live up to this expectation: he "plays" the waiter, he "plays" his own being. The obligation to be what he is thus becomes a play, a performance, and the freedom of the "Pour-soi" to transcend his contingent condition (being-a-waiter) shows forth as the freedom to play, to perform.

Can the example be generalized so that the transcendence of the *Cogito*, the realization of its freedom, shows forth as a permanent and ubiquitous play, a "jouer à être"? Sartre strongly suggests such generalization, although he does not make the concept of "jouer a l'être" the guiding idea of his analysis. But at least at one decisive place, he does link it with the general condition of man. The essential contingency of human existence coagulates in the fact that man is and remains his past, and that this past prevents him once and for all from freely creating his being.

> [The past is] the fact which cannot determine the content of my motivations but which passes through them with its contingence because they can neither suppress nor change it. The past is rather that which the motivations necessarily carry with them and modify. ... This is what causes me, at each instant, *not to be* a diplomat or a sailor, but rather a professor, although I can only play this being without ever being able to rejoin it (EN, pp. 162ff.).

But if man can only play his being, then the freedom of the "Pour-soi" is in reality nothing but his ability to act a prescribed role in a play in which neither his part nor its interpretation is of his own free choosing. The *Cogito*'s transcendence, instead of showing forth as the very root of man's power over himself and his world, would appear as the very token of his being for others. Moreover, and most important, his liberty would lie, not in the "free" transcendence of the *Cogito* but rather in its negation: in the cancellation of that performance in which he has to play permanently the "Pour-soi" while actually being-for-others. But the negation of the "Pour-soi" is the "En-soi," the negation of the *Cogito* is the state of being a thing, nature. The analysis is thus driven into the sphere of reification: this sphere seems to contain the possibility of a freedom and satisfaction which are quite different from that of the *Cogito* and its activity.

The state of reification as the lever for the liberation of man appears in Sartre's philosophy on two different levels: (1) on the level of the individual existence as the "attitude of (sexual) desire," (2) on the socio-historical level as the revolutionary attitude of the proletariat. Sartre does not establish the link between these two levels: whereas the first is intrinsically connected with the main philosophical argument, the second remains extraneous to it and is developed only outside *L'Être et le Néant*, in the article "Matérialisme et Revolution."

According to Sartre, "le désir" is essentially "le désir sexuel." To him, sexuality is not "un accident contingent lié à notre nature physiologique," but a fundamental structure of the "Pour-soi" in its being-for-others (EN, pp. 452ff.). He had previously described the two chief types of human relations in terms of sexual relations (sadism and masochism); now sexuality becomes the force which cancels the entire apparatus of existentialist freedom, activity, and morality.

"Le désir" becomes this force first by virtue of the fact that it is the negation of all activity, all "performance": "Le désir n'est pas désir de faire" (EN, p. 454).

Whatever activity the desire may engender, all "technique amoureuse," accrues to it from outside. The desire itself is "purement et simplement désir d'un objet transcendant," namely, "désir d'un corps." And this object is desired purely and simply as what it is and appears, in its brute "facticité."

In describing the "désir sexuel" and its object, Sartre emphasizes the characteristics which make this relation the very opposite of the "Pour-soi" and its activity:

> . . . in sexual desire consciousness is as though dulled; one appears to let oneself be pervaded by the mere facticity (of one's existence as body), to cease fleeing from it, and to glide into a passive ascent to desire (EN, p. 457).

This is the coming-to-rest of the transcending *Cogito*, the paralysis of its freedom, "projects," and performances. And the same force which cancels the incessant performance of the "Pour-soi" also cancels its alienation. The "désir sexuel" reveals its object as stripped of all the attitudes, gestures, and affiliations which make it a standardized instrument, reveals the "corps comme chair" and thereby "comme révélation fascinante de la facticité" (EN, p. 458). Enslavement and repression are cancelled, not in the sphere of purposeful, "projective" activity, but in the sphere of the "corps vécu comme chair," in the "trame d'inertie" (EN, p. 458). By the same token, the image of fulfillment and satisfaction is, not in the ever transcending "Pour-soi," but in its own negation, in its pure "être-là," in the fascination of its being an object (for itself and for others). Reification itself thus turns into liberation.

The "désir sexuel" accomplishes this negation of the negation not as a mere relapse into animal nature, but as a free and liberating human relation. In other words, the "désir sexuel" is what it is only as activity of the "Pour-soi," an activity, however, which is rather the negation of all activity and which aims at the liberation of the pure presence to its object. This activity is "la caresse":

Desire expresses itself through caress as thought does through language (EN, p. 459). The breaking of the reified world, the revelation of the "Chair... comme contingence pure de la présence" is only brought about by the "caresse":

> Caress causes the Other to be born as flesh for me and for himself. ...Caress reveals the flesh by divesting the body of its action, by isolating it from the possibilities which surround it... (EN, p. 459).

It is thus in complete isolation from its possibilities, oblivious of its freedom and responsibility, divested of all its performances and achievements, in being a pure "object" ("corps vécu comme chair") that the *Ego* finds itself in the Other. The relationships among men have become relationships among things, but this fact is no longer concealed and distorted by societal fetishes and ideologies. Reification no longer serves to perpetuate exploitation and toil but is in its entirety determined by the "pleasure principle."

Moreover, the fundamental change in the existential structure caused by the "désir sexuel" affects not only the individuals concerned but also their (objective) world. The "désir sexuel" has, according to Sartre, a genuinely cognitive function: it reveals the (objective) world in a new form.

> If my body... is no longer felt to be the instrument which can be used by any other instrument, that is, as the synthetic organization of my acts in the world, if it is lived as flesh, it is then, as reverberation of my flesh, that I seize the objects in the world. This means that I make myself passive in relationship to them.... A contact as caress means that my perception is not utilization of an object and not the transcending of the present with a view to a goal. To perceive an object, in the attitude of desire, is to caress myself with it (EN, p. 461).

The "attitude désirante" thus releases the objective world as well as the *Ego* from domination and manipulation, cancels their "instrumentality," and, in doing so, reveals their own pure presence, their "chair."

We have seen that the fixation on the property relation permeates Sartre's entire book: not only the relation between the "Pour-soi" and "En-soi," but also the fundamental relationships between the "Pour-soi" and "l'autrui," the inter-human relationships are eventually interpreted in terms of "appropriation." Finally, the "désir sexuel" is the attempt to appropriate freely the liberty of the Other. That all these appropriations turn out to be futile and self-defeating only renews and perpetuates the attempt to appropriate. And the one point, the one moment which appears as fulfillment, possession, is where and when man becomes a thing: body, flesh; and his free activity becomes complete inertia: caressing the body as thing. The *Ego*, thus far separated from the "things" and therefore dominating and exploiting them, now has become a "thing" itself—but the thing, in turn, has been freed to its own pure existence. The Cartesian gap between the two substances is bridged in that both have changed their substantiality. The *Ego* has lost its character of being "Pour-soi," set off from and against everything other-than-the *Ego*, and its objects have assumed a subjectivity of their own. The "attitude désirante" thus reveals (the possibility of) a world in which the individual is in complete harmony with the whole, a world which is at the same time the very negation of that which gave the *Ego* freedom only to enforce its free submission to necessity. With the indication of this form of the "réalité humaine," Existentialism cancels its own fundamental conception.

In the sphere of the individual existence, the cancellation is only a temporary one: the free satisfaction afforded in the "attitude désirante" is bound to end in new frustration. Confined within the circle of sadistic and masochistic relationships, man is driven back into the transcending activity of the "Pour-soi." But the image which has guided Sartre's analysis to seek the reality of freedom in the sphere of reification and alienation also leads him into the socio-historical sphere. He tests his conception in a critical discussion of Historical Materialism.

IV

In Sartre's interpretation of the socio-historical sphere, the reification of the subject (which, in the private sphere, appeared as the "corps vécu comme chair") manifests itself in the existence of the industrial worker. The modern entrepreneur tends to reduce the worker to the state of a thing by assimilating his behaviour to [that of] properties (TM, 10, p. 15).

In view of the brute mechanization of the worker and his work, in view of his complete subjugation to the capitalistic machine process, it would be ridiculous to preach him the "internal" liberty which the philosophers have preached throughout the centuries:

> The revolutionary himself...distrusts freedom. And rightly so. There has never been lack of prophets to proclaim to him that he was free, and each time in order to cheat him (TM, 10, p. 14).

Sartre mentions in this connection the Stoic concept of freedom, Christian liberty, and Bergson's idea of freedom:

> They all come back to a certain internal liberty which man can preserve in any situation whatsoever. This internal liberty is nothing but an idealistic mystification... (TM, 10, p. 14).

It would seem that Sartre's own ontological concept of freedom would well be covered by this verdict of "idealistic mystification," and L'Être et le Néant provides little ground for evading it. Now he recognizes the fact that, in the empirical reality, man's existence is organized in such a way that his freedom is totally "alienated," and that nothing short of a revolutionary change in the social structure can restore the development of his liberty (TM, 9, pp. 15–16). If this is true, if, by the organization of society, human freedom can be alienated to such an extent that it all but ceases to exist, then the content of human freedom is determined, not by the structure of the "Pour-soi," but by the specific historical forces which shape the human society. However, Sartre tries to rescue his idea of freedom from Historical Materialism. He accepts the revolution as the only way to the liberation of mankind, but he insists that the revolutionary solution presupposes man's freedom to *seize* this solution, in other words, that man must be free *"prior"* to his liberation. Sartre maintains that this presupposition destroys the basis of materialism, according to which man is wholly determined by the material world. But according to Historical Materialism, the revolution remains an act of freedom—in spite of all material determination. Historical Materialism has recognized this freedom in the important role of the maturity of the revolutionary consciousness. Marx's constant emphasis on the material determination of the consciousness in all its manifestations points up the relationships between the subject and his world as they actually prevail in the capitalist society, where freedom has shrunk to the possibility of recognizing and seizing the necessity for liberation.

In the concrete historical reality, the freedom of the "Pour-soi," to whose glorification Sartre devotes his entire book, is thus nothing but one of the preconditions for the possibility of freedom—it is not freedom itself. Moreover, isolated from the specific historical context in which alone the "transcendence" of the subject may become a precondition of freedom, and hypostatized into the ontological form of the subject as such, this transcendental liberty becomes the very token of enslavement. The anti-fascist who is tortured to death may retain his moral and intellectual freedom to "transcend" this situation: he is still tortured to death. Human freedom is the very negation of that transcendental liberty in which Sartre sees its realization. In L'Être et le Néant this negation appeared only in the "attitude désirante": it was the loss of the "Pour-soi," its reification in the "corps vécu comme chair" which suggested a new idea of freedom and happiness.

Similarly, in Sartre's interpretation of the socio-historical sphere, it is the existence, not of the free but of the reified subject which points the way toward real liberation. The wage labourer, whose existence is that of a thing, and whose activity is essentially action on things, conceives of his liberation naturally as a change in the relationship between man and things. Sartre interprets the process between capital and wage labour in terms of the Hegelian process between master and servant. The labourer, who works in the service of the entrepreneur on the means of production, transforms, through his labour, these means into the instruments for his liberation. True, his labour is imposed upon him, and he is deprived of its products, but "within these limitations," his labour confers upon him "la mâitrise sur les choses":

The worker sees himself as the possibility of modifying endlessly the form of material objects by acting on them in accordance with certain universal rules. In other words, it is the determinateness of matter which offers him the first view of his freedom.... He transcends his state of slavery through his action on things, and things give back to him, by the very rigidity of their bondage, the image of a tangible freedom which consists of modifying them. And since

the outline of tangible freedom appears to him shackled to deter-
minism, it is not surprising that he visualizes the relationship of
man to man, which appears to him as that of tyrannic liberty to
humbled obedience, replaced by a relationship of man to thing,
and finally, since, from another point of view, the man who controls
things is in turn a thing himself, by the relationship of thing to thing
(TM, 10, pp. 15–16).

Sartre maintains that the materialistic conception of freedom is itself
the victim of reification in so far as it conceives the liberated world in
terms of a new relationship among things, a new organization of things.
As the liberation originates in the process of labour, it remains defined
by this process, and the liberated society appears only as "une entreprise
harmonieuse d'exploitation du monde" (TM, 10, p. 17). The result
would simply be "a more rational organization of society" (TM, 10, p. 21)
—not the realization of human freedom and happiness.

This critique is still under the influence of "idealistic mystifica-
tions." The "more rational organization of society," which Sartre belit-
tles as "simplement," is the very precondition of freedom. It means
the abolition of exploitation and repression in all their forms. And since
exploitation and repression are rooted in the material structure of society, their abolition requires a change in this structure: a more rational
organization of the relationships of production. In Historical Materialism, this organization of the liberated society is so little "defined by
labour" ("définie par le travail") that Marx once formulated the Communist goal as the "abolition of labour," and the shortening of the working day as the precondition for the establishment of the "realm of
freedom." The formula conveys the image of the unfettered satisfaction
of the human faculties and desires, thus suggesting the essential identity of freedom and happiness which is at the core of materialism.

Sartre notes that throughout history, materialism was linked with a
revolutionary attitude:

No matter how far back I go, I find it [materialistic faith] linked with
the revolutionary attitude (TM, 9, pp. 15–16).

Indeed, the materialist faith was revolutionary in so far as it was materialistic, that is to say, as it shifted the definition of human freedom from
the sphere of consciousness to that of material satisfaction, from toil to

enjoyment, from the moral to the pleasure principle. The idealistic phi-losophy has made freedom into something frightening and tyrannic, bound up with repression, resignation, scarcity, and frustration. Behind the idealistic concept of freedom lurked the demand for an incessant moral and practical performance, an enterprise the profits of which were to be invested ever again in the same activity—an activity which was really rewarding only for a very small part of the population. The materialistic conception of freedom implies the discontinuation of this activity and performance: it makes the reality of freedom a pleasure. Prior to the achievement of this "utopian" goal, materialism teaches man the necessities which determine his life in order to break them by his liberation. And his liberation is nothing less than the abolition of repression.

Sartre hits upon the revolutionary function of the materialistic prin-ciple in his interpretation of the "attitude désirante": there, and only there, is his concept of freedom identical with the abolition of repres-sion. But the tendencies which make for the destruction of his idealis-tic conception remain confined within the framework of philosophy and do not lead to the destruction of the ideology itself. Consequently, in Sartre's work, they manifest themselves only as a disintegration of the traditional philosophical "style." This disintegration is expressed in his rejection of the "esprit de sérieux" (seriousness).

V

According to Sartre, the "esprit de sérieux" must be banned from phi-losophy because, by taking the "réalité humaine" as a totality of objec-tive relationships, to be understood and evaluated in terms of objective standards, the "esprit de sérieux" offends against the free play of sub-jective forces which is the very essence of the "réalité humaine." By its very "style" philosophy thus fails to gain the adequate approach to its subject. In contrast, the existentialist style is designed to assert, already through the mode of presentation, the absolutely free movement of the *Cogito*, the "Pour-soi," the creative subject. Its "jouer à être" is to be re-produced by the philosophical style. Existentialism plays with every affirmation until it shows forth as negation, qualifies every statement until it turns into its opposite, extends every position to absurdity, makes liberty into compulsion and compulsion into liberty, choice into necessity and necessity into choice, passes from philosophy to *belles lettres* and vice versa, mixes ontology and sexology, etc. The heavy seriousness of Hegel and Heidegger is translated into artistic play. The ontological analysis includes a series of "scènes amoureuses," and the existentialist novel sets forth philosophical theses in italics.

This disintegration of the philosophical style reflects the inner contradictions of all existential philosophy: the concrete human existence cannot be understood in terms of philosophy. The contradiction derives from the historical conditions under which Western philosophy has developed and to which it remained committed throughout its development. The separation of the intellectual from the material production, of leisure and the leisure class from the underlying population, of theory from practice caused a fundamental gap between the terms of philosophy and the terms of existence. When Aristotle insisted that philosophy presupposed the establishment of the arts directed to the necessities of life, he defined not only the situation of the philosopher but of philosophy itself. The content of the basic philosophical concepts implies a degree of freedom from the necessities of life which is enjoyed only by a small number of men. The general concepts which aim at the structures and forms of being transcend the realm of necessity and the life of those who are confined to this realm. Their existence is not on the philosophical level. Conversely philosophy does not possess the conceptual instruments for comprehending their existence, which is the concreteness of the "réalité humaine." The concepts which do adequately describe this concreteness are not the exemplifications and particularizations of any philosophical concept. The existence of a slave or of a factory worker or of a sales clerk is not an "example" of the concept of being or freedom or life or man. The latter concepts may well be "applicable" to such forms of existence and "cover" them by their scope, but this coverage refers only to an irrelevant part or aspect of the reality. The philosophical concepts abstract necessarily from the concrete existence, and they abstract from its very content and essence; their generality transcends the existence *qualitatively*, into a different *genus*. Man as such, as "kind," is the genuine theme of philosophy; his *hic et nunc* is the ὕλη (matter, stuff) which remains outside the realm of philosophy. Aristotle's dictum that man is an ultimate indivisible kind (ἔσχατον ἄτομον; ἄτομον ειδος; ἄτομον τώ γένε), which defies further concretization pronounces the inner impossibility of all existential philosophy.

Against its intentions and efforts, Existentialism demonstrates the truth of Aristotle's statement. We have seen how, in Sartre's philosophy, the concept of the "Pour-soi" vacillates between that of the individual subject and that of the universal *Ego* or consciousness. Most of the essential qualities which he attributes to the "Pour-soi" are qualities of man as a *genus*. As such, they are *not* the essential qualities of man's concrete existence. Sartre makes reference to Marx's early writings, but not to Marx's statement that man, in his concrete historical existence, is not (yet) the realization of the *genus* man. This proposition states the fact that the historical forms of society have crippled the development of the general human faculties, of the *humanitas*. The concept of the *genus* man is thus at the same time the concept of the abstract-universal and of the *ideal* man—but is *not* the concept of the "réalité humaine."

But if the "réalité humaine" is not the concretization of the *genus* man, it is equally indescribable in terms of the individual. For the same historical conditions which crippled the realization of the *genus* man also crippled the realization of his individuality. The activities, attitudes, and efforts which circumscribe his concrete existence are, in the last analysis, not his but those of his class, profession, position, society. In this sense is the life of the individual indeed the life of the universal, but this universal is a configuration of specific historical forces, made up by the various groups, interests, institutions, etc., which form the social reality. The concepts which actually reach the concrete existence must therefore derive from a theory of society. Hegel's philosophy comes so close to the structure of the concrete existence because he interprets it in terms of the historical universal, but because he sees in this universal only the manifestation of the Idea he remains within the realm of philosophical abstraction. One step more toward concretization would have meant a transgression beyond philosophy itself.

Such transgression occurred in the opposition to Hegel's philosophy. Kierkegaard and Marx are frequently claimed as the origins of existential philosophy. But neither Kierkegaard nor Marx wrote existential philosophy. When they came to grips with the concrete existence, they abandoned and repudiated philosophy. Kierkegaard comes to the conclusion that the situation of man can be comprehended and "solved" only by theology and religion. For Marx, the conception of the "réalité humaine" is the critique of political economy and the theory of the socialist revolution. The opposition against Hegel pronounces the essential inadequacy of philosophy in the face of the concrete human existence.

Since then, the gap between the terms of philosophy and those of existence has widened. The experience of the totalitarian organization of the human existence forbids to conceive freedom in any other form than that of a free society.

Postscript

Existentialism "leads men to understand that reality alone counts, that dreams, expectations, and hopes only permit the definition of a man as a deceived dream, an abortive hope, useless expectation . . ." (EH, p. 58). These phrases are frighteningly ambivalent. "Reality alone counts" — as what? Such a statement could be the motto of total conformism; or worse: of a healthy acceptance of reality. But it can also show the direction which Sartre's own thought has since taken: the way of radical contradiction. For this direction reality is what must be overthrown so that human existence can begin.

It was said in a note to *L'Être et le Néant* that a morality of liberation and deliverance was possible, but that it would require a "radical conversion." Sartre's writings and the stands he has taken over the last two decades are a conversion of this kind. In Sartre's concept pure ontology and phenomenology recede before the invasion of real history, the dispute with Marxism and the adoption of the dialectic. Philosophy becomes politics because no philosophical concept can be thought out and developed without incorporating within itself the inhumanity which is today organized by the rulers and accepted by the ruled. In this politicized philosophy the basic existentialist concept is rescued through the consciousness which declares war on this reality — in the knowledge that the reality will remain victor. For how long? This question, which has no answer, does not alter the validity of the position which is today the only possible one for the thinking person. In his famous Preface to Fanon's *Wretched of the Earth*, in his declarations against the colonial wars in Vietnam and Santo Domingo, Sartre has fulfilled his promise of a "morality of liberation." If, as he fears, he has become an "institution," then it would be an institution in which conscience and truth have found refuge.

Notes

Publisher's note: This essay was written in English and first published in *Philosophy and Phenomenological Research*, vol. VIII, no. 3, 1948. The version printed above follows the original, except for the Postscript which was rewritten as a separate section by Marcuse for the essay's republication in German in his *Kultur und Gesellschaft*, vol. 2, Frankfurt, 1965. The translations from the French are those prepared by Beatrice Braude for Marcuse in 1948.

1. A. Camus, *Le Mythe de Sisyphe*, Paris, 1946, pp. 83ff.

2. Ibid., pp. 89ff.

3. In *Les lettres françaises*, 24 November, 1945. Cf. also Sartre, *L'existentialisme est un humanisme*, Paris, 1946, p. 17 (henceforth referenced in text thus: EH).

4. "Matérialisme et Révolution" in *Les Temps modernes*, I, 9 and 10, Paris, June and July 1946 (henceforth referenced in text thus: TM, 9, 10).

5. Unless otherwise stated, "existentialist" and "Existentialism" refer only to Sartre's philosophy.

6. *L'Être et le Néant*, Paris, 1943, p. 38 (henceforth referenced in text thus: EN).

FREEDOM AND FREUD'S THEORY
OF INSTINCTS (1956)

This essay was first delivered as a lecture in 1956 at events commemorating the centenary of Freud's birth, and thus it represents Marcuse's thinking at the time he wrote his book on Freud, *Eros and Civilization* (1955). It takes up again one of the constant themes in Marcuse's thought: the concept of freedom. In "Foundations of Historical Materialism," as we have seen, the concept of freedom is approached from the standpoint of the labor process. In this essay the standpoint is the theory of instincts—more specifically, the notion that what is commonly called "progress" in civilization is based on repression of the individual's instinctual striving for pleasure and fulfillment. Freud called this the "reality principle," the subjection of the individual's needs for sensual gratification to the project of building the edifice of order—the ever-expanding scope of bureaucratic institutions and the economy.

In this process, as Marcuse interprets Freud's theory, "the individual becomes, *in his very nature,* the subject-object of socially useful labor, of the domination of men and nature." The underlying rationale of the civilizing process is the sacrifice of generations in the course of laying the foundations for universal freedom and, ultimately, for a release from the sway of the reality principle in the "free play of human capacities." But, Marcuse asks, how long must this process go on? Why do we never seem to actually arrive at the point where we can say: We now have enough. We can stop taking the economy to new heights of production and productivity. We can finally relax and enjoy what has been built over the years by so many who did not get the chance to enjoy it.

A discussion of Freudian theory from the standpoint of political science and philosophy requires some justification—in part because Freud repeatedly emphasized the scientific and empirical character of his work. The justification must be two-fold: first, it must show that the structure of Freudian theory is open to and in fact *encourages* consideration in political terms, that this theory, which appears to be purely biological, is fundamentally social and historical. Second, it must show on the one hand to what extent psychology today is an essential part of political science, and on the other hand to what extent the Freudian theory of instincts (which is the only thing we will be concerned with here) makes it possible to understand the hidden nature of certain decisive tendencies in current politics.

We will begin with the second aspect of the justification. Our concern is not with introducing psychological concepts into political science or with explaining political processes in psychological terms. That would mean attempting to explain what is basic in terms of what is based on it. Rather, psychology in its inner structure must reveal itself to be political. The psyche appears more and more immediately to be a piece of the social totality, so that individuation is almost synonymous with apathy and even with guilt, but also with the principle of negation, of possible revolution. Moreover, the totality of which the psyche is a part becomes to an increasing extent less "society" than "politics." That is, society has fallen prey to and become identified with domination.

We must identify at the outset what we mean by "domination," because the content of this notion is central to Freudian instinct theory. Domination is in effect whenever the individual's goals and purposes and the means of striving for and attaining them are prescribed to him and performed by him as something prescribed. Domination can be exercised by men, by nature, by things—it can also be internal, exercised by the individual on himself, and appear in the form of autonomy. This second form plays a decisive role in Freudian instinct theory: the super-ego absorbs the authoritarian models, the father and his representatives, and makes their commands and prohibitions its own laws, the individual's conscience. Mastery of drives becomes the individual's own accomplishment—autonomy.

Under these circumstances, however, freedom becomes an impossible concept, for there is nothing that is not prescribed for the individual in some way or other. And in fact freedom can be defined only within the framework of domination, if previous history is to provide a guide to the definition of freedom. Freedom is *a form of domination*: the one in which the means provided satisfy the needs of the individual with a minimum of displeasure and renunciation. In this sense freedom is completely historical, and the degree of freedom can be determined only historically; capacities and needs as well as the minimum of renunciation differ depending on the level of cultural development and are subject to objective conditions. But it is precisely the fact of being objectively, historically conditioned that makes the distinction between freedom and domination transcend any merely subjective valuation: like human needs and capacities themselves, the means of satisfying the needs produced at a particular level of culture are socially given facts, present in material and mental productive forces and in the possibilities for their application. Civilization can use these possibilities in the interest of individual gratification of needs and so will be organized under the aspect of freedom. Under optimal conditions domination is reduced to a rational division of labor and experience; freedom and happiness converge. On the other hand, individual satisfaction itself may be subordinated to a social need that limits and diverts these possibilities; in that case the social and the individual needs become separate, and civilization is operating through domination.

Hitherto existing culture has been organized in the form of domination insofar as social needs have been determined by the interests of the ruling groups at any given time, and this interest has defined the needs of other groups and the means and limitations of their satisfactions. Contemporary civilization has developed social wealth to a point where the renunciations and burdens placed on individuals seem more and more unnecessary and irrational. The irrationality of unfreedom is most crassly expressed in the intensified subjection of individuals to the enormous apparatus of production and distribution, in the deprivatization of free time, in the almost indistinguishable fusion of constructive and destructive social labor. And it is precisely this fusion that is the condition of the constantly increasing productivity and domination of nature which keeps individuals—or at least the majority of them in the advanced countries—living in increasing comfort. Thus irrationality becomes the form of social *reason*, becomes the rational universal. Psychologically—and that is all that concerns us here—the difference between domination and freedom is becoming smaller. The individual reproduces on the deepest level, in his instinctual structure, the values and behavior patterns that serve to maintain domination, while domination becomes increasingly less autonomous, less "personal," more objective and universal. What actually dominates is the economic, political, and cultural apparatus, which has become an indivisible unity constructed by social labor.

To be sure, the individual has always reproduced domination from within himself, and to the extent that domination represented and developed the whole, this reproduction has been of service to rational self-preservation and self-development. From the outset the whole has asserted itself in the sacrifice of the happiness and the freedom of a great part of mankind; it has always contained a self-contradiction, which has been embodied in the political and spiritual forces striving toward a different form of life. What is peculiar to the present stage is the neutralization of this contradiction—the mastering of the tension between the given form of life and its negation, a refusal in the name of the greater freedom which is historically possible. Where the neutralization of this contradiction is now most advanced, the possible is scarcely still known and desired, especially by those on whose knowing and willing its realization depends, those who alone could make it something really possible. In the most technically advanced centers of the contemporary world, society has been hammered into a unity as never before; what is possible is defined and realized by the forces that have brought about this unity; the future is to remain theirs, and individuals are to desire and bring about this future "in freedom."

"In freedom"—for compulsion presupposes a contradiction that can express itself in resistance. The totalitarian state is only one of the forms—a form perhaps already obsolete—in which the battle against the historical possibility of liberation takes place. The other, the democratic form, rejects terror because it is strong and rich enough to preserve and reproduce itself without terror: most individuals are in fact better off in this form. But what determines its historical direction is not this fact, but the way it organizes and utilizes the productive forces at its disposal. It, too, maintains society at the attained level, despite all technical progress. It, too, works against the new forms of freedom that are

FREEDOM AND FREUD'S THEORY OF INSTINCTS 163

historically possible. In this sense its rationality, too, is regressive, although it works with more painless and more comfortable means and methods. But that it does so should not repress the consciousness that in the democratic form freedom is played off against its complete realization, reality against possibility.

To compare potential freedom with existing freedom, to see the latter in the light of the former, presupposes that at the present stage of civilization much of the toil, renunciation, and regulation imposed upon men is no longer justified by scarcity, the struggle for existence, poverty, and weakness. Society could afford a high degree of instinctual liberation without losing what it has accomplished or putting a stop to its progress. The basic trend of such liberation, as indicated by Freudian theory, would be the recovery of a large part of the instinctual energy diverted to alienated labor, and its release for the fulfillment of the autonomously developing needs of individuals. That would in fact also be *desublimation*—but a desublimation that would not destroy the "spiritualized" manifestations of human energy but rather take them as projects for and possibilities of happy satisfaction. The result would be not a reversion to the prehistory of civilization but rather a fundamental change in the content and goal of civilization, in the principle of progress. I shall try to explain this elsewhere;[1] here I should simply like to point out that the realization of this possibility presupposes fundamentally changed social and cultural institutions. In the existing culture that progression appears as a catastrophe, and the battle against it as a necessity, with the result that the forces tending toward it are paralyzed.

Freudian instinct theory reveals this neutralization of the dynamic of freedom in terms of psychology, and Freud made visible its necessity, its consequences for the individual, and its limits. We will formulate these dimensions in the form of theses, using but also going beyond the concepts of Freudian instinct theory.

Within the framework of civilization which has become historical reality, freedom is possibly only on the basis of unfreedom, that is, on the basis of instinctual suppression. For in terms of its instinctual structure, the organism is directed toward procuring pleasure; it is dominated by the *pleasure principle*: the instincts strive for pleasurable release of tension, for painless satisfaction of needs. They resist delay of gratification, limitation and sublimation of pleasure, non-libidinal work. But culture *is* sublimation: postponed, methodically controlled satisfaction which presupposes unhappiness. The "struggle for existence," "scarcity," and cooperation all compel renunciation and repression in the interest of security, order, and living together. Cultural progress consists in the ever greater and more conscious production of the technical, material, and intellectual conditions of progress—in work, itself unsatisfying, on the means of satisfaction. Freedom in civilization has its internal limit in the necessity of gaining and maintaining labor power in the organism—of transforming him from a subject-object of pleasure into a subject-object of work. This is the social content of the overcoming of the pleasure principle through the *reality principle*, which becomes from earliest childhood the dominant principle in the psychic processes. Only this transformation, which leaves an unhealable wound in men, makes them fit for society and thus for life, for without secure cooperation it is impossible to survive in a hostile and niggardly environment. It is only this traumatic transformation, which is an "alienation" of man from nature in the authentic sense, an alienation from his own nature, that makes man capable of enjoyment; only the instinct that has been restrained and mastered raises the merely natural satisfaction of need to pleasure that is experienced and comprehended—to happiness.

But from then on all happiness is only of a sort that is consonant with social restrictions, and man's growing freedom is based on unfreedom. According to Freud's theory this intertwining is inevitable and indissoluble. In order to understand this we must pursue his theory of instincts a little further. In doing so we will proceed from the late version of the theory, developed after 1920. It is the metapsychological, even metaphysical version, but perhaps precisely for that reason it is also the one that contains the deepest and most revolutionary nucleus of Freudian theory.

The organism develops through the activity of two original basic instincts: the *life* instinct (sexuality, which Freud for the most part now calls *Eros*) and the *death* instinct, the destructive instinct. While the former strives for the binding of living substance into ever larger and more permanent units, the death instinct desires regression to the condition before birth, without needs and thus without pain. It strives for the annihilation of life, for reversion to inorganic matter. The organism equipped with such an antagonistic instinctual structure finds itself in an environment which is too poor and too hostile for the immediate gratification of the life instincts. Eros desires life under the pleasure principle, but the environment stands in the way of this goal. Thus as soon as the life instinct has subjected the death instinct to itself (a subjection which is simultaneous with the beginning and the continuation of life), the environment compels a decisive modification of the instincts: in part they are diverted from their original goal or inhibited on the way to it, in part the area of their activity is limited and their direction is changed.[2] The result of this modification is gratification which is inhibited, delayed, and vicarious but also secure, useful, and relatively lasting.

Thus the psychic dynamic takes the form of a constant struggle of three basic forces: Eros, the death instinct, and the outside world. Corresponding to these three forces are the three basic principles which according to Freud determine the functions of the psychic apparatus: the *pleasure principle*, the *Nirvana principle*, and the *reality principle*. If the pleasure principle stands for the unlimited unfolding of the life instinct, and the Nirvana principle for regression into the painless condition before birth, then the reality principle signifies the totality of the modifications of those instincts compelled by the outside world; it signifies "reason" as reality itself.

It seems that there is a dichotomy hidden behind the tripartite division: if the death instinct presses for the annihilation of life because life is the predominance of displeasure, tension, and need, then the Nirvana principle too would be a form of the pleasure principle, and the death instinct would be dangerously close to Eros. On the other hand, Eros itself seems to partake of the nature of the death instinct: the striving for pacification, for making pleasure eternal, indicates an instinctual resistance in Eros as well to the continual appearance of new tensions, to giving up a pleasurable equilibrium once reached. This resistance, if not hostile to life, is nevertheless static and thus "antagonistic to progress." Freud saw the original unity of the two opposing instincts: he spoke of the *"conservative nature"* common to them, of the "inner weight" and "inertia" of all life. He rejected this thought—in fear, one might almost say—and maintained the duality of Eros and the death instinct, the pleasure principle and the Nirvana principle, despite the difficulty, which he emphasized several times, of demonstrating any drives in the organism other than originally libidinous ones. It is the effective "mixture" of the two fundamental instincts that defines life: although forced into the service of Eros, the death instinct retains the energy proper to it, except that this destructive energy is diverted from the organism itself and directed toward the outside world in the form of socially useful aggression — toward nature and sanctioned enemies — or, in the form of conscience, of morality, it is used by the super-ego for the socially useful mastery of one's own drives.

The instincts of destruction become of service to the life instincts in this form, but only in that the latter are decisively transformed. Freud devoted the major portion of his work to analyzing the transformations of Eros; here we shall emphasize only what is decisive for the fate of freedom. Eros as the life instinct is sexuality, and sexuality in its original function is "deriving pleasure from the zones of the body," no more and no less. Freud expressly adds: a pleasure which only "afterwards is placed in the service of reproduction."[3] This indicates the polymorphous-perverse character of sexuality: in terms of their object, the instincts are indifferent with respect to one's own and other bodies; above all they are not localized in specific parts of the body or limited to special functions. The primacy of genital sexuality and of reproduction, which then becomes reproduction in monogamous marriage, is to a certain extent a subsequent development — a late achievement of the reality principle, that is, a historical achievement of human society in its necessary struggle against the pleasure principle, which is not compatible with society. Originally[4] the organism in its totality and in all its activities and relationships is a potential field for sexuality, dominated by the pleasure principle. And precisely for this reason it must be *desexualized* in order to carry out unpleasurable work, in order, in fact, to live in a context of unpleasurable work.

Here we can bring out only the two most important aspects of the process of desexualization which Freud describes: first the blocking off of the so-called "partial instincts," that is, of pre- and non-genital sexuality, which proceed from the body as a total erogenous zone. The partial instincts either lose their independence, become subservient to genitality and thereby to reproduction by being made into preliminary stages, or they become sublimated and, if there is resistance, suppressed and tabooed as perversions. Second, sexuality and the sexual object are desensualized in "love"—the ethical taming and inhibiting of Eros. This is one of the greatest achievements of civilization—and one of the latest. It alone makes the patriarchal monogamous family the healthy "nucleus" of society.

The overcoming of the Oedipus complex is the precondition for this. In this process Eros, which originally includes everything, is reduced to the special function of genital sexuality and its accompaniments. Eroticism is limited to the socially acceptable minimum. Now Eros is no longer the life instinct governing the whole organism and striving to become the formative principle for the human and natural environment; it has become a private matter for which there is neither time nor place in the necessary social relations of men, labor relations, and Eros becomes "general" only as the reproductive function. The suppression of instincts—for sublimation is also suppression—becomes the basic condition of life in civilized society.

This biological-psychological transformation determines the fundamental experience of human existence and the goal of human life. Life is experienced as a struggle with one's self and the environment; it is suffered and won by conquests. Its substance is unpleasure, not pleasure. Happiness is a reward, relaxation, coincidence, a moment—in any case, not the goal of existence. That goal is rather *labor*. And labor is essentially alienated labor. Only in privileged situations does man work "for himself" in his occupation, does he satisfy his own needs, sublimated and unsublimated, in his occupation; normally he is busy all day long carrying out a prescribed social function, while his self-fulfillment, if there is any, is limited to a scanty free time. The social structuring of time is patterned on the structuring of the instincts completed in childhood; only the limitation of Eros makes possible the limitation of free, that is, pleasurable time to a minimum deducted from full-time labor. And time, like existence itself, is divided into the primary content "alienated labor" and the secondary content "non-labor."

But the structuring of the instincts that dethrones the pleasure principle also makes possible ethics, which has become increasingly more decisive in the development of Western civilization. The individual reproduces *instinctively* the cultural negation of the pleasure principle, renunciation, the pathos of labor: in the repressively modified instincts social legislation becomes the individual's own legislation; the necessary unfreedom appears as an act of his autonomy and thus as freedom. If the Freudian theory of the instincts had stopped here, it would be little more than the psychological grounding of the idealist concept of freedom, which in turn had given a philosophical foundation to the facts of cultural domination. This philosophical concept defines freedom in opposition to pleasure, so that the control, even the suppression of instinctual sensuous aims appears to be a condition of the possibility of freedom. For Kant, freedom is essentially moral — inner, intelligible — freedom and as such it is *compulsion:* "The less man can be physically compelled but the more he can rather be morally compelled (through the mere mental representation of duty), the more free he is."[5] The step from the realm of necessity to the realm of freedom here is progress from physical to moral compulsion, but the object of the compulsion remains the same: man as a member of the "sensuous world." And the moral compulsion is not only moral; it has its own very physical institutions. From the family to the factory to the army, they surround the individual as the effective embodiments of the reality principle. Political freedom is developed on this double basis of moral compulsion: wrung from absolutism in bloody street conflicts and battles, it is set up, secured, and neutralized in the self-discipline and self-renunciation of individuals. They have learned that their inalienable freedom is subject to duties not the least of which is the suppression of instinctual drives. Moral and physical compulsion have a common denominator — *domination.*

Domination is the internal logic of the development of civilization. In acknowledging it, Freud is at one with idealistic ethics and with liberal-bourgeois politics. Freedom must contain compulsion: scarcity, the struggle for existence, and the amoral nature of the instincts make the suppression of instinctual drives indispensable; the alternative is progress or barbarism. It must be emphasized again that for Freud the most fundamental reason for the necessity to suppress the instincts is the integral claim of the pleasure principle, that is, the fact that the organism is constitutionally directed toward calm through fulfillment, gratification, peace. The "conservative nature" of the instincts makes them unproductive in the deepest sense: unproductive for the alienated productivity that is the motor of cultural progress, so unproductive that even the self-preservation of the organism is not an original goal as long as self-preservation means predominance of displeasure. In Freud's late instinct theory there is no longer an independent drive for self-preservation: it is a manifestation either of Eros or of aggression. For this reason unproductiveness and conservatism must be overcome if the species is to develop a civilized communal life. Calm and peace and the pleasure principle are worth nothing in the struggle for existence: "The program for becoming happy which the pleasure principle presses upon us cannot be fulfilled."[6]

The repressive transformation of the instincts becomes the biological constitution of the organism: history rules even in the instinctual structure; culture becomes nature as soon as the individual learns to affirm and to reproduce the reality principle from within himself, through his instincts. In limiting Eros to the partial function of sexuality and making the destructive instinct useful, the individual becomes, *in his very nature*, the subject-object of socially useful labor, of the domination of men and nature. Technology too is born of suppression; even the highest achievements for making human existence less burdensome bear witness to their origin in the rape of nature and in the deadening of human nature. "Individual freedom is not a product of civilization."[7]

As soon as civilized society establishes itself the repressive transformation of the instincts becomes the psychological basis of a *threefold domination*: first, domination over one's self, over one's own nature, over the sensual drives that want only pleasure and gratification; second, domination of the labor achieved by such disciplined and controlled individuals; and third, domination of outward nature, science, and technology. And to domination subdivided in this way belongs the *threefold freedom* proper to it: first, freedom from the mere necessity of satisfying one's drives, that is, freedom for renunciation and thus for socially acceptable pleasure—moral freedom; second, freedom from arbitrary violence and from the anarchy of the struggle for existence, social freedom characterized by the division of labor, with legal rights and duties—political freedom; and third, freedom from the power of nature, that is, the mastery of nature, freedom to change the world through human reason—intellectual freedom.

The psychic substance common to these three aspects of freedom is *unfreedom:* domination of one's instincts, domination that society makes into second nature and that perpetuates the institutions of domination. But civilized unfreedom is oppression of a particular kind: it is rational unfreedom, rational domination. It is rational to the extent that it makes possible the ascent from a human animal to a human being, from nature to civilization. But does it remain rational when civilization has developed completely?

This is the point at which the Freudian theory of the instincts questions the development of civilization. The question arose in the course of psychoanalytic practice, of clinical experience, which for Freud opened the way to theory. Thus it is in the individual and from the point of view of the individual—and in fact from the point of view of the sick, neurotic individual—that civilization is put into question. The sickness is one's individual fate, private history; but in psychoanalysis the private reveals itself to be a particular instance of the general destiny, of the traumatic wound that the repressive transformation of the instincts has inflicted on man. When Freud then asks what civilization has made of man, he is contrasting civilization not with the idea of some "natural" condition but rather with the historically developing needs of individuals and with the possibilities for their fulfillment.

Freud's answer has already been indicated in what has been said. The more civilization progresses, the more powerful its apparatus for the development and gratification of social needs becomes, the more oppressive are the sacrifices that it has to impose on individuals in order to maintain the necessary instinctual structure.

The thesis contained in the Freudian theory asserts that repression increases with cultural progress because the aggression to be suppressed increases. The assertion seems more than questionable when we compare present freedoms with previous ones. Sexual morality is certainly much more relaxed than it was in the nineteenth century. Certainly the patriarchal authority structure and with it the family as the agency of education, of "socialization" of the individual, has been considerably weakened. Certainly political liberties in the Western world are much more widespread than they were previously, even though the substance of the fascist period is alive in them again and there is no need to prove the growth of aggression. Nevertheless, when we consider the greater liberality of public and private morality, the essential connection that, according to Freud, existed between these facts and the instinctual dynamic is by no means immediately evident. But the present situation appears in another light when we apply the Freudian categories to it more concretely.

There are two orientations for this examination of Freudian instinct theory. The first is in terms of the *reification and automatization of the ego.* According to Freudian instinct theory, the reality principle works primarily through the processes that occur between the id, the ego, and the superego, between the unconscious, the conscious, and the outside world. The ego, or rather the conscious part of the ego, fights a battle on two fronts, against the id and against the outside world, with frequently shifting alliances. Essentially, the struggle centers on the degree of instinctual freedom to be allowed and the modifications, sublimations, and repressions to be carried out. The conscious ego plays a leading role in this struggle. The decision is really *its* decision; it is, at least in the normal case of the mature individual, the responsible master of the psychic processes. But this mastery has undergone a crucial change. Franz Alexander pointed out that the ego becomes "corporeal," so to speak, and that its reactions to the outside world and to the instinctual desires emerging from the id become increasingly "automatic." The conscious processes of confrontation are replaced to an increasing degree by immediate, almost physical reactions in which comprehending consciousness, thought, and even one's own feelings play a very small role. It is as though the free space which the individual has at his disposal for his psychic processes has been greatly narrowed down; it is no longer possible for something like an individual psyche with its own demands and decisions to develop; the space is occupied by public, social forces. This reduction of the relatively autonomous ego is empirically observable in people's frozen gestures, and in the growing passivity of leisure-time activities, which become more and more inescapably deprivatized, centralized, universalized in the bad sense, and as such controlled. This process is the psychic correlate of the social overpowering of the opposition, the impotence of criticism, technical coordination, and the permanent mobilization of the collective.

The second change is the *strengthening* of *extra-familial* authority. The social development that has dethroned the individual as an eco-

nomic subject has also reduced, to an extreme degree, the individualistic function of the family in favor of more effective powers. The
younger generation is taught the reality principle less through the
family than outside the family; it learns socially useful reactions and
ways of behaving outside of the protected private sphere of the family.
The modern father is not a very effective representative of the reality
principle, and the loosening of sexual morality makes it easier to overcome the Oedipus complex: the struggle against the father loses much
of its decisive psychological significance. But the effect of this is to
strengthen rather than to weaken the omnipotence of domination.
Precisely insofar as the family was something private it stood against
public power or at least was different from it; the more the family is now
controlled by public power, that is, the more the models and examples
are taken from outside it, the more unified and uninterrupted becomes
the "socialization" of the young generation in the interest of public
power, as a part of public power. Here too the psychic space in which
independence and difference could emerge is limited and occupied.

In order to make the historical function of these psychic changes evident, we must try to see them in connection with contemporary political structures. The defining characteristic of these structures has been
called *mass democracy*. Without discussing whether we are justified in
using this concept, we will outline its main components briefly: in mass
democracy the real elements of politics are no longer identifiable individual groups but rather unified—or politically integrated—*totalities*.
There are two dominant units; first, the giant production-and-distribu-
tion apparatus of modern industry, and second, the masses which serve
this apparatus. Having control of the apparatus, or even of its key positions, means having control of the masses in such a way, in fact, that
this control seems to result automatically from the division of labor, to
be its technical result, the rationale of the functioning apparatus that
spans and maintains the whole society. Thus domination appears as a
technical-administrative quality, and this quality fuses the different
groups that hold the key positions in the apparatus—economic, political, military—into a technical-administrative collective that represents
the whole.

On the other hand, the groups that serve the apparatus are united
into the masses, the people, through a technical necessity; the people

become the object of administration even where they, the "sovereign," delegate power freely and control it democratically.

This technical-administrative collectivization appears as the expression of objective reason, that is, as the form in which the whole reproduces and extends itself. All freedoms are predetermined and preformed by it and subordinated not so much to political force as to the rational demands of the apparatus. The latter encompasses the public and private existence of individuals, of those who administer it as well as those who are administered, it encompasses work time and free time, service and relaxation, nature and culture. But in doing so the apparatus invades the inner sphere of the person himself, his instincts and his intelligence, and this occurs differently than in the earlier stages of the development: it no longer occurs primarily as the intervention of a brutal external, personal, or natural force, no longer even as the free working of competition, of the economy, but rather as completely objectified technological reason, which appears doubly rational, methodically controlled — and legitimized.

Thus the masses are no longer simply those who are dominated, but rather the governed who are *no longer in opposition*, or whose opposition itself is integrated into the positive whole, as a calculable and manipulable corrective that demands improvements in the apparatus. What was previously a political subject has become an object, and the antagonistic interests that were previously irreconcilable seem to have passed over into a true collective interest.

With this, however, the political picture as a whole has been transformed. There is no longer an autonomous subject across from the object, a subject that governs and in doing so pursues its own definable interests and goals. *Domination tends to become neutral, interchangeable*, without the totality itself being changed by this change; domination is dependent only on the capacity and the drive to maintain and extend the apparatus as a whole. One visible political expression of this neutralization is the increasing resemblance in the most advanced countries of political parties previously opposed to one another, of their strategy and their goals, the growing unification of political language and political symbols, and the supranational and even supracontinental unification that is taking place despite all resistance and that does not stop even at countries with very different political systems. Might the neutralization of contradictions and the tendency to increasing international resemblance finally determine the relationship of the two opposing total systems, those of the Western and Eastern worlds? There are signs of this.

This political digression may help to illuminate the historical function of the psychic dynamic uncovered by Freud. The political collectivization has its counterpart in the neutralization of the psychic structure, which was briefly described above: the unification of the ego and the superego through which the ego's free confrontation with paternal authority is absorbed by social reason. To the technical-administrative quality of domination correspond the automatization and reification of the ego, in which free actions become rigidified to reactions.

But the ego that has been robbed of its independent power to structure its instincts, and delivered over to the superego is all the more a subject of destruction and all the less a subject of Eros. For the superego is the social agent of repression and the locus of the socially useful destruction stored up in the psyche. *Thus it seems that the psychic atoms of contemporary society are themselves as explosive as is social productivity.* Behind the technical-administrative rational quality of the unification appears the danger of the irrationality that has still not been mastered—in Freud's language, the harshness of the sacrifice that existing civilization must demand of individuals.

As productivity increases, the taboos and instinctual prohibitions on which social productivity rests have to be guarded with ever greater anxiety. Might we say, going beyond Freud, that this is so because the temptation to enjoy this increasing productivity in freedom and happiness becomes increasingly strong and increasingly rational? In any case Freud speaks of an "intensification of the feeling of guilt" in the progress of civilization, of its increase "perhaps to extremes that the individual finds hard to tolerate."[8] And he sees in this feeling of guilt the "expression of the conflict of ambivalence, of the perpetual struggle between Eros and the destructive or death instinct."[9] This is Freud's revolutionary insight: the conflict that is decisive for the fate of civilization is that between the reality of repression and the almost equally real possibility of doing away with repression, between the increase of Eros necessary for civilization and the equally necessary suppression of its claims for pleasure. To the extent that the emancipation of Eros can be more and more clearly envisaged as social wealth increases, its repression becomes harsher and harsher. And thus just as this repression weakens Eros' power to bind the death instinct, it also releases destructive energy from its bonds and frees aggression to a hitherto unknown extent, which in turn makes more intensive control and manipulation a political necessity.

This is the fatal dialectic of civilization, which, according to Freud, has no solution—just as the struggle between Eros and the death instinct, productivity and destruction has no solution. But if we are justified in seeing in this conflict the contradiction between socially necessary oppression and the historical possibility of going beyond it, then the increasing "feeling of guilt" would be characterized by the same contradiction: the guilt then lies not only in the continued existence of prohibited instinctual impulses—hostility toward the father and desire for the mother—but also in the acceptance and even complicity with suppression, that is, in reinstating, internalizing, and defying paternal authority and thus domination as such. What on more primitive cultural levels was—perhaps—not only a social but also a biological necessity for the further development of the species has become, at the height of civilization, a merely social, political "necessity" for maintaining the status quo. The incest taboo was the historical and structural *prima causa* for the whole chain of taboos and repressions that characterize patriarchal-monogamous society. These perpetuate the subordination of gratification to a productivity that transcends itself and destroys itself, and perpetuates the mutilation of Eros, of the life instincts. Hence the feeling of guilt about a freedom that one has both missed and betrayed.

Freud's definition of the conflict in civilization as the expression of the eternal struggle between Eros and the death instinct points to an internal contradiction in Freudian theory, which contradiction, in turn, as a genuine one, contains the possibility of its own solution, a possibility that psychoanalysis has almost repressed. Freud emphasizes that "civilization obeys an inner erotic impulse that tells it to unite men in an increasingly intimately bound mass."[10] If this is true, how can what Freud repeatedly emphasized as the amoral and asocial, even antimoral and anti-social nature of Eros be at the same time one that "creates civilization"? How can the integral claim of the pleasure principle, which outweighs even the drive for self-preservation, how can the polymorphous-perverse character of sexuality be an erotic impulse to civilization? It does not help to assign the two sides of the contradiction to two successive stages of development; Freud ascribes both sides to the original nature of Eros. Instead we must sustain the contradiction itself and find in it the way to its solution.

When Freud ascribes the goal of "uniting the organic in ever greater units,"[11] of "producing and preserving ever greater units,"[12] to the sexual drives, this striving is at work in every process that preserves life, from the first union of the germ cells to the formation of cultural communities: society and nation. This drive stands under the aegis of the pleasure principle: it is precisely the polymorphous character of sexuality that drives beyond the special function to which it is limited, toward gaining more intensive and extensive pleasure, toward the generation of libidinous ties with one's fellow men, the production of a libidinous, that is, happy environment. Civilization arises from pleasure: we must hold fast to this thesis in all its provocativeness. Freud writes: "The same process occurs in the social relations of men that psychoanalytic research has become familiar with in regard to the course of development of individual libido. Libido involves itself in gratifying the major needs of life and chooses for its first objects the persons who participate in this activity. And as with the individual, so in the development of mankind as a whole, love alone, in the sense of turning from egoism to altruism, has acted as the force of civilization."[13] It is Eros, not Agape, it is the drive that has not yet been split into sublimated and unsublimated energy, from which this effect proceeds. The *work* that has contributed so essentially to the development of man from animal is *originally libidinous*. Freud states expressly that sexual as well as sublimated love is "connected to communal labor."[14] Man begins working because he finds pleasure in work, not only after work, pleasure in the play of his faculties and the fulfillment of his life needs, not as a means of life but as life itself. Man begins the cultivation of nature and of himself, cooperation, in order to secure and perpetuate the gaining of pleasure. It is perhaps Géza Róheim who has most penetratingly presented and tried to prove this thesis.

If this is so, however, the Freudian conception of the relationship between civilization and the dynamic of the instincts is in need of a decisive correction. The conflict between the pleasure principle and the reality principle would then be neither biologically necessary nor insoluble nor soluble only through a repressive transformation of the instincts. And the repressive solution would then be not a natural process extended into history and compelled by an ineluctable struggle for existence, weakness, and hostility, but rather a socio-historical process which has become part of nature. The traumatic transformation of the organism into an instrument of alienated labor is *not* the psychic condition of civilization as such but only of civilization as domination, that is, of a specific form of civilization. Constitutional unfreedom would not be the condition of freedom in civilization but rather only of freedom in a civilization organized on the basis of domination, which in fact is what existing civilization is.

Freud actually did derive the fate of the instincts from that of domination: it is the despotism of the primal father that forces the development of the instincts into the path which then becomes the psychological foundation for rational, domination-based civilization, which, however, never abandoned its roots in the original domination. Since the rebellion of the sons and brothers against the primal father[15] and the reestablishment and internalization of paternal authority, domination, religion, and morality have been intimately connected, and in such a way that the latter provide the psychological foundation for the permanence and the legitimized organization—the "reason"—of domination but at the same time make domination universal. Just as all share in the guilt, the rebellion, so all must make sacrifices, including those who now rule. The masters, like the servants, submit to limitations on their instinctual gratification, on pleasure. But just as repression of the instincts makes every servant "master in his own house," so it also reproduces masters over all houses: with instinctual repression social domination fortifies its position as universal reason. This takes place in the *organization of labor.*

The development of domination through the organization of labor is a process the study of which belongs to political economy rather than psychology. But the somatic-psychic preconditions for this development which Freud uncovered make it possible to pinpoint the hypothetical point at which civilization based on instinctual repression stops being historically "rational" and reproducing historical reason. To demonstrate that this is possible let me summarize again the main factors in the dynamic of the instincts insofar as they are decisive for the labor process: first, repressive modifications of sexuality make the organism free to be used as an instrument of unpleasurable but socially useful labor. Second, if this labor is a lifelong chief occupation, that is, has become the universal means of life, then the original direction of the instincts is so distorted that the content of life is no longer gratification but rather working toward it. Third, in this way civilization reproduces itself on an increasingly extended scale. The energy won from sexuality and sublimated constantly increases the psychic "investment fund" for the increasing productivity of labor (technical progress). Fourth, increasing productivity of labor increases the possibility of enjoyment and thus the potential reversal of the socially compelled relationship between labor and enjoyment, labor time and free time. But the domination reproduced in the existing relationships also reproduces sublimation on an increasing scale: the goods produced for enjoyment remain commodities, the enjoyment of which presupposes further labor within existing relationships. Gratification remains a by-product of ungratifying labor. Increasing productivity itself becomes the necessity which it was to eliminate. Thus, fifth, the sacrifices that socialized individuals have imposed on themselves since the fall of the primal father become increasingly more irrational the more obviously reason has fulfilled its purpose and eliminated the original state of need. And the guilt which the sacrifices were to expiate through the deification and internalization of the father (religion and morality) remains unexpiated, because with the reestablishment of patriarchal authority, although in the form of rational universality, the—suppressed —wish for its annihilation remains alive. Indeed, the guilt becomes increasingly oppressive as this domination reveals its archaic character in the light of historical possibilities for liberation.

At this stage of development unfreedom appears no longer as the fundamental condition of rational freedom but rather as a limitation on freedom. The achievements of domination-based civilization have undermined the necessity for unfreedom; the degree of domination of nature and of social wealth attained makes it possible to reduce ungratifying labor to a minimum; quantity is transformed into quality, free time can become the content of life, and work can become the free play of human capacities. In this way the repressive structure of the instincts would be explosively transformed: the instinctual energies that would no longer be caught up in ungratifying work would become free and, as Eros, would strive to universalize libidinous relationships and develop a libidinous civilization. But although in the light of this possibility the necessity of instinctual repression appears irrational, it remains not only a social but also a biological necessity for men in existing society. For the repression of the instincts reproduced renunciation in the individuals themselves, and the apparatus of need-gratification that they have constructed reproduces the individuals themselves in the form of labor power.

We have already said that the Freudian theory of the instincts in its fundamental conception seems to represent the psychological counterpart of the ethical-idealist notion of freedom. Despite Freud's mechanistic-materialist notion of the soul, freedom contains its own repression, its own unfreedom, because without this unfreedom man would fall back to the animal level: "Individual freedom is not a product of civilization." And just as idealist ethics interprets the freedom that suppresses sensuousness as an ontological structure and sees in it the "essence" of human freedom, so Freud sees in the repression of the instincts both a cultural and a natural necessity: scarcity, the struggle for existence, and the anarchical character of the instincts place limits on freedom which cannot be trespassed. We can now follow these parallels further. A second essential moment of the idealist notion of freedom, most clearly expressed in existential philosophy, is transcendence: human freedom is the possibility, even the necessity, of going beyond, negating every given situation in existence, because in relation to men's possibilities every situation itself is negativity, a barrier, "something other." Human existence thus seems, to use Sartre's notion, an eternal "project," which never reaches fulfillment, plenitude, rest: the contradiction between in-itself and for-itself can never be solved in a real being-in-and-for-itself. This negativity of the notion of freedom also finds its psychological formulation in Freud's instinct theory.

This becomes evident when we remember the "conservative nature" of the instincts, which produces the lifelong conflict between the pleasure principle and the reality principle. The basic instincts are striving essentially for gratification, perpetuation of pleasure, but the fulfillment of this striving would be the *death* of man, both his natural and his socio-historical death: natural death in being the condition before birth, historical death in being the state before civilization. Sublimation is the psychological transcendence in which civilized freedom consists, the negation of a negativity which itself still remains negative—not only because it is repression of sensuality but also because it perpetuates itself as transcendence: the productivity of renunciation, which spurs itself on endlessly. But what in idealist ethics remains wrapped up and concealed in an ontological structure and in this form is transfigured as the crown of humanity appears in Freud as a traumatic wound, a disease that culture has inflicted on man and that cries out for healing. Increasing destruction and constriction, growing anxiety, "discontent with civilization" that grows out of the suppression of the wish for happiness, out of the sacrifice of the possibility of happiness—all this is not the other side of civilized freedom but its inner logic, and must be controlled and supervised all the more strictly the nearer civilization, in progressing, brings the possibility of happiness and the more it transforms a utopian fantasy into an undertaking that can be directed by science and knowledge.

Thus Freud reveals the actual negativity of freedom, and in refusing to transfigure it idealistically he preserves the idea of another possible freedom in which the repression of the instincts would be abolished along with political oppression, while the achievements of repression would be preserved. In Freud there is nothing like a return to nature or to natural man: the process of civilization is irreversible. If instinctual repression can be done away with to the point where the existing relationship of labor and enjoyment can be reversed, the archaic sublimation of erotic energy can be revoked. If, therefore, sensuousness and reason, happiness and freedom can be brought into harmony or even unity, this is possible only at the height of the development of civilization, where the state of absolute need and lack could be done away with, technically at least, and where the struggle for existence no longer need be a struggle for the means of existence.

Freud was more than skeptical with regard to this possibility. He was all the more so in that he had seen the profound connection between growing productivity and growing destruction, between increasing control of nature and increasing control of men, long before the atom and hydrogen bombs and before that total mobilization that began with the period of fascism and evidently has not yet reached its peak. He saw that men must be kept in line with ever better and more effective means the greater social wealth becomes, the wealth that would be able to satisfy their freely—not manipulated—developing needs. This is perhaps the final reason for Freud's assertion that the progress of civilization has intensified guilt feeling to almost unbearable heights—the feeling of guilt about the prohibited instinctual wishes that are still active despite almost lifelong repression. He maintained that these forbidden and living instinctual impulses are directed in the final instance toward the father and mother; but in his late work they are distinguished increasingly clearly from their first biological-psychological form. The feeling of guilt is now defined as "the expression of the conflict of ambivalence, of the eternal struggle between Eros and the destruction or death instinct."[16] And a puzzling statement reads: "What began with the father is completed in the masses."[17] Civilization obeys "an inner erotic impulse" when it unites men in "intimately connected" communities; it obeys the pleasure principle. But Eros is connected to the death instinct, the pleasure principle to the Nirvana principle. The conflict has to be fought out—and "as long as this community knows only the form of the family," it expresses itself in the Oedipus complex. To understand the full import of the Freudian conception one must be aware of the way the forces are distributed in this conflict. The father, in forbidding the son the mother he desires, represents Eros, which restricts the regression of the death instinct— and thereby, repressive Eros, which limits the pleasure principle to pleasure compatible with life but also with society, and thus releases destructive energy. There is a corresponding ambivalence of love and hate in the relationship to the father. The mother is the goal of Eros and of the death instinct: behind the sexual wish stands the wish for regression to the condition before birth, the undifferentiated union of the pleasure principle and the Nirvana principle *on this side* of the reality principle and thus without ambivalence, pure libido. The erotic impulse to civilization then extends beyond the family and joins greater and greater social groups, the conflict becomes intensified "in forms that depend on the past": paternal domination extends itself triumphantly and thus the ambivalence conflict does too. At the height of civilization it plays itself out in and against the masses, who have incorporated the father into themselves. And the more universal domination becomes, the more universal becomes the destruction that it releases. The conflict between Eros and the death instinct belongs to the innermost essence of the development of civilization, *as long as it occurs in forms that "depend on the past."*

Thus the thought Freud expresses so often is emphasized again — that the history of mankind is still dominated by "archaic" powers, that prehistory and early history are still at work in us. The "return of the repressed" takes place at the fearful turning points of history: in the hatred of and rebellion against the father, in the deification and restoration of paternal authority. The erotic impulses to civilization that strive for the union of happiness and freedom fall prey to domination over and over again, and protest suffocates in destruction. Only seldom and cautiously did Freud express the hope that civilization would finally realize at some date the freedom that it could have realized for so long and thus conquer the archaic powers. *Civilization and Its Discontents* closes with the words: "Men have brought their powers of subduing the forces of nature to such a pitch that by using them they could now very easily exterminate one another to the last man. They know this — hence arises a great part of their current unrest, their dejection, their mood of apprehension. And now it may be expected that the other of the two 'heavenly forces,' eternal Eros, will put forth his strength so as to maintain himself alongside of his equally immortal adversary."[18]

That was written in 1930. In the time that has passed since then there has been truly no trace of the opponent's growing retaliation, of the approach of that happy freedom, of Eros as creator of civilization. Or does perhaps the increasing activity of destruction, which presents an ever more rational face, indicate that civilization is proceeding toward a catastrophe that will pull the archaic forces down with it in its collapse and thus clear the way to a higher stage?

Notes

1. See "Progress and Freud's Theory of Instincts," pp. 28–43 in *Five Lectures: Psychoanalysis, Politics, and Utopia,* trans. by J. Shapiro and S. Weber (Boston: Beacon Press, 1970).

2. The "plasticity" of the instincts which this theory presupposes should suffice to refute the notion that the instincts are essentially unalterable biological substrata: only the "energy" of the instincts and—to some extent—their "localization" remain fundamentally unchanged.

3. Sigmund Freud, "Abriss der Psychoanalyse" (Outline of Psychoanalysis), *Gesammelte Werke*, 18 vols. (London and Frankfurt: S. Fischer Verlag, 1940–1968), 17:75. All subsequent references to the collected works of Freud are taken from this edition.

4. The notion of "origin" as Freud uses it has simultaneously structural—functional—and temporal, ontogenetic, and phylogenetic significance. The "original" structure of the instincts was the one which dominated in the prehistory of the species. It is transformed during the course of history but continues to be effective as a substratum, preconscious and unconscious, in the history of the individual and the species—most obviously so in early childhood. The idea that mankind, in general and in its individuals, is still dominated by "archaic" powers is one of Freud's most profound insights.

5. Immanuel Kant, "Metaphysische Anfangsgründe der Tugendlehre," *Die Metaphysik der Sitten*, in two parts (Königsberg: Nicolovius, 1797), 2:6.

6. Sigmund Freud, "Das Unbehagen in der Kultur" (Civilization and Its Discontents), *Gesammelte Werke*, 14:442.

7. Ibid., 14:455.

8. Ibid., 14:493.

9. Ibid., 14:492.

10. Ibid.

11. Sigmund Freud, "Jenseits des Lustprinzips" (Beyond the Pleasure Principle), *Gesammelte Werke*, 13:45.

12. Sigmund Freud, "Abriss der Psychoanalyse" (Outline of Psychoanalysis), *Gesammelte Werke*, 17:71.

13. Sigmund Freud, "Massenpsychologie und Ich-Analyse" (Group Psychology and the Analysis of the Ego), *Gesammelte Werke*, 13:112.

14. Ibid., 13:113.

15. See *Five Lectures*, pp. 28–43.

16. Sigmund Freud, "Das Unbehagen in der Kultur" (Civilization and Its Discontents), *Gesammelte Werke*, 14:492.

17. Ibid., 14:492–93.

18. Sigmund Freud, *Civilization and Its Discontents* (New York: Doubleday, Anchor edition, 1958), p. 105.

PART III

Philosophical Critique

PHILOSOPHICAL INTERLUDE (1955)

This text is drawn from Marcuse's book *Eros and Civilization*. It offers a brief account of the fate of reason in Western philosophy since the Greeks. Reason, Marcuse argues, has been pulled in two different directions throughout this long history. On the one hand, it is bound to the struggle with nature and becomes an instrument of domination of both human beings and things. On the other hand, the concept of reason contains an implicit aspiration for reconciliation with itself and the world. The struggle to harmonize "the Logos of alienation" with "the Logos of gratification" shapes the history of philosophy.

Here Marcuse traces this history primarily through a brief comment on Aristotle and lengthier analyses of the contrasting texts of Hegel and Nietzsche. Aristotle's logic becomes the basis of rational domination while his image of God as a self-thinking thought is the model of reason reconciled. The two concepts of reason appear in Hegel in his accounts of the master-slave dialectic and the Absolute. For Hegel, history begins with the struggle for domination and culminates in a thinking which remembers and heals the wounds of its own development. This thinking, which he calls "Absolute," remains purely spiritual and as such cannot redeem the horror of actual history.

With Nietzsche the concept of reason undergoes a radical transformation. According to Marcuse, Nietzsche denounces the Logos of alienation in his concept of the Will to Power but this denunciation is ambiguous and has left the impression that Nietzsche is a philosopher of domination. His intent, however, is to go beyond will to affirmation. His goal is to reconcile humanity with its finite condition, to unleash the potential for joy in existence that is wasted in resentment and hatred of life. The doctrine of the eternal return postulates that history will repeat its course indefinitely, challenging us to acceptance of what time has wrought. The circularity of the self-thinking thought, the Absolute, appears in this image of eternal return but it is no longer a matter of thinking alone. Marcuse interprets it as an image of the transcendence of the opposition of reason and instinct, necessity and fulfillment.

• • •

As the scientific rationality of Western civilization began to bear its full fruit, it became increasingly conscious of its psychical implications. The ego which undertook the rational transformation of the human and natural environment revealed itself as an essentially aggressive, offensive subject, whose thoughts and actions were designed for mastering objects. It was a subject *against* an object. This *a priori* antagonistic experience defined the *ego cogitans* as well as the *ego agens*. Nature (its own as well as the external world) were "given" to the ego as something that had to be fought, conquered, and even violated—such was the precondition for self-preservation and self-development.

The struggle begins with the perpetual internal conquest of the "lower" faculties of the individual: his sensuous and appetitive faculties. Their subjugation is, at least since Plato, regarded as a constitutive element of human reason, which is thus in its very function repressive. The struggle culminates in the conquest of external nature, which must be perpetually attacked, curbed, and exploited in order to yield to human needs. The ego experiences being as "provocation,"[1] as "project";[2] it experiences each existential condition as a restraint that has to be overcome, transformed into another one. The ego becomes preconditioned for mastering action and productivity even prior to any specific occasion that calls for such an attitude. Max Scheler has pointed out that the "conscious or unconscious impulse or will to power over nature is the *primum movens*" in the relation of the modern individual to being, and that it structurally precedes modern science and technology —a "pre- and a-logical" antecedent before scientific thought and intuition.[3] Nature is *a priori* experienced by an organism bent to domination and therefore experienced as susceptible to mastery and control.[4]

And consequently work is *a priori* power and provocation in the struggle with nature; it is overcoming of resistance. In such work-attitude, the images of the objective world appear as "symbols for points of *aggression*"; action appears as domination, and reality *per se* as "resistance."[5] Scheler calls this mode of thought "knowledge geared to domination and achievement" and sees in it the specific mode of knowledge which has guided the development of modern civilization.[6] It has shaped the predominant notion not only of the ego, the thinking and acting subject, but also of its objective world—the notion of being as such.

Whatever the implications of the original Greek conception of Logos as the essence of being, since the canonization of the Aristotelian logic the term merges with the idea of ordering, classifying, mastering reason. And this idea of reason becomes increasingly antagonistic to those faculties and attitudes which are receptive rather than productive, which tend toward gratification rather than transcendence—which remain strongly committed to the pleasure principle. They appear as the unreasonable and irrational that must be conquered and contained in order to serve the progress of reason. Reason is to insure, through the ever more effective transformation and exploitation of nature, the fulfillment of the human potentialities. But in the process the end seems to recede before the means: the time devoted to alienated labor absorbs the time for individual needs—and defines the needs themselves. The Logos shows forth as the logic of domination. When logic then reduces the units of thought to signs and symbols, the laws of thought have finally become techniques of calculation and manipulation.

But the logic of domination does not triumph unchallenged. The philosophy which epitomizes the antagonistic relation between subject and object also retains the image of their reconciliation. The restless labor of the transcending subject terminates in the ultimate unity of subject and object: the idea of "being-in-and-for-itself," existing in its own fulfillment. The Logos of gratification contradicts the Logos of alienation: the effort to harmonize the two animates the inner history of Western metaphysics. It obtains its classical formulation in the Aristotelian hierarchy of the modes of being, which culminates in the *nous theos*: its existence is no longer defined and confined by anything other than itself but is entirely itself in all states and conditions. The ascending curve of becoming is bent in the circle which moves in itself; past, present, and future are enclosed in the ring. According to Aristotle, this mode of being is reserved to the god; and the movement of thought, pure thinking, is its sole "empirical" approximation. Otherwise the empirical world does not partake of such fulfillment; only a yearning, "Eros-like," connects this world with its end-in-itself. The Aristotelian conception is not a religious one. The *nous theos* is, as it were, *part* of the universe, neither its creator nor its lord nor its savior, but a mode of being in which all potentiality is actuality, in which the "project" of being has been fulfilled.

The Aristotelian conception remains alive through all subsequent transformations. When, at the end of the Age of Reason, with Hegel, Western thought makes its last and greatest attempt to demonstrate the validity of its categories and of the principles which govern its world, it concludes again with the *nous theos*. Again, fulfillment is relegated to the absolute idea and to absolute knowledge. Again, the movement of the circle ends the painful process of destructive and productive transcendence. Now the circle comprises the whole: all alienation is justified and at the same time canceled in the universal ring of reason which is the world. But now philosophy comprehends the concrete historical ground on which the edifice of reason is erected.

The *Phenomenology of the Spirit* unfolds the structure of reason as the structure of domination—and as the overcoming of domination. Reason develops through the developing self-consciousness of man who conquers the natural and historical world and makes it the material of his self-realization. When mere consciousness reaches the stage of self-consciousness, it finds itself as *ego*, and the ego is first *desire*: it can become conscious of itself only through satisfying itself in and by an "other." But such satisfaction involves the "negation" of the other, for the ego has to prove itself by truly "being-for-itself" *against* all "otherness."[7] This is the notion of the individual which must constantly assert and affirm himself in order to be real, which is set off against the world as his "negativity," as *denying* his freedom, so that he can exist only by incessantly winning and testing his existence *against* something or some-one which contests it. The ego must become *free*, but if the world has the "character of negativity," then the ego's freedom depends on being "recognized," "acknowledged" as master—and such recognition can only be tendered by another ego, another self-conscious subject. Objects are not alive; the overcoming of their resistance cannot satisfy or "test" the power of the ego: "Self-consciousness can attain its satisfaction only in another self-consciousness." The aggressive attitude toward the object-world, the domination of nature, thus ultimately aims at the domination of man by man. It is aggressiveness toward the other subjects: satisfaction of the ego is conditioned upon its "negative relation" to another ego:

> The relation of both self-consciousnesses is in this way so constituted that they prove themselves and each other through a life-and-death struggle....And it is solely by risking life, that freedom is obtained...[8]

Freedom involves the risk of life, not because it involves liberation from servitude, but because the very content of human freedom is defined by the mutual "negative relation" to the other. And since this negative relation affects the totality of life, freedom can be "tested" only by staking life itself. Death and anxiety—not as "fear for this element or that, not for this or that moment of time," but as fear for one's 'entire being'"[9] —are the essential terms of human freedom *and* satisfaction. From the negative structure of self-consciousness results the relation of master and servant, domination and servitude. This relation is the consequence of the specific nature of self-consciousness and the consequence of its specific attitude toward the other (object and subject).

But the *Phenomenology of the Spirit* would not be the self-interpretation of Western civilization if it were nothing more than the development of the logic of domination. The *Phenomenology of the Spirit* leads to the overcoming of that form of freedom which derives from the antagonistic relation to the other. And the true mode of freedom is, not the incessant activity of conquest, but its coming to rest in the transparent knowledge and gratification of being. The ontological climate which prevails at the end of the *Phenomenology* is the very opposite of the Promethean dynamic:

The wounds of the Spirit heal without leaving scars; the deed is not everlasting; the Spirit takes it back into itself, and the aspect of particularity (individuality) present in it ... immediately passes away.[10]

Mutual acknowledgment and recognition are still the test for the reality of freedom, but the terms are now forgiveness and reconciliation:

The word of reconciliation is the (objectively) existent Spirit which apprehends in its opposite the pure knowledge of itself *qua* universal essence ... a mutual recognition which is Absolute Spirit.[11]

These formulations occur at the decisive place where Hegel's analysis of the manifestations of the spirit has reached the position of the "self-conscious spirit"—its being-in-and-for-itself. Here, the "negative relation to the other" is ultimately, in the existence of the spirit as *nous*, transformed into productivity which is receptivity, activity which is fulfillment. Hegel's presentation of his system in his *Encyclopedia* ends on the word "enjoys." The philosophy of Western civilization culminates in the idea that the truth lies in the negation of the principle that governs this civilization—negation in the twofold sense that freedom appears as real only in the idea, and that the endlessly projecting and transcending productivity of being comes to fruition in the perpetual peace of self-conscious receptivity.

The *Phenomenology of the Spirit* throughout preserves the tension between the ontological and the historical content: the manifestations of the spirit *are* the main stages of Western civilization, but these historical manifestations remain affected with negativity; the spirit comes to itself only in and as absolute knowledge. It is at the same time the true form of thought and the true form of being. Being is in its very essence reason. But the highest form of reason is, to Hegel, almost the opposite of the prevailing form: it is attained and sustained fulfillment, the transparent unity of subject and object, of the universal and the individual—a dynamic rather than static unity in which all becoming is free self-externalization *(Entäusserung)*, release and "enjoyment" of potentialities. The labor of history comes to rest in history: alienation is canceled, and with it transcendence and the flux of time. The spirit "overcomes its temporal form; negates Time."[12] But the "end" of history recaptures its content: the force which accomplishes the conquest of time is remembrance (re-collection). Absolute knowledge, in which the spirit attains its truth, is the spirit "entering into its real self, whereby it abandons its (extraneous) existence and entrusts its Gestalt to remembrance."[13] Being is no longer the painful transcendence toward the future but the peaceful recapture of the past. Remembrance, which has preserved everything that was; is "the inner and the actually higher form of the substance."[14]

The fact that remembrance here appears as the decisive existential category for the highest form of being indicates the inner trend of Hegel's philosophy. Hegel replaces the idea of progress with that of a cyclical development which moves, self-sufficient, in the reproduction and consummation of what *is*. This development presupposes the entire history of man (his subjective and objective world) and the comprehension of his history—the remembrance of his past. The past remains present; it is the very life of the spirit; what has been decides on what is. Freedom implies reconciliation—redemption of the past. If the past is just left behind and forgotten, there will be no end to destructive transgression. Somehow the progress of transgression must be arrested. Hegel thought that "the wounds of the spirit heal without leaving scars." He believed that, on the attained level of civilization, with the triumph of reason, freedom had become a reality. But neither the state nor society embodies the ultimate form of freedom. No matter how rationally they are organized, they are still afflicted with unfreedom. True freedom is only in the idea. Liberation thus is a spiritual event. Hegel's dialectic remains within the framework set by the established reality principle.

Western philosophy ends with the idea with which it began. At the beginning and at the end, in Aristotle and in Hegel, the supreme mode of being, the ultimate form of reason and freedom, appear as *nous*, spirit, *Geist*. At the end and at the beginning, the empirical world remains in negativity—the stuff and the tools of the spirit, or of its representatives on earth. In reality, neither remembrance nor absolute knowledge redeems that which was and is. Still, this philosophy testifies not only to the reality principle which governs the empirical world, but also to its negation. The consummation of being is, not the ascending curve, but the closing of the circle: the *re-turn* from alienation. Philosophy could conceive of such a state only as that of pure thought.

Between the beginning and the end is the development of reason as the logic of domination—progress through alienation. The repressed liberation is upheld: in the idea and in the ideal.

After Hegel, the mainstream of Western philosophy is exhausted. The Logos of domination has built its system, and what follows is epilogue: philosophy survives as a special (and not very vital) function in the academic establishment. The new principles of thought develop outside this establishment: they are qualitatively novel and committed to a different form of reason, to a different reality principle. In metaphysical terms, the change is expressed by the fact that the essence of being is no longer conceived as Logos. And, with this change in the basic experience of being, the logic of domination is challenged. When Schopenhauer defines the essence of being as *will*, it shows forth as insatiable want and aggression which must be redeemed at all cost. To Schopenhauer, they are redeemable only in their absolute negation; will itself must come to rest—to an end. But the ideal of Nirvana contains the affirmation: the end is fulfillment, gratification. Nirvana is the image of the pleasure principle. As such it emerges, still in a repressive form, in Richard Wagner's music drama: repressive because (as in any good theology and morality) fulfillment here demands the sacrifice of earthly happiness. The *principium individuationis* itself is said to be at fault—fulfillment is only beyond its realm; the most orgastic *Liebestod* still celebrates the most orgastic renunciation.

Only Nietzsche's philosophy surmounts the ontological tradition, but his indictment of the Logos as repression and perversion of the will-to-power is so highly ambiguous that it has often blocked the understanding. First the indictment itself is ambiguous. Historically, the Logos of domination released rather than repressed the will-to-power; it was the *direction* of this will that was repressive—toward productive renunciation which made man the slave of his labor and the enemy of his own gratification. Moreover, the will-to-power is not Nietzsche's last word: "Will—this is the liberator and joybringer: thus I taught you, my friends! But now this also learn: the Will itself is still a prisoner."[15] Will is still a prisoner because it has no power over time: the past not only remains unliberated but, unliberated, continues to mar all liberation. Unless the power of time over life is broken, there can be no freedom:

the fact that time does not "recur" sustains the wound of bad conscience: it breeds vengeance and the need for punishment, which in
turn perpetuate the past and the sickness to death. With the triumph of
Christian morality, the life instincts were perverted and constrained;
bad conscience was linked with a "guilt against God." In the human
instincts were implanted "hostility, rebellion, insurrection against
the 'master,' 'father,' the primal ancestor and origin of the world."[16]
Repression and deprivation were thus justified and affirmed; they were
made into the masterful and aggressive forces which determined the
human existence. With their growing social utilization, progress became of necessity progressive repression. On this road, there is no alternative, and no spiritual and transcendental freedom can compensate
for the repressive foundations of culture. The "wounds of the spirit," if
they heal at all, do leave scars. The past becomes master over the present, and life a tribute to death:

> And now cloud upon cloud rolled over the Spirit, until at last mad-
> ness preached: "all things pass away, therefore all things deserve to
> pass away!" "And this is justice itself, this law of Time, that it must
> devour its children": thus preached madness.[17]

Nietzsche exposes the gigantic fallacy on which Western philosophy and morality were built—namely, the transformation of facts into
essences, of historical into metaphysical conditions. The weakness and
despondency of man, the inequality of power and wealth, injustice and
suffering were attributed to some transcendental crime and guilt; rebellion became the original sin, disobedience against God; and the striving for gratification was concupiscence. Moreover, this whole series of
fallacies culminated in the deification of time: because everything in
the empirical world is passing, man is in his very essence a finite being,
and death is in the very essence of life. Only the higher values are eternal, and therefore really real: the inner man, faith, and love which does
not ask and does not desire. Nietzsche's attempt to uncover the historical roots of these transformations elucidates their twofold function: to
pacify, compensate, and justify the underprivileged of the earth, and to
protect those who made and left them underprivileged. The achievement snowballed and enveloped the masters and the slaves, the rulers
and the ruled, in that upsurge of productive repression which advanced
Western civilization to ever higher levels of efficacy. However, growing

efficacy involved growing degeneration of the life instincts—the decline of man.

Nietzsche's critique is distinguished from all academic social psychology by the position from which it is undertaken: Nietzsche speaks in the name of a reality principle fundamentally antagonistic to that of Western civilization. The traditional form of reason is rejected on the basis of the experience of being-as-end-in-itself—as joy *(Lust)* and enjoyment. The struggle against time is waged from this position: the tyranny of becoming over being must be broken if man is to come to himself in a world which is truly his own. As long as there is the uncomprehended and unconquered flux of time—senseless loss, the painful "it was" that will never be again—being contains the seed of destruction which perverts good to evil and vice versa. Man comes to himself only when the transcendence has been conquered—when eternity has become present in the here and now. Nietzsche's conception terminates in the vision of the closed circle—not progress, but the "eternal return":

> All things pass, all things return; eternally turns the wheel of Being. All things die, all things blossom again, eternal is the year of Being. All things break, all things are joined anew; eternally the house of Being builds itself the same. All things part, all things welcome each other again; eternally the ring of Being abides by itself. In each Now, Being begins; round each Here turns the sphere of There. The center is everywhere. Bent is the path of eternity.[18]

The closed circle has appeared before: in Aristotle and Hegel, as the symbol of being-as-end-in-itself. But while Aristotle reserved it to the *nous theos,* while Hegel identified it with the absolute idea, Nietzsche envisages the eternal return of the finite exactly as it is—in its full concreteness and finiteness. This is the total affirmation of the life instincts, repelling all escape and negation. The eternal return is the will and vision of an *erotic* attitude toward being for which necessity and fulfillment coincide.

> Shield of necessity!
> Star-summit of Being!
> Not reached by any wish,

not soiled by any No,
eternal Yes of Being:
I affirm you eternally,
for I love you, eternity.[19]

Eternity, long since the ultimate consolation of an alienated existence, had been made into an instrument of repression by its relegation to a transcendental world—unreal reward for real suffering. Here, eternity is reclaimed for the fair earth—as the eternal return of its children, of the lily and the rose, of the sun on the mountains and lakes, of the lover and the beloved, of the fear for their life, of pain and happiness. Death *is*; it is conquered only if it is followed by the real rebirth of everything that was before death here on earth—not as a mere repetition but as willed and wanted re-creation. The eternal return thus includes the return of suffering, but suffering as a means for more gratification, for the aggrandizement of joy.[20] The horror of pain derives from the "instinct of weakness," from the fact that pain overwhelms and becomes final and fatal. Suffering can be affirmed if man's "power is sufficiently strong"[21] to make pain a stimulus for affirmation—a link in the chain of joy. The doctrine of the eternal return obtains all its meaning from the central proposition that "joy wants eternity"—wants itself and all things to be everlasting.

Nietzsche's philosophy contains enough elements of the terrible past: his celebration of pain and power perpetuates features of the morality which he strives to overcome. However, the image of a new reality principle breaks the repressive context and anticipates the liberation from the archaic heritage. "The earth has all too long been a madhouse!"[22] For Nietzsche, the liberation depends on the reversal of the sense of guilt; mankind must come to associate the bad conscience not with the affirmation but with the denial of the life instincts, not with the rebellion but with the acceptance of the repressive ideals.[23]

We have suggested certain nodal points in the development of Western philosophy which reveal the historical limitations of its system of reason—and the effort to surpass this system. The struggle appears in the antagonism between becoming and being, between the ascending curve and the closed circle, progress and eternal return, transcendence and rest in fulfillment.[24] It is the struggle between the logic of domination and the will to gratification. Both assert their claims for defining the reality principle. The traditional ontology is contested: against the conception of being in terms of Logos rises the conception of being in a-logical terms: will and joy. This countertrend strives to formulate its own Logos: the logic of gratification.

In its most advanced positions, Freud's theory partakes of this philosophical dynamic. His metapsychology, at tempting to define the essence of being, defines it as Eros—in contrast to its traditional definition as Logos. The death instinct affirms the principle of non-being (the negation of being) against Eros (the principle of being). The ubiquitous fusion of the two principles in Freud's conception corresponds to the traditional metaphysical fusion of being and non-being. To be sure, Freud's conception of Eros refers only to organic life. However, inorganic matter is, as the "end" of the death instinct, so inherently linked to organic matter that (as suggested above) it seems permissible to give his conception a general ontological meaning. Being is essentially the striving for pleasure. This striving becomes an "aim" in the human existence: the erotic impulse to combine living substance into ever larger and more durable units is the instinctual source of civilization. The sex instincts are *life* instincts: the impulse to preserve and enrich life by mastering nature in accordance with the developing vital needs is originally an erotic impulse. Ananke is experienced as the barrier against the satisfaction of the life instincts, which seek pleasure, not security. And the "struggle for existence" is originally a struggle for pleasure: culture begins with the collective implementation of this aim. Later, however, the struggle for existence is organized in the interest of domination: the erotic basis of culture is transformed. When philosophy conceives the essence of being as Logos, it is already the Logos of domination—commanding, mastering, directing reason, to which man and nature are to be subjected.

Freud's interpretation of being in terms of Eros recaptures the early stage of Plato's philosophy, which conceived of culture not as the repressive sublimation but as the free self-development of Eros. As early as Plato, this conception appears as an archaic-mythical residue. Eros is being absorbed into Logos, and Logos is reason which subdues the instincts. The history of ontology reflects the reality principle which governs the world ever more exclusively: The insights contained in the metaphysical notion of Eros were driven underground. They survived, in eschatological distortion, in many heretic movements, in the hedonistic philosophy. Their history has still to be written—as has the history of the transformation of Eros in Agape.[25] Freud's own theory follows the general trend: in his work, the rationality of the predominant reality principle supersedes the metaphysical speculations on Eros.

Notes

1. Gaston Bachelard, *L'Eau et les Rêves* (Paris: José Corti, 1942), p. 214.

2. J. P. Sartre, *L'Etre et le Néant* (Paris: Gallimard, 1946), passim.

3. *Die Wissensformen und die Gesellschaft* (Leipzig, 1926), pp. 234–235.

4. Ibid., pp. 298–299. Scheler refers to "herrschaftswilliges Lebewesen."

5. Ibid., pp. 459, 461.

6. *Die Formen des Wissens und die Bildung* (Bonn, 1925), p. 33. Scheler's phrase is "Herrschafts- und Leistungswissen."

7. This and the following according to the *Phenomenology* (B, IV, A).

8. *The Philosophy of Hegel*, ed. Carl J. Friedrich (New York: Modern Library, 1953), p. 402.

9. Ibid., p. 407.

10. "Die Wunden des Geistes heilen, ohne dass Narben bleiben; die Tat ist nicht das Unvergängliche, sondern wird von dem Geiste in sich zurückgenommen, und die Seite der Einzelheit... ist das unmittelbar Verschwindende." *The Phenomenology of the Mind*, transl. J. B. Baillie (London: Sven Sonnenschein, 1910), II, 679. (Translation changed.)

11. "Das Wort der Versöhnung ist der daseiende Geist, der das reine Wissen seiner selbst als allgemeines Wesen in seinem Gegenteile... anschaut,—ein gegenseitiges Anerkennen, welches der absolute Geist ist." Ibid., p. 680 (with a minor change in translation).

12. "...hebt seine Zeitform auf; tilgt die Zeit." Ibid., p. 821.

13. "...sein Insichgehen, in welchem er sein Dasein verlässt und seine Gestalt der Erinnerung übergibt." Ibid. No English translation can render the connotation of the German term which takes *Er-innerung* as "turning into oneself," *re-turn* from externalization.

14. "...das Innere und die in der Tat höhere Form der Substanz."

15. *Thus Spake Zarathustra*, Part II ("On Redemption"), in *The Portable Nietzsche*, transl. Walter Kaufmann (New York: Viking Press, 1954), p. 251. (Translation here and in the following quotations changed in part.)

16. *The Genealogy of Morals*, Section II:22.

17. *Thus Spake Zarathustra*, p. 25.

18. Ibid., Part III ("The Convalescent"), pp. 329–30.

19. "Ruhm und Ewigkeit," in *Werke* (Leipzig: Alfred Kröner, 1919), VIII, 436 (my translation).

20. Ibid., XIV, 301.

21. Ibid., p. 295.

22. *The Genealogy of Morals*, Section II, 22.

23. Ibid., 24.

24. The two antagonistic conceptions of time outlined here are discussed by Mircea Eliade in his book *The Myth of the Eternal Return* (London: Routledge and Kegan Paul, 1955). He contrasts the "cyclical" with the "linear" notion of time, the former characteristic of "traditional" (predominantly primitive) civilizations, the latter of "modern man."

25. See Anders Nygren, *Agape and Eros* (Philadelphia: Westminster Press, 1953).

THE AFFIRMATIVE CHARACTER
OF CULTURE (1937)

One of the hallmarks of the Frankfurt School's distinctive approach, worked out in the 1930s as the group was—literally—on the run from the Nazis, was its emphasis on culture. To be sure, this was in part a reaction against the worst features of "automatic Marxism," namely, a crude conception of "base and superstructure," proposing that material life (the economy) determined the forms of social and intellectual life. But even more important was the conviction that the revolutionary theory of the day was radically deficient in how it presented the sphere of "consciousness," and the importance of that sphere for finding the right pathway to human freedom. The second defining characteristic of this approach was its historical method: present-day society, in terms of its limitations as well as its future possibilities, can only be understood as the result of previous stages of development.

Marcuse's early essays on this general theme are both breathtaking in their scope and sharply focused on specific lines of cultural development. Broadly speaking, they contrast the enduring spirit of "negativity" —the struggle of thinkers and opposition forces to overcome limited forms of freedom—with the powerful currents of authoritarianism in culture, which strive to make us believe that acceptance of those limitations is in our best interests.

The essay that follows, published in 1937, approaches this theme in terms of the place of art in social life. "Affirmative culture" refers to the higher culture of the bourgeois era, and especially its art, which depicts

a world of beauty and fulfillment denied by the realities of capitalist social life. While art idealizes and glorifies a better world, individuals struggle relentlessly for survival and money in everyday social and economic
life. The concept of the soul and, in a later time, of personality, identify
the residue of inner selfhood that is fulfilled only in the contemplation of
art since the demand for happiness is frustrated by the repressive organization of society. Overcoming the split between ideal values and
degraded reality remains the task of a general transformation of the social world.

●　●　●

The doctrine that all human knowledge is oriented toward practice belonged to the nucleus of ancient philosophy. It was Aristotle's view that
the truths arrived at through knowledge should direct practice in daily
life as in the arts and sciences. In their struggle for existence, men need
the effort of knowledge, the search for truth, because what is good, ben-
eficial, and right for them is not immediately evident. Artisan and merchant, captain and physician, general and statesman—each must have
correct knowledge in his field in order to be capable of acting as the
changing situation demands.

While Aristotle maintained the practical character of every instance of knowledge, he made a significant distinction between forms
of knowledge. He ordered them, as it were, in a hierarchy of value
whose nadir is functional acquaintance with the necessities of everyday
life and whose zenith is philosophical knowledge. The latter has no
purpose outside itself. Rather, it occurs only for its own sake and to afford men felicity. Within this hierarchy there is a fundamental break
between the necessary and useful on the one hand and the "beautiful"
on the other. "The whole of life is further divided into two parts, business and leisure, war and peace, and of actions some aim at what is necessary and useful, and some at what is beautiful [τά καλά]."[1] Since this
division is not itself questioned, and since, together with other regions
of the "beautiful," "pure" theory congeals into an independent activity
alongside and above other activities, philosophy's original demand
disintegrates: the demand that practice be guided by known truths.
Separating the useful and necessary from the beautiful and from enjoyment initiated a development that abandons the field to the materi-

alism of bourgeois practice on the one hand and to the appeasement of happiness and the mind within the preserve of "culture" on the other.

One theme continually recurs in the reasons given for the relegation of the highest form of knowledge and of pleasure to pure, purposeless theory: the world of necessity, of everyday provision for life, is inconstant, insecure, unfree—not merely in fact, but in essence. Disposal over material goods is never entirely the work of human industry and wisdom, for it is subject to the rule of contingency. The individual who places his highest goal, happiness, in these goods makes himself the slave of men and things. He surrenders his freedom. Wealth and well-being do not come or persist due to his autonomous decision but rather through the changeable fortune of opaque circumstances. Man thus subjects his existence to a purpose situated outside him. Of itself, such an external purpose can vitiate and enslave men only if the material conditions of life are poorly ordered, that is, if their reproduction is regulated through the anarchy of opposing social interests. In this order the preservation of the common existence is incompatible with individual happiness and freedom. Insofar as philosophy is concerned with man's happiness—and the theory of classical antiquity held it to be the highest good—it cannot find it in the established material organization of life. That is why it must transcend this order's facticity.

Along with metaphysics, epistemology, and ethics, this transcendence also affects psychology. Like the extrapsychic[2] world, the human soul is divided into a lower and a higher region. The history of the soul transpires between the poles of sensuality[3] and reason. The devaluation of sensuality results from the same motives as that of the material world: because sensuality is a realm of anarchy, of inconstancy, and of unfreedom. Sensual pleasure is not in itself bad. It is bad because, like man's lower activities, it is fulfilled in a bad order. The "lower parts of the soul" drive man to covet gain and possessions, purchase and sale. He is led to "admire and value nothing but wealth and its possessors."[4] Accordingly the "appetitive" part of the soul, which is oriented toward sensual pleasure, is also termed by Plato the "money-loving" part, "because money is the principal means of satisfying desires of this kind."[5]

All the ontological classifications of ancient idealism express the badness of a social reality in which knowledge of the truth about human existence is no longer incorporated into practice. The world of the true, the good, and the beautiful is in fact an "ideal" world insofar as it lies beyond the existing conditions of life, beyond a form of existence in which the majority of men either work as slaves or spend their life in commerce, with only a small group having the opportunity of being concerned with anything more than the provision and preservation of the necessary. When the reproduction of material life takes place under the rule of the commodity form and continually renews the poverty of class society, then the good, beautiful, and true are transcendent to this life. And if everything requisite to preserving and securing material life is produced in this form, then whatever lies beyond it is certainly "superfluous." What is of authentic import to man, the highest truths, the highest goods, and the highest joys, is separated in significance from the necessary by an abyss. They are a "luxury." Aristotle did not conceal this state of affairs. "First philosophy," which includes the highest good and the highest pleasure, is a function of the leisure of the few, for whom all necessities of life are already adequately taken care of. "Pure theory" is appropriated as the profession of an elite and cordoned off with iron chains from the majority of mankind. Aristotle did not assert that the good, the beautiful, and the true are universally valid and obligatory values which should also permeate and transfigure "from above" the realm of necessity, of the material provision for life. Only when this claim is raised are we in the presence of the concept of culture that became central to bourgeois practice and its corresponding weltanschauung. The ancient theory of the higher value of truths above the realm of necessity includes as well the "higher" level of society. For these truths are supposed to have their abode in the ruling social strata, whose dominant status is in turn confirmed by the theory insofar as concern with the highest truths is supposed to be their profession.

In Aristotelian philosophy, ancient theory is precisely at the point where idealism retreats in the face of social contradictions and expresses them as ontological conditions. Platonic philosophy still contended with the social order of commercial Athens. Plato's idealism is interlaced with motifs of social criticism. What appears as facticity from the standpoint of the Ideas is the material world in which men and things encounter one another as commodities. The just order of the soul is destroyed by the passion for wealth which leaves a man not a moment of leisure to attend to anything beyond his personal fortunes. So long as a citizen's whole soul is wrapped up in these, he cannot give a thought to anything but the day's takings.[6]

And the authentic, basic demand of idealism is that this material world be transformed and improved in accordance with the truths yielded by knowledge of the Ideas. Plato's answer to this demand is his program for a reorganization of society. This program reveals what Plato sees as the root of evil. He demands, for the ruling strata, the abolition of private property (even in women and children) and the prohibition of trade. This same program, however, tries to root the contradictions of class society in the depths of human nature, thereby perpetuating them. While the majority of the members of the state are engaged for their entire lives in the cheerless business of providing for the necessities of life, enjoyment of the true, the good, and the beautiful is reserved for a small elite. Although Aristotle still lets ethics terminate in politics, for him the reorganization of society no longer occupies a central role in philosophy. To the extent to which he is more "realistic" than Plato, his idealism is more resigned in the face of the historical tasks of mankind. The true philosopher is for him no longer essentially the true statesman. The distance between facticity and Idea has increased precisely because they are conceived of as in closer relationship. The purport of idealism, viz. the realization of the Idea, dissipates. The history of idealism is also the history of its coming to terms with the established order.

Behind the ontological and epistemological separation of the realm of the senses and the realm of Ideas, of sensuousness and reason, of necessity and beauty, stands not only the rejection of a bad historical form of existence, but also its exoneration. The material world (i.e. the manifold forms of the respective "lower" member of this relation) is in itself mere matter, mere potentiality, akin more to Non-Being than to Being. It becomes real only insofar as it partakes of the "higher" world. In all these forms the material world remains bare matter or stuff for something outside it which alone gives it value. All and any truth, goodness, and beauty can accrue to it only "from above" by the grace of the Idea. All activity relating to the material provision of life remains in its essence untrue, bad, and ugly. Even with these characteristics, however, such activity is as necessary as matter is for the Idea. The misery of slave labor, the degradation of men and things to commodities, the joylessness and lowliness in which the totality of the material conditions of existence continuously reproduces itself, all these do not fall within the sphere of interest of idealist philosophy, for they are not yet the actual reality that constitutes the object of this philosophy. Due to its irrevocably material quality, material practice is exonerated from responsibility for the true, good, and beautiful, which is instead taken care of by the pursuit of theory. The ontological cleavage of ideal from material values tranquilizes idealism in all that regards the material processes of life. In idealism, a specific historical form of the division of labor and of social stratification takes on the eternal, metaphysical form of the relationship of necessity and beauty, of matter and Idea.

In the bourgeois epoch the theory of the relationship between necessity and beauty, labor and enjoyment, underwent decisive changes. First, the view that concern with the highest values is appropriated as a profession by particular social strata disappears. In its place emerges the thesis of the universality and universal validity of "culture." With good conscience, the theory of antiquity had expressed the fact that most men had to spend their lives providing for necessities while a small number devoted themselves to enjoyment and truth. Although the fact has not changed, the good conscience has disappeared. Free competition places individuals in the relation of buyers and sellers of labor power. The pure abstractness to which men are reduced in their social relations extends as well to intercourse with ideas. It is no longer supposed to be the case that some are born to and suited to labor and others to leisure, some to necessity and others to beauty. Just as each individual's relation to the market is immediate (without his personal qualities and needs being relevant except as commodities), so his relations to God, to beauty, to goodness, and to truth are relations of immediacy. As abstract beings, all men are supposed to participate equally in these values. As in material practice the product separates itself from the producers and becomes independent as the universal reified form of the "commodity," so in cultural practice a work and its content congeal into universally valid "values." By their very nature the truth of a philosophical judgment, the goodness of a moral action, and the beauty of a work of art should appeal to everyone, relate to everyone, be binding upon everyone. Without distinction of sex or birth, regardless of their position in the process of production, individuals must subordinate themselves to cultural values. They must absorb them into their lives and let their existence be permeated and transfigured by them. "Civilization" is animated and inspired by "culture."

This is not the place to discuss the various attempts to define culture. There is a concept of culture that can serve as an important instrument of social research because it expresses the implication of the mind in the historical process of society. It signifies the totality of social life in a given situation, insofar as both the areas of ideational reproduction (culture in the narrower sense, the "spiritual world") and of material reproduction ("civilization") form a historically distinguishable and comprehensible unity.[7] There is, however, another fairly widespread usage of the concept of culture, in which the spiritual world is lifted out of its social context, making culture a (false) collective noun and attributing (false) universality to it. This second concept of culture (clearly seen in such expressions as "national culture," "Germanic culture," or "Roman culture") plays off the spiritual world against the material world by holding up culture as the realm of authentic values and self-contained ends in opposition to the world of social utility and means. Through the use of this concept, culture is distinguished from civilization and sociologically and valuationally removed from the social process.[8] This concept itself has developed on the basis of a specific historical form of culture, which is termed "affirmative culture" in what follows. By affirmative culture is meant that culture of the bourgeois epoch which led in the course of its own development to the segregation from civilization of the mental and spiritual world as an independent realm of value that is also considered superior to civilization. Its decisive characteristic is the assertion of a universally obligatory, eternally better and more valuable world that must be unconditionally affirmed: a world essentially different from the factual world of the daily struggle for existence, yet realizable by every individual for himself "from within," without any transformation of the state of fact. It is only in this culture that cultural activities and objects gain that value which elevates them above the everyday sphere. Their reception becomes an act of celebration and exaltation.

Although the distinction between civilization and culture may have joined only recently the mental equipment of the social and cultural sciences, the state of affairs that it expresses has long been characteristic of the conduct of life and the weltanschauung of the bourgeois era. "Civilization and culture" is not simply a translation of the ancient relation of purposeful and purposeless, necessary and beautiful. As the purposeless and beautiful were internalized and, along with the qualities of binding universal validity and sublime beauty, made into the cultural values of the bourgeoisie, a realm of apparent unity and apparent freedom was constructed within culture in which the antagonistic relations of existence were supposed to be stabilized and pacified. Culture affirms and conceals the new conditions of social life.

In antiquity, the world of the beautiful beyond necessity was essentially a world of happiness and enjoyment. The ancient theory had never doubted that men's concern was ultimately their worldly gratification, their happiness. Ultimately, not immediately; for man's first concern is the struggle for the preservation and protection of mere existence. In view of the meager development of the productive forces in the ancient economy, it never occurred to philosophy that material practice could ever be fashioned in such a way that it would itself contain the space and time for happiness. Anxiety stands at the source of all idealistic doctrines that look for the highest felicity in ideational practice: anxiety about the uncertainty of all the conditions of life, about the contingency of loss, of dependence, and of poverty, but anxiety also about satiation, ennui, and envy of men and the gods. Nonetheless, anxiety about happiness, which drove philosophy to separate beauty and necessity, preserves the demand for happiness even within the separated sphere. Happiness becomes a preserve, in order for it to be able to be present at all. What man is to find in the philosophical knowledge of the true, the good, and the beautiful is ultimate pleasure, which has all the opposite characteristics of material facticity: permanence in change, purity amidst impurity, freedom amidst unfreedom.

The abstract individual who emerges as the subject of practice at the beginning of the bourgeois epoch also becomes the bearer of a new claim to happiness, merely on the basis of the new constellation of social forces. No longer acting as the representative or delegate of higher social bodies, each separate individual is supposed to take the provision of his needs and the fulfillment of his wants into his own hands and be in immediate relation to his "vocation," to his purpose and goals, without the social, ecclesiastical, and political mediations of feudalism. In this situation the individual was allotted more room for individual requirements and satisfactions: room which developing capitalist production began to fill with more and more objects of possible satisfaction in the form of commodities. To this extent, the bourgeois liberation of the individual made possible a new happiness.

But the universality of this happiness is immediately canceled, since the abstract equality of men realizes itself in capitalist production as concrete inequality. Only a small number of men dispose of the purchasing power required for the quantity of goods necessary in order to secure happiness. Equality does not extend to the conditions for attaining the means. For the strata of the rural and urban proletariat, on whom the bourgeoisie depended in their struggle against the feudal powers, abstract equality could have meaning only as real equality. For the bourgeoisie, when it came to power, abstract equality sufficed for the flourishing of real individual freedom and real individual happiness, since it already disposed of the material conditions that could bring about such satisfaction. Indeed, stopping at the stage of abstract freedom belonged to the conditions of bourgeois rule, which would have been endangered by a transition from abstract to concrete universality. On the other hand, the bourgeoisie could not give up the general character of its demand (that equality be extended to all men) without denouncing itself and openly proclaiming to the ruled strata that, for the majority, everything was still the same with regard to the improvement of the conditions of life. Such a concession became even less likely as growing social wealth made the real fulfillment of this general demand possible while there was in contrast the relatively increasing poverty of the poor in city and country. Thus the demand became a postulate, and its object a mere idea. The vocation of man, to whom general fulfillment is denied in the material world, is hypostatized as an ideal.

The rising bourgeois groups had based their demand for a new social freedom on the universality of human reason. Against the belief in the divinely instituted eternity of a restrictive order they maintained their belief in progress, in a better future. But reason and freedom did not extend beyond these groups' interest, which came into increasing opposition to the interest of the majority. To accusing questions the bourgeoisie gave a decisive answer: affirmative culture. The latter is fundamentally idealist. To the need of the isolated individual it responds with general humanity, to bodily misery with the beauty of the soul, to external bondage with internal freedom, to brutal egoism with the duty of the realm of virtue. Whereas during the period of the militant rise of the new society all of these ideas had a progressive character by pointing beyond the attained organization of existence, they entered increasingly into the service of the suppression of the discontented masses and of mere self-justifying exaltation, once bourgeois rule began to be stabilized. They concealed the physical and psychic vitiation of the individual.

But bourgeois idealism is not merely ideology, for it expresses a correct objective content. It contains not only the justification of the established form of existence, but also the pain of its establishment: not only quiescence about what is, but also remembrance of what could be. By making suffering and sorrow into eternal, universal forces, great bourgeois art has continually shattered in the hearts of men the facile resignation of everyday life. By painting in the luminous colors of this world the beauty of men and things and transmundane happiness, it has planted real longing alongside poor consolation and false consecration in the soil of bourgeois life. This art raised pain and sorrow, desperation and loneliness, to the level of metaphysical powers and set individuals against one another and the gods in the nakedness of physical immediacy, beyond all social mediations. This exaggeration contains the higher truth that such a world cannot be changed piecemeal, but only through its destruction. Classical bourgeois art put its ideal forms at such a distance from everyday occurrence that those whose suffering and hope reside in daily life could only rediscover themselves through a leap into a totally other world. In this way art nourished the belief that all previous history had been only the dark and tragic prehistory of a coming existence. And philosophy took this idea seriously enough to be concerned about its realization. Hegel's system is the last protest against the degradation of the idea: against playing officiously with the mind as though it were an object that really has nothing to do with human history. At least idealism maintained that the materialism of bourgeois practice is not the last word and that mankind must be led beyond it. Thus idealism belongs to a more progressive stage of development than later positivism, which in fighting metaphysical ideas eliminates not only their metaphysical character, but their content as well. It thus links itself inevitably to the status quo.

Culture is supposed to assume concern for the individual's claim to happiness. But the social antagonisms at the root of culture let it admit this claim only in an internalized and rationalized form. In a society that reproduces itself through economic competition, the mere demand for a happier social existence constitutes rebellion. For if men value the enjoyment of worldly happiness, then they certainly cannot value acquisitive activity, profit, and the authority of the economic powers that preserve the existence of this society. The claim to happiness has a dangerous ring in an order that for the majority means need, privation, and toil. The contradictions of such an order provide the impetus to the idealization of that claim. But the real gratification of individuals cannot be contained by an idealistic dynamic which either continually postpones gratification or transmutes it into striving for the unattained. It can only be realized *against* idealist culture, and only *against* this culture is it propagated as a general demand: the demand for a real transformation of the material conditions of existence, for a new life, for a new form of labor and of enjoyment. Thus it has remained active in the revolutionary groups that have fought the expanding new system of injustice since the waning of the Middle Ages. And while idealism surrenders the earth to bourgeois society and makes its ideas unreal by finding satisfaction in heaven and the soul, materialist philosophy takes seriously the concern for happiness and fights for its realization in history. In the philosophy of the Enlightenment, this connection becomes clear.

> False philosophy can, like theology, promise us an eternal happiness and, cradling us in beautiful chimeras, lead us there at the expense of our days or our pleasure. Quite different and wiser, true philosophy affords only a temporal happiness. It sows roses and flowers in our path and teaches us to pick them.[9]

Idealist philosophy, too, admits the centrality of human happiness. But in its controversy with stoicism, the Enlightenment adopted precisely

that form of the claim to happiness which is incompatible with idealism and with which affirmative culture cannot deal:

> And how we shall be anti-Stoics! These philosophers are strict, sad,
> and hard; we shall be tender, joyful, and agreeable. All soul, they
> abstract from their body; all body, we shall abstract from our soul.
> They show themselves inaccessible to pleasure and pain; we shall
> be proud to feel both the one and the other. Aiming at the sublime,
> they elevate themselves above all occurrences and believe them-
> selves to be truly men only insofar as they cease to exist. Ourselves,
> we shall not control what governs us, although circumstances will
> not command our feelings. By acknowledging their lordship and
> our bondage, we shall try to make them agreeable to us, in the con-
> viction that it is here that the happiness of life resides. Finally, we
> shall believe ourselves that much happier, the more we feel nature,
> humanity, and all social virtues. We shall recognize none but these,
> nor any life other than this one.[10]

In its idea of pure humanity, affirmative culture took up the historical
demand for the general liberation of the individual. "If we consider
mankind as we know it according to the laws which it embodies, we
find nothing higher in man than humanity."[11] This concept is meant
to comprise everything that is directed toward "man's noble education
to reason and freedom, to more refined senses and instincts, to the most
delicate and the heartiest health, to the fulfillment and domination of
the earth."[12] All human laws and forms of government are to have the
exclusive purpose of "enabling man, free from attack by others, to exercise his powers and acquire a more beautiful and freer enjoyment of
life."[13] The highest point which man can attain is a community of free
and rational persons in which each has the same opportunity to unfold
and fulfill all of his powers. The concept of the person, in which the
struggle against repressive collectivities has remained active through
the present, disregards social conflicts and conventions and addresses itself to all individuals. No one relieves the individual of the burden of
his existence, but no one prescribes his rights and sphere of action — no
one except the "law in his own breast."

Nature intended that man generate entirely out of himself everything going beyond the mechanical organization of his animal existence, and that he partake of no other happiness or perfection than
that which he provides for himself, free of instinct, by means of his
own reason.[14]

All wealth and all poverty derive from him and react back upon him.
Each individual is immediate to himself: without worldly or heavenly
mediations. And this immediacy also holds for his relations to others.
The clearest representation of this idea of the person is to be found in
classical literature since Shakespeare. In its dramas, individuals are so
close to one another that between them there is nothing that is in principle ineffable or inexpressible. Verse makes possible what has already
become impossible in prosaic reality. In poetry men can transcend all
social isolation and distance and speak of the first and last things. They
overcome the factual loneliness in the glow of great and beautiful
words; they may even let loneliness appear in its metaphysical beauty.
Criminal and saint, prince and servant, sage and fool, rich and poor
join in discussion whose free flow is supposed to give rise to truth. The
unity represented by art and the pure humanity of its persons are unreal; they are the counterimage of what occurs in social reality. The
critical and revolutionary force of the ideal, which in its very unreality
keeps alive the best desires of men amidst a bad reality, becomes clearest in those times when the satiated social strata have accomplished
the betrayal of their own ideals. The ideal, to be sure, was conceived
in such a fashion that its regressive and apologetic, rather than its progressive and critical, characteristics predominated. Its realization is
supposed to be effected through the cultural education of individuals.
Culture means not so much a better world as a nobler one: a world
to be brought about not through the overthrow of the material order of
life but through events in the individual's soul. Humanity becomes an
inner state. Freedom, goodness, and beauty become spiritual qualities:
understanding for everything human, knowledge about the greatness of
all times, appreciation of everything difficult and sublime, respect for
history in which all of this has become what it is. This inner state is to
be the source of action that does not come into conflict with the given
order. Culture belongs not to him who comprehends the truths of hu-

manity as a battle cry, but to him in whom they have become a posture which leads to a mode of proper behavior: exhibiting harmony and reflectiveness even in daily routine. Culture should ennoble the given by permeating it, rather than putting something new in its place. It thus exalts the individual without freeing him from his factual debasement. Culture speaks of the dignity of "man" without concerning itself with a concretely more dignified status for men. The beauty of culture is above all an inner beauty and can only reach the external world from within. Its realm is essentially a realm of the *soul*.

That culture is a matter of spiritual *(seelisch)* values is constitutive of the affirmative concept of culture at least since Herder. Spiritual values belong to the definition of culture in contrast to mere civilization. Alfred Weber was merely summing up a conceptual scheme with a long history when he wrote:

> Culture . . . is merely spiritual expression and spiritual will and thus the expression and will of an "essence" that lies behind all intellectual mastery of existence, of a "soul" that, in its striving for expression and in its willing, pays no regard to purposiveness and utility. . . . From this follows the concept of culture as the prevailing form in which the spiritual is expressed and released in the materially and spiritually given substance of existence.[15]

The soul posited by this interpretation is other and more than the totality of psychic forces and mechanisms (such as might be the object of empirical psychology). Rather, this noncorporeal being of man is asserted as the real substance of the individual.

The character of the soul as substance has since Descartes been founded upon the uniqueness of the ego as *res cogitans*. While the entire world outside the ego becomes in principle one of measurable matter with calculable motion, the ego is the only dimension of reality to evade the materialistic rationality of the rising bourgeoisie. By coming into opposition to the corporeal world as a substance differing from it in essence, the ego is subjected to a remarkable division into two regions. The ego as the subject of thought (*mens*, mind) remains, in the independence of self-certainty, on this side of the being of matter—its a priori, as it were—while Descartes attempts to explain materialistically the ego as soul *(anima)*, as the subject of "passions" (love and hate, joy and

sorrow, shame, jealousy, regret, gratitude, and so forth). The passions of
the soul are traced to blood circulation and its transformation in the
brain. This reduction does not quite succeed. To be sure, all muscular
movements and sense perceptions are thought to depend on the nerves,
which "are like small filaments or small pipes that all come from the
brain," but the nerves themselves contain "a certain very fine air or
wind called animal spirits."[16] Despite this immaterial residue, the tendency of the interpretation is clear: the ego is either mind (thought,
cogito me cogitare) or, insofar as it is not merely thought *(cogitatio)*, it is
no longer authentically ego, but rather corporeal. In the latter case, the
properties and activities ascribed to it belonged to *res extensa*.[17] Yet they
do not quite admit of being dissolved into matter. The soul remains an
unmastered intermediate realm between the unshakable self-certainty
of pure thought and the mathematical and physical certainty of material being. Already in the original project of rationalism there is no
room in the system for what is later considered actually to compose the
soul, viz. the individual's feelings, appetites, desires, and instincts. The
position within rationalism of empirical psychology, i.e. of the discipline really dealing with the human soul, is characteristic, for it exists
although reason is unable to legitimate it.

Kant polemized against the treatment of empirical psychology
within rational metaphysics (by Baumgarten). Empirical psychology must be "completely banished from the domain of metaphysics; it
is indeed already completely excluded by the very idea of the latter science." But, he goes on, "in conformity, however, with scholastic usage
we must allow it some sort of a place (although as an episode only) in
metaphysics, and this from economical motives, because it is not yet so
rich as to be able to form a subject of study by itself, and yet is too important to be entirely excluded and forced to settle elsewhere.... It is
thus merely a stranger who is taken in for a short while until he finds
a home of his own, in a complete anthropology."[18] And in his metaphysics lectures of 1792–93 Kant expressed himself even more scep-
tically about this "stranger": "Is an empirical psychology possible as
science? No—our knowledge of the soul is entirely too limited."[19]

Rationalism's estrangement from the soul points to an important
state of affairs. For in fact the soul does not enter into the social labor
process. Concrete labor is reduced to abstract labor that makes possible

the exchange of the products of labor as commodities. The idea of the soul seems to allude to those areas of life which cannot be managed by the abstract reason of bourgeois practice. It is as though the processing of matter is accomplished only by a part of the *res cogitans*: by technical reason. Beginning with the division of labor in manufacture and brought to completion in machine industry, "the intellectual *[geistigen]* potencies of the material process of production" come into opposition to the immediate producers as "the property of another and as a power that rules them."[20] To the extent that thought is not immediately technical reason, it has freed itself since Descartes from conscious connection with social practice and tolerates the reification that it itself promotes. When in this practice human relations appear as material relations, as the very laws of things, philosophy abandons the individual to this appearance by retreating and re-establishing itself at the level of the transcendental constitution of the world in pure subjectivity. Transcendental philosophy does not make contact with reification, for it investigates only the process of cognition of the immemorially *(je schon)* reified world.

The soul is not comprehended by the dichotomy of *res cogitans* and *res extensa*, for it cannot be understood merely as one or the other. Kant destroyed rational psychology without arriving at an empirical psychology. For Hegel, every single attribute of the soul is comprehended from the standpoint of mind *(Geist)*, into which the soul passes over *(übergeht)*; for mind reveals itself to be the soul's true content. The soul is essentially characterized by its "not yet being mind."[21] Where Hegel treats psychology, i.e. the human soul, in his doctrine of subjective mind, the guiding principle is no longer soul but mind. Hegel deals with the soul principally as part of "anthropology," where it is still completely "bound to the attributes of nature."[22] He examines planetary life on a general scale, natural racial distinctions, the ages of man, magic, somnambulism, various forms of psychopathic self-images, and—only for a few pages—the "real soul." For him the latter is nothing but the transition to the ego of consciousness, wherewith the anthropological doctrine of soul is already left behind, and the phenomenology of mind arrived at. The soul is thus allotted to physiological anthropology on the one hand and the philosophy of mind on the other. Even in the greatest system of bourgeois rationalism there is no place for the independence of the soul. The authentic objects of psychology, feelings, instincts, and will, are conceived only as forms of the existence of mind.

With its concept of the soul, however, affirmative culture means precisely what is not mind. Indeed, the concept of soul comes into ever sharper contradiction to the concept of mind. What is meant by soul "is forever inaccessible to the lucid mind, to the understanding, or to empirical, factual research.... One could sooner dissect with a knife a theme by Beethoven or dissolve it with an acid than analyze the soul with the means of abstract thought."[23] In the idea of the soul, the noncorporeal faculties, activities, and properties of man (according to the traditional classifications, reason, will, and appetite) are combined in an indivisible unity that manifestly endures through all of the individual's behavior and, indeed, constitutes his individuality.

The concept of the soul typical of affirmative culture was not developed by philosophy, and the examples from Descartes, Kant, and Hegel were intended only to illustrate philosophy's embarrassment with regard to the soul.[24] This concept found its first positive expression in the literature of the Renaissance. Here the soul is in the first instance an unexplored part of the world to be discovered and enjoyed. To it are extended those demands with whose proclamation the new society accompanied the rational domination of the world by liberated man: freedom and the intrinsic worth of the individual. The riches of the soul, of the "inner life," were thus the correlate of the new-found riches of external life. Interest in the neglected "individual, incomparable, living states" of the soul belonged to the program of "living out one's life fully and entirely."[25] Concern with the soul "reacts upon the increasing differentiation of individualities and augments man's consciousness of enjoying life with a natural development rooted in man's essence."[26] Seen from the standpoint of the consummated affirmative culture of the eighteenth and nineteenth centuries, this spiritual demand appears as an unfulfilled promise. The idea of "natural development" remains, but it signifies primarily inner development. In the external world the soul cannot freely "live itself out." The organization of this world by the capitalist labor process has turned the development of the individual into economic competition and left the satisfaction of his needs to the commodity market. Affirmative culture uses the soul as a protest against reification, only to succumb to it in the end. The soul is sheltered as the only area of life that has not been drawn into the social labor process.

> The word "soul" gives the higher man a feeling of his inner existence, separated from all that is real or has evolved, a very definite feeling of the most secret and genuine potentialities of his life, his destiny, his history. In the early stages of the languages of all cultures, the word "soul" is a sign that encompasses everything that is not world.[27]

And in this—negative—quality it now becomes the only still immaculate guarantor of bourgeois ideals. The soul glorifies resignation. The ideal that man, individual, irreplaceable man, beyond all natural and social distinctions, be the ultimate end; that truth, goodness, and justice hold between men; that all human weaknesses be expiated by humanity—this ideal can be represented, in a society determined by the economic law of value, only by the soul and as spiritual occurrence. All else is inhuman and discredited. The soul alone obviously has no exchange value. The value of the soul does not enter into the body in such a way as to congeal into an object and become a commodity. There can be a beautiful soul in an ugly body, a healthy one in a sick body, a noble one in a common body—and vice versa. There is a kernel of truth in the proposition that what happens to the body cannot affect the soul. But in the established order this truth has taken on a terrible form. The freedom of the soul was used to excuse the poverty, martyrdom, and bondage of the body. It served the ideological surrender of existence to the economy of capitalism. Correctly understood, however, spiritual freedom does not mean the participation of man in an eternal beyond where everything is righted when the individual can no longer benefit from it. Rather, it anticipates the higher truth that in this world a form of social existence is possible in which the economy does not preempt the entire life of individuals. Man does not live by bread alone; this truth is thoroughly falsified by the interpretation that spiritual nourishment is an adequate substitute for too little bread.

The soul appears to escape reification just as it does the law of value. As a matter of fact, it can almost be defined by the assertion that through its means all reified relations are dissolved into human relations and negated. The soul institutes an all-encompassing inner community of men that spans the centuries. "The first thought in the first human soul links up with the last thought in the last human soul."[28] In the realm of culture spiritual education and spiritual greatness overcome the inequality and unfreedom of everyday competition, for men participate in culture as free and equal beings. He who looks to the soul sees through economic relations to men in themselves. Where the soul speaks, the contingent position and merit of men in the social process are transcended. Love breaks through barriers between rich and poor, high and lowly. Friendship keeps faith even with the outcast and despised, and truth raises its voice even before the tyrant's throne. Despite all social obstacles and encroachments, the soul develops in the individual's interior. The most cramped surroundings are large enough to expand into an infinite environment for the soul. In its classical era, affirmative culture continually poetized the soul in such a manner.

The individual's soul is first set off from, and against, his body. Its adoption as the decisive area of life can have two meanings: the release of sensuality (as the irrelevant area of life) or, to the contrary, the subjection of sensuality to the domination of the soul. Affirmative culture unequivocally took the second course. Release of sensuality would be release of enjoyment, which presupposes the absence of guilty conscience and the real possibility of gratification. In bourgeois society, such a trend is increasingly opposed by the necessity of disciplining discontented masses. The internalization of enjoyment through spiritualization therefore becomes one of the decisive tasks of cultural education. By being incorporated into spiritual life, sensuality is to be harnessed and transfigured. From the coupling of sensuality and the soul proceeds the bourgeois idea of love.

The spiritualization of sensuality fuses matter with heaven and death with eternity. The weaker the belief in a heavenly beyond, the stronger the veneration of the spiritual beyond. The idea of love absorbs the longing for the permanence of worldly happiness, for the blessing of the unconditional, for the conquest of termination. In bourgeois poetry, lovers love in opposition to everyday inconstancy, to the demands of reality, to the subjugation of the individual, and to death. Death does not come from outside, but from love itself. The liberation of the individual was effected in a society based not on solidarity but on conflict of interests among individuals. The individual has the character of an independent, self-sufficient monad. His relation to the (human and nonhuman) world is either abstractly immediate (the individual constitutes the world immemorially in itself as knowing, feeling, and willing ego) or abstractly mediated (i.e. determined by the blind laws of the production of commodities and of the market). In neither case is the monadic isolation of the individual overcome. To do so would mean the establishment of real solidarity and presupposes the replacement of individualist society by a higher form of social existence.

The idea of love, however, requires that the individual overcome monadic isolation and find fulfillment through the surrender of individuality in the unconditional solidarity of two persons. In a society in which conflict of interest is the *principium individuationis*, this complete surrender can appear in pure form only in death. For only death eliminates all of the external conditions that destroy permanent solidarity and in the struggle with which individuals wear themselves out. It appears not as the cessation of existence in nothingness, but rather as the only possible consummation of love and thus as its deepest significance.

While in art love is elevated to tragedy, it threatens to become mere duty and habit in everyday bourgeois life. Love contains the individualistic principle of the new society: it demands exclusiveness. The latter appears in the requirement of unconditional fidelity which, originating in the soul, should also be obligatory for sensuality. But the spiritualization of sensuality demands of the latter what it cannot achieve: withdrawal from change and fluctuation and absorption into the unity and indivisibility of the person. Just at this point, inwardness and outwardness, potentiality and reality are supposed to be found in a preestablished harmony which the anarchic principle of society destroys everywhere. This contradiction makes exclusive fidelity untrue and vitiates sensuality, which finds an outlet in the furtive improprieties of the petit bourgeois.

Purely private relationships such as love and friendship are the only realm in which the dominion of the soul is supposed to be immediately confirmed in reality. Otherwise the soul has primarily the function of elevating men to the ideal without urging the latter's realization. The soul has a tranquilizing effect. Because it is exempted from reification, it suffers from it least, consequently meeting it with the least resistance. Since the soul's meaning and worth do not fall within historical reality, it can maintain itself unharmed in a bad reality. Spiritual joys are cheaper than bodily ones; they are less dangerous and are granted more willingly. An essential difference between the soul and the mind is that the former is not oriented toward critical knowledge of truth. The soul can understand what the mind must condemn. Conceptual knowledge attempts to distinguish the one from the other and resolves contradiction only on the basis of the "dispassionately proceeding necessity of the object," while the soul rapidly reconciles all "external" antitheses in some "internal" unity. If there is a Western, Germanic, Faustian soul, then a Western, Germanic, and Faustian culture belongs to it, and feudal, capitalist, and socialist societies are nothing but manifestations of such souls. Their firm antitheses dissolve into the beautiful and profound unity of culture. The reconciliatory nature of the soul manifests itself clearly where psychology is made the organon of the social and cultural sciences, without foundation in a theory of society that penetrates behind culture. The soul has a strong affinity with historicism. As early as Herder we find the idea that the soul, freed from rationalism, should be capable of universal empathy *(einfühlen)*. He adjures the soul,

> Entire nature of the soul that rules all things, that models all other inclinations and psychic forces after itself and tinges even the most indifferent actions—in order to feel these, do not answer in words, but penetrate into the epoch, into the region of heaven, into all of history, feel yourself into everything.... [29]

With its property of universal empathy the soul devalues the distinction between true and false, good and bad, or rational and irrational that can be made through the analysis of social reality with regard to the attainable potentialities of the organization of material existence. Every historical epoch, then, as Ranke stated, manifests but another facet of the same human spirit. Each one possesses its own meaning, "and its value rests not on what results from it, but on its very existence, on its own self." [30] Soul has nothing to do with the correctness of what it expresses. It can do honor to a bad cause (as in Dostoevski's case). [31] In the struggle for a better human future, profound and refined souls may stand aside or on the wrong side. The soul takes fright at the hard truth of theory, which points up the necessity of changing an impoverished form of existence. How can an external transformation determine the authentic, inner substance of man? Soul lets one be soft and compliant, submitting to the facts; for, after all, they do not really matter. In this way the soul was able to become a useful factor in the technique of mass domination when, in the epoch of authoritarian states, all available forces had to be mobilized against a real transformation of social existence. With the help of the soul, the bourgeoisie in advanced capitalist society buried its ideals of an earlier period. That soul is of the essence makes a good slogan when only power is of the essence.

But the soul really is essential—as the unexpressed, unfulfilled life of the individual. The culture of souls absorbed in a false form those forces and wants which could find no place in everyday life. The cultural ideal assimilated men's longing for a happier life: for humanity, goodness, joy, truth, and solidarity. Only, in this ideal, they are all furnished with the affirmative accent of belonging to a higher, purer, nonprosaic world. They are either internalized as the duty of the individual soul (to achieve what is constantly betrayed in the external existence of the whole) or represented as objects of art (whereby their reality is relegated to a realm essentially different from that of everyday life). There is a good reason for the exemplification of the cultural ideal in art, for only in art has bourgeois society tolerated its own ideals and taken them seriously as a general demand. What counts as utopia, fantasy, and rebellion in the world of fact is allowed in art. There affirmative culture has displayed the forgotten truths over which "realism" triumphs in daily life. The medium of beauty decontaminates truth and sets it apart from the present. What occurs in art occurs with no obligation. When this beautiful world is not completely represented as something long past (the classic artistic portrayal of victorious humanity, Goethe's *Iphigenie*, is a "historical" drama), it is deprived of concrete relevance by the magic of beauty.

In the medium of beauty, men have been permitted to partake of happiness. But even beauty has been affirmed with good conscience only in the ideal of art, for it contains a dangerous violence that threatens the given form of existence. The immediate sensuousness of beauty immediately suggests sensual happiness. According to Hume the power to stimulate pleasure belongs to the essential character of beauty. Pleasure is not merely a by-product of beauty, but constitutes its very essence.[32] And for Nietzsche beauty reawakens "aphrodisiac bliss." He polemizes against Kant's definition of the beautiful as the object of completely disinterested pleasure (Wohlgefallen) and opposes to it Stendhal's assertion that beauty is "une promesse de bonheur."[33] Therein lies its danger in a society that must rationalize and regulate happiness. Beauty is fundamentally shameless.[34] It displays what may not be promised openly and what is denied the majority. In the region of mere sensuality, separated from its connection with the ideal, beauty falls prey to the general devaluation of this sphere. Loosed from all spiritual and mental demands, beauty may be enjoyed in good conscience only in well delimited areas, with the awareness that it is only for a short period of relaxation or dissipation.

Bourgeois society has liberated individuals, but as persons who are to keep themselves in check. From the beginning, the prohibition of pleasure was a condition of freedom. A society split into classes can afford to make man into a means of pleasure only in the form of bondage and exploitation. Since in the new order the regulated classes rendered services not immediately, with their persons, but only mediated by the production of surplus value for the market, it was considered inhuman to exploit an underling's body as a source of pleasure, i.e., to use men directly as means (Kant). On the other hand, harnessing their bodies and intelligence for profit was considered a natural activation of freedom. Correspondingly, for the poor, hiring oneself out to work in a factory became a moral duty, while hiring out one's body as a means to pleasure was depravity and "prostitution." Also, in this society, poverty is a condition of profit and power, yet dependence takes place in the medium of abstract freedom. The sale of labor power is supposed to occur due to the poor man's own decision. He labors in the service of his employer, while he may keep for himself and cultivate as a sacred preserve the abstraction that is his person-in-itself, separated from its socially valuable functions. He is supposed to keep it pure. The prohibition against marketing the body not merely as an instrument of labor but as an instrument of pleasure as well is one of the chief social and psychological roots of bourgeois patriarchal ideology. Here reification has firm limits important to the system. Nonetheless, insofar as the body becomes a commodity as a manifestation or bearer of the sexual function, this occurs subject to general contempt. The taboo is violated. This holds not only for prostitution but for all production of pleasure that does not occur for reasons of "social hygiene" in the service of reproduction.

Those social strata, however, which are kept back in semi-medieval forms, pushed to the lowest margin of society, and thoroughly demoralized, provide, even in these circumstances, an anticipatory memory. When the body has completely become an object, a beautiful thing, it can foreshadow a new happiness. In suffering the most extreme reification man triumphs over reification. The artistry of the beautiful body, its effortless agility and relaxation, which can be displayed today only in the circus, vaudeville, and burlesque, herald the joy to which men will attain in being liberated from the ideal, once mankind, having become a true subject, succeeds in the mastery of matter. When all links to the affirmative ideal have been dissolved, when in the context of an existence marked by knowledge it becomes possible to have real enjoyment without any rationalization and without the least puritanical guilt feeling, when sensuality, in other words, is entirely released by the soul, then the first glimmer of a new culture emerges.

But in affirmative culture, the "soulless" regions do not belong to culture. Like every other commodity of the sphere of civilization, they are openly abandoned to the economic law of value. Only spiritual beauty and spiritual enjoyment are left in culture. According to Shaftesbury, it follows from the inability of animals to know and enjoy beauty

> "that neither can man by the same sense or brutish part conceive or enjoy beauty; but all the beauty and good he enjoys is in a nobler way, and by the help of what is noblest, his mind and reason.". . . When you place a joy elsewhere than in the mind, the enjoyment itself will be no beautiful subject, nor of any graceful or agreeable appearance.[35]

Only in the medium of ideal beauty, in art, was happiness permitted to be reproduced as a cultural value in the totality of social life. Not so in the two areas of culture which in other respects share with art in the representation of ideal truth: philosophy and religion. In its idealist trend, philosophy became increasingly distrustful of happiness, and religion accorded it a place only in the hereafter. Ideal beauty was the form in which yearning could be expressed and happiness enjoyed. Thus art became the presage of possible truth. Classical German aesthetics comprehended the relation between beauty and truth in the idea of an aesthetic education of the human species. Schiller says that the "political problem" of a better organization of society "must take the path through the aesthetic realm, because it is through beauty that one arrives at freedom."[36] And in his poem "*Die Künstler*" ("The Artists") he expresses the relation between the established and the coming culture in the lines: "What we have here perceived as beauty / We shall some day encounter as truth" ("*Was wir als Schönheit hier empfunden / Wird einst als Wahrheit uns entgegen gehn*"). With respect to the extent of socially permitted truth and to the form of attained happiness, art is the highest and most representative area within affirmative culture. "Culture: dominion of art over life"—this was Nietzsche's definition.[37] What entitles art to this unique role?

Unlike the truth of theory, the beauty of art is compatible with the bad present, despite and within which it can afford happiness. True theory recognizes the misery and lack of happiness prevailing in the established order. Even when it shows the way to transformation, it offers no consolation that reconciles one to the present. In a world without happiness, however, happiness cannot but be a consolation: the consolation of a beautiful moment in an interminable chain of misfortune. The enjoyment of happiness is compressed into a momentary episode. But the moment embodies the bitterness of its disappearance. Given the isolation of lone individuals, there is no one in whom one's own happiness can be preserved after the moment passes, no one who is not subject to the same isolation. Ephemerality which does not leave behind solidarity among the survivors must be eternalized in order to become at all bearable. For it recurs in every moment of existence and in each one, as it were, it anticipates death. Because every moment comprehends death, the beautiful moment must be eternalized in order to make possible anything like happiness. In the happiness it proffers, affirmative culture eternalizes the beautiful moment; it immortalizes the ephemeral.

One of the decisive social tasks of affirmative culture is based on this contradiction between the insufferable mutability of a bad existence and the need for happiness in order to make such existence bearable. Within this existence the resolution can be only illusory. And the possibility of a solution rests precisely on the character of artistic beauty as *illusion*. On the one hand the enjoyment of happiness is permitted only in spiritualized, idealized form. On the other, idealization annuls the meaning of happiness. For the ideal cannot be enjoyed, since all pleasure is foreign to it and would destroy the rigor and purity that must adhere to it in idealless reality if it is to be able to carry out its internalizing, disciplining function. The ideal emulated by the person who renounces his instincts and places himself under the categorical imperative of duty (this Kantian ideal is merely the epitome of all affirmative tendencies of culture) is insensitive to happiness. It can provide neither happiness nor consolation since it never affords gratification in the present. If the individual is ever to come under the power of the ideal to the extent of believing that his concrete longings and needs are to be found in it—found moreover in a state of fulfillment and gratification, then the ideal must give the illusion of granting present satisfaction. It is this illusory reality that neither philosophy nor religion can attain. Only art achieves it—in the medium of beauty. Goethe disclosed the deceptive and consoling role of beauty when he wrote:

> The human mind finds itself in a glorious state when it admires, when it worships, when it exalts an object and is exalted by it. Only it cannot long abide in this condition. The universal left it cold, the ideal elevated it above itself. Now, however, it would like to return to itself. It would like to enjoy again the earlier inclination that it cherished toward the individual without returning to a state of limitation, and does not want to let the significant, that which exalts the mind, depart. What would become of the mind in this condition if beauty did not intervene and happily solve the riddle! Only beauty gives life and warmth to the scientific; and by moderating the high and significant and showering it with heavenly charm, beauty brings us closer to it. A beautiful work of art has come full circle; it is now a sort of individual that we can embrace with affection, that we can appropriate.[38]

What is decisive in this connection is not that art represents ideal reality, but that it represents it as beautiful reality. Beauty gives the ideal the character of the charming, the gladdening, and the gratifying—of happiness. It alone perfects the illusion of art. For only through it does the illusory world arouse the appearance of familiarity, of being present; in short, of reality. Illusion *(Schein)* really enables something to appear *(erscheinen)*: in the beauty of the work of art, longing is momentarily fulfilled. The percipient experiences happiness. And once it has taken form in the work, the beautiful moment can be continually repeated. It is eternalized in the art work. In artistic enjoyment, the percipient can always reproduce such happiness.

Affirmative culture was the historical form in which were preserved those human wants which surpassed the material reproduction of existence. To that extent, what is true of the form of social reality to which it belonged holds for it as well: right is on its side. Certainly, it exonerated "external conditions" from responsibility for the "vocation of man," thus stabilizing their injustice. But it also held up to them as a task the image of a better order. The image is distorted, and the distortion falsified all cultural values of the bourgeoisie. Nevertheless it is an image of happiness. There is an element of earthly delight in the works of great bourgeois art, even when they portray heaven. The individual enjoys beauty, goodness, splendor, peace, and victorious joy. He even enjoys pain and suffering, cruelty and crime. He experiences liberation. And he understands, and encounters understanding for and in response to, his instincts and demands. Reification is transpierced in private. In art one does not have to be "realistic," for man is at stake, not his occupation or status. Suffering is suffering and joy is joy. The world appears as what it is behind the commodity form: a landscape is really a landscape, a man really a man, a thing really a thing.

In the form of existence to which affirmative culture belongs, "happiness in existing... is possible only as happiness in illusion."[39] But this illusion has a real effect, producing satisfaction. The latter's meaning, though, is decisively altered; it enters the service of the status quo. The rebellious idea becomes an accessory in justification. The truth of a higher world, of a higher good than material existence, conceals the truth that a better material existence can be created in which such happiness is realized. In affirmative culture even unhappiness becomes a means of subordination and acquiescence. By exhibiting the beautiful as present, art pacifies rebellious desire. Together with the other cultural areas it has contributed to the great educational achievement of so disciplining the liberated individual, for whom the new freedom has brought a new form of bondage, that he tolerates the unfreedom of social existence. The potentiality of a richer life, a potentiality disclosed with the help of modern thought, and the impoverished actual form of life have come into open opposition, repeatedly compelling this thought to internalize its own demands and deflect its own conclusions. It took a centuries-long education to help make bearable the daily reproduced shock that arises from the contradiction between the constant sermon of the inalienable freedom, majesty, and dignity of the person, the magnificence and autonomy of reason, the goodness of humanity and of impartial charity and justice, on the one hand, and the general degradation of the majority of mankind, the irrationality of the social life process, the victory of the labor market over humanity, and of profit over charity, on the other. "The entire counterfeit of transcendence and of the hereafter has grown up on the basis of an *impoverished* life . . ."[40] but the injection of cultural happiness into unhappiness and the spiritualization of sensuality mitigate the misery and the sickness of that life to a "healthy" work capacity. This is the real miracle of affirmative culture. Men can feel themselves happy even without being so at all. The effect of illusion renders incorrect even one's own assertion that one is happy. The individual, thrown back upon himself, learns to bear and, in a certain sense, to love his isolation. Factual loneliness is sublimated to metaphysical loneliness and, as such, is accorded the entire aura and rapture of inner plenitude alongside external poverty. In its idea of personality affirmative culture reproduces and glorifies individuals' social isolation and impoverishment.

The personality is the bearer of the cultural ideal. It is supposed to represent happiness in the form in which this culture proclaims it as the highest good: private harmony amidst general anarchy, joyful activity amidst bitter labor. The personality has absorbed everything good and cast off or refined everything bad. It matters not that man lives. What matters is only that he live as well as possible. That is one of the precepts of affirmative culture. "Well" here refers essentially to culture: participating in spiritual and mental values, patterning individual existence after the humanity of the soul and the breadth of the mind. The happiness of unrationalized enjoyment has been omitted from the ideal of felicity. The latter may not violate the laws of the established order and, indeed, does not need to violate them, for it is to be realized immanently. The personality, which in developed affirmative culture is supposed to be the "highest happiness" of man, must respect the foundations of the status quo: deference to given relations of domination belongs to its virtues. It may only kick over the traces if it remains conscious of what it is doing and takes it back afterward.

It was not always so. Formerly, at the beginning of the new era, the personality showed another face. Like the soul whose completed human embodiment it was supposed to be, it belonged in the first instance to the ideology of the bourgeois liberation of the individual. The person was the source of all forces and properties that made the individual capable of mastering his fate and shaping his environment in accordance with his needs. Jacob Burckhardt depicted this idea of the personality in his description of the "uomo universale" of the Renaissance.[41] If the individual was addressed as a personality, this was to emphasize that all that he made of himself he owed only to himself, not to his ancestors, his social status, or God. The distinguishing mark of the personality was not soul (in the sense of the "beautiful soul") but power, influence, fame: a life as extensive and as full of deeds as possible.

In the concept of personality which has been representative of affirmative culture since Kant, there is nothing left of this expansive activism. The personality remains lord of its existence only as a spiritual and ethical subject. "Freedom and independence from the mechanism of nature as a whole," which is now the token of its nature,[42] is only an "intelligible" freedom that accepts the given circumstances of life as the material of duty. Space for external fulfillment has shrunk; space for inner fulfillment has expanded considerably. The individual has learned to place all demands primarily upon himself. The rule of the soul has become more exacting inwardly and more modest outwardly. The person is no longer a springboard for attacking the world, but rather a protected line of retreat behind the front. In its inwardness, as an ethical person, it is the individual's only secure possession, the only one he can never lose.[43] It is no longer the source of conquest, but of renunciation. Personality characterizes above all him who renounces, who ekes out fulfillment within given conditions, no matter how poor they might be. He finds happiness in the Establishment. But even in this impoverished form, the idea of personality contains a progressive aspect: the individual is still the ultimate concern. To be sure, culture individuates men to the isolation of self-contained personalities whose fulfillment lies within themselves. But this corresponds to a method of discipline still liberal in nature, for it exempts a concrete region of private life from domination. It lets the individual subsist as a person as long as he does not disturb the labor process, and lets the immanent laws of this labor process, i.e. economic forces, take care of men's social integration.

Notes

This essay was prompted by Max Horkheimer's remarks about "affirmative culture" and the "false idealism" of modern culture. Cf. *Zeitschrift für Sozialforschung*, V (1936), p. 219.

1. Aristotle *Politics* 1333 a 30ff., trans. by Benjamin Jowett in *The Basic Works of Aristotle*, Richard McKeon, ed. (New York: Random House, 1941), p. 1298 (with change in translation).

2. *Translator's note:* While "*Seele*" has an adjectival form, "*seelisch*," its English counterpart "soul" does not. I have used "psychic" or "spiritual," depending on the context. Accordingly, although the word "*geistig*" means both "spiritual" and "mental," in the present essay I have rendered it as "mental," and "spiritual" refers to a quality of "soul," not of "mind."

3. *Translator's note:* "*Sinnlich*" means simultaneously "sensual," which stresses its appetitive aspect, and "sensuous," which stresses its aesthetic aspect. I have translated it in each case according to the emphasis of the context, but both meanings are always implied. For further discussion, see Herbert Marcuse, *Eros and Civilization* (Boston: Beacon Press, 1955), pp. 166–67.

4. Plato *Republ.* 553 in *The Republic of Plato*, trans. by Francis M. Cornford (New York: Oxford, 1945), p. 277. Cf. *Republ.* 525.

5. Ibid., pp. 306–307.

6. Plato *Leges* 831, trans. by A. E. Taylor in *The Collected Dialogues of Plato*, Edith Hamilton and Huntington Cairns, eds. (New York: Bollingen Foundation-Pantheon Books, 1964), p. 1397. Cf. J. Brake, *Wirtschaften und Charakter in der antiken Bildung* (Frankfurt am Main, 1935), pp. 124ff.

7. See *Studien über Autorität und Familie* ("Schriften des Instituts für Sozialforschung," V [Paris, 1936]), pp. 7ff.

8. Spengler interprets the relationship of culture and civilization not as simultaneity, but as "necessary organic succession." Civilization is the inevitable

fate and end of every culture. See *Der Untergang des Abendlandes*, 23d to 32d editions (Munich, 1920), I, pp. 43–44. Such reformulation does not modify the above-mentioned traditional evaluation of culture and civilization.

9. La Mettrie, "Discours sur le Bonheur," *Oeuvres Philosophiques* (Berlin, 1775), II, p. 102.

10. Ibid., pp. 86–87.

11. Herder, *Ideen zur Philosophie der Geschichte der Menschheit* in *Werke*, Bernhard Suphan, ed. (Berlin, 1877–1913), XIV, p. 208.

12. Ibid., XIII, p. 154.

13. Ibid., XIV, p. 209.

14. Kant, *Idee zu einer allgemeinen Geschichte in weltbürgerlicher Absicht* in *Werke*, Ernst Cassirer, ed. (Berlin, 1912ff.), IV, p. 153.

15. Alfred Weber, "Prinzipielles zur Kultursoziologie," *Archiv für Sozialwissenschaft*, XLVII (1920–21), pp. 29ff. See also Georg Simmel, "Der Begriff und die Tragödie der Kultur," where "the soul's way to itself" is described as the fundamental fact of culture [in *Philosophische Kultur* (Leipzig, 1919), p. 222]. Spengler characterizes culture as "the realization of the spiritually possible"; op. cit., p. 418.

16. Descartes, *Traité des Passions*, François Mizrachi, ed. (Paris: Union Générale d'Editions, 1965), p. 39.

17. See Descartes' reply to Gassendi's objections to the second Meditation, *Meditationen über die Grundlagen der Philosophie*, trans. by A. Buchenau (Leipzig, 1915), pp. 327–28.

18. Kant, *Critique of Pure Reason*, trans. by Norman Kemp Smith (London: Macmillan, 1958), p. 664 (with changes in translation).

19. *Die Philosophischen Hauptvorlesungen Immanuel Kants*, A. Kowalewski, ed. (Munich and Leipzig, 1924), p. 602.

20. Marx, *Das Kapital*, Meissner, ed. (Hamburg, n.d.), I. p. 326.

21. Hegel, *Enzyklopädie der philosophischen Wissenschaften*, II, par. 388.

22. Ibid., par. 387, addendum.

23. Spengler, op. cit., p. 406.

24. Characteristic is the introduction of the concept of the soul in Herbart's psychology: The soul is "not anywhere or anytime" and has "absolutely no predispositions and faculties either to receive or produce anything." "The simple nature of the soul is fully unknown and forever remains so; it is as little an object of speculative as of empirical psychology." Herbart, *Lehrbuch zur Psychologie* in *Sämtliche Werke*, Hartenstein, ed. (Leipzig, 1850), V, pp. 108–109.

25. Wilhelm Dilthey on Petrarca in "Weltanschauung und Analyse des Menschen seit Renaissance und Reformation," *Gesammelte Schriften* (Leipzig,

1914), II, p. 20. See also Dilthey's analysis of the transition from metaphysical to "descriptive and analytical" psychology in the thought of L. Vives, ibid., pp. 423ff.

26. Ibid., p. 18.

27. Spengler, op. cit., p. 407.

28. Herder, *Abhandlung über den Ursprung der Sprache*, op. cit., V, p. 135.

29. Herder, *Auch eine Philosophie der Geschichte zur Bildung der Menschheit*, ibid., p. 503.

30. Ranke, *Über die Epochen der neueren Geschichte*, in *Das politische Gespräch und andere Schriften zur Wissenschaftslehre*, Erich Rothacker, ed. (Halle, 1925), pp. 61–62.

31. On the quietist character of spiritual demands in Dostoevski see L. Löwenthal, "Die Auffassung Dostojewskis im Vorkriegsdeutschland," *Zeitschrift für Sozialforschung*, III (1934), p. 363.

32. David Hume, *A Treatise of Human Nature*, L. A. Selby-Bigge, ed. (Oxford, 1928), p. 301.

33. Nietzsche, *Werke* (large 8-vol. ed., 1917), XVI, p. 233, and VII, p. 408.

34. Goethe, *Faust II*, Phorkias: "Old is the saying, yet noble and true its meaning still, that shame and beauty never hand in hand traverse earth's green path." *Werke* (Cotta Jubiläumsausgabe), XIII, p. 159.

35. "The Moralists, a Philosophical Rhapsody" in *Characteristics of Men, Manners, Opinions, Times, etc.* by the Right Honourable Anthony Earl of Shaftesbury, John M. Robertson, ed. (in two volumes; New York: E. P. Dutton & Co., 1900), II, p. 143.

36. Schiller, *Über die ästhetische Erziehung des Menschen*, end of the second letter.

37. Nietzsche, op. cit., X, p. 245.

38. Goethe, *Der Sammler und die Seinigen*, toward the end of the sixth letter.

39. Nietzsche, op. cit., XIV, p. 366.

40. Ibid., VIII, p. 41.

41. *Die Kultur der Renaissance in Italien*, 11th ed., L. Geiger, ed. (Leipzig, 1913), especially I, pp. 150ff.

42. Kant, *Kritik der praktischen Vernunft*, op. cit., V, p. 95.

43. Goethe once expressed as follows the quality "only" that is present in the idea of personality: "People are always carping at the personality, reasonably and boldly. But what do you have that gladdens you aside from your beloved personality, of whatever sort it be?" "Zahme Xenien," *Werke*, IV, p. 54.

NATURE AND REVOLUTION (1972)

This essay first appeared as a chapter in the 1972 volume, *Counterrevolution and Revolt*. It is marked by Marcuse's reflections on the tumultuous events of the late 1960s and early 1970s, as they played out on university campuses, in protest marches, and in the attempts to construct alternative lifestyles. As was his common practice, he interpreted those events through the lenses of the intellectual traditions of Western philosophy, Marxism, and Freud's theory of civilization. The essay contains Marcuse's most extensive remarks on what may be called a "philosophy of nature." He contends that there is more to the world of nature than the economic benefits we extract from the materials of the earth's crust and transform with our technologies, more also than is revealed by the natural sciences.

This obsession with transforming the natural environment and its resources into goods blinds us to the other side of humanity's interaction with nature—nature as the source and foundation of our sensibility, the richness of experience made available to us through our senses. This side of our experience of nature is primarily one of aesthetic form, the sense of beauty and intrinsic value that arises in us when we contemplate the colors, shapes, movements, textures, and surfaces of the natural environment and its plant and animal inhabitants.

Although most of the essay treats these ideas at a high level of generality, there are also some specific applications, for example, the contention that we have a duty to make a "concerted effort to reduce

consistently the suffering which man imposes on the animal world."
Marcuse also seeks to show how and why reaffirming this other experience of nature is vitally important for the idea of human freedom itself,
and for the necessary transformations of social institutions and the relations between men and women.

•   •   •

I

The novel historical pattern of the coming revolution is perhaps best
reflected in the role played by a new sensibility in radically changing
the "style" of the opposition. I have sketched out this new dimension in
An Essay on Liberation; here I shall attempt to indicate what is at stake,
namely, a new relation between man and nature—his own, and external nature. The radical transformation of nature becomes an integral
part of the radical transformation of society. Far from being a mere
"psychological" phenomenon in groups or individuals, the new sensibility is the medium in which social change becomes an individual
need, the mediation between the political practice of "changing the
world" and the drive for personal liberation.

What is happening is the discovery (or rather, rediscovery) of nature
as an ally in the struggle against the exploitative societies in which
the violation of nature aggravates the violation of man. The discovery of
the liberating forces of nature and their vital role in the construction
of a free society becomes a new force in social change.

What is involved in the liberation of nature as a vehicle of the liberation of man?

This notion refers to (1) *human* nature: man's primary impulses and
senses as foundation of his rationality and experience and (2) *external*
nature: man's existential environment, the "struggle with nature" in
which he forms his society. It must be stressed from the beginning that,
in both of these manifestations, nature is a historical entity: man encounters nature as transformed by society, subjected to a specific rationality which became, to an ever-increasing extent, technological,
instrumentalist rationality, bent to the requirements of capitalism. And
this rationality was also brought to bear on man's own nature, on his primary drives. To recall only two characteristic contemporary forms of
the adaptation of primary drives to the needs of the established system:

the social steering of *aggressiveness* through transferring the aggressive act to technical instruments, thus reducing the sense of guilt; and the social steering of *sexuality* through controlled desublimation, the plastic beauty industry, which leads to a reduction of the sense of guilt and thus promotes "legitimate" satisfaction.

Nature is a part of history, an object of history; therefore, "liberation of nature" cannot mean returning to a pretechnological stage, but advancing to the use of the achievements of technological civilization for freeing man and nature from the destructive abuse of science and technology in the service of exploitation. Then, certain lost qualities of artisan work may well reappear on the new technological base.

In the established society, nature itself, ever more effectively controlled, has in turn become another dimension for the control of man: the extended arm of society and its power. Commercialized nature, polluted nature, militarized nature cut down the life environment of man, not only in an ecological but also in a very existential sense. It blocks the erotic cathexis (and transformation) of his environment: it deprives man from finding himself in nature, beyond and this side of alienation; it also prevents him from recognizing nature as a *subject* in its own right—a subject with which to live in a common human universe. This deprivation is not undone by the opening of nature to massive fun and togetherness, spontaneous as well as organized—a release of frustration which only adds to the violation of nature.

Liberation of nature is the recovery of the life-enhancing forces in nature, the sensuous aesthetic qualities which are foreign to a life wasted in unending competitive performances: they suggest the new qualities of *freedom*. No wonder then that the "spirit of capitalism" rejects or ridicules the idea of liberated nature, that it relegates this idea to the poetic imagination. Nature, if not left alone and protected as "reservation," is treated in an aggressively scientific way: it is there for the sake of domination; it is value-free matter, material. This notion of nature is a *historical* a priori, pertaining to a specific form of society. A free society may well have a very different a priori and a very different object; the development of the scientific concepts may be grounded in an experience of nature as a totality of life to be protected and "cultivated," and technology would apply this science to the reconstruction of the environment of life.

Domination of man through the domination of nature: the concrete link between the liberation of man and that of nature has become manifest today in the role which the ecology drive plays in the radical movement. The pollution of air and water, the noise, the encroachment of industry and commerce on open natural space have the physical weight of enslavement, imprisonment. The struggle against them is a political struggle; it is obvious to what extent the violation of nature is inseparable from the economy of capitalism. At the same time, however, the political function of ecology is easily "neutralized" and serves the beautification of the Establishment. Still, the physical pollution practiced by the system must be combated here and now—just as its mental pollution. To drive ecology to the point where it is no longer containable within the capitalist framework means first extending the drive *within* the capitalist framework.[1]

The relation between nature and freedom is rarely made explicit in social theory. In Marxism too, nature is predominantly an object, the adversary in man's "struggle with nature," the field for the ever more rational development of the productive forces.[2] But in this form, nature appears as that which capitalism has *made* of nature: matter, raw material for the expanding and exploiting administration of men and things. Does this image of nature conform to that of a free society? Is nature only a productive force—or does it also exist *"for its own sake"* and, in *this* mode of existence, for *man?*

In the treatment of *human* nature, Marxism shows a similar tendency to minimize the role of the natural basis in social change—a tendency which contrasts sharply with the earlier writings of Marx. To be sure, "human nature" would be different under socialism to the degree to which men and women would, for the first time in history, develop and fulfill their own needs and faculties in association with each other. But this change is to come about almost as a by-product of the new socialist institutions. Marxist emphasis on the development of political consciousness shows little concern with the roots of liberation in individuals, i.e., with the roots of social relationships there where individuals most directly and profoundly experience their world and themselves: in their *sensibility,* in their instinctual needs.

In *An Essay on Liberation,* I suggested that without a change in this dimension, the old Adam would be reproduced in the new society, and that the construction of a free society *presupposes* a break with the familiar experience of the world: with the mutilated sensibility. Conditioned and "contained" by the rationality of the established system, sense experience tends to "immunize" man against the very unfamiliar experience of the possibilities of human freedom. The development of a radical, nonconformist sensibility assumes vital political importance in view of the unprecedented extent of social control perfected by advanced capitalism: a control which reaches down into the instinctual and physiological level of existence. Conversely, resistance and rebellion, too, tend to activate and operate on this level.

"Radical sensibility": the concept stresses the active, constitutive role of the senses in shaping reason, that is to say, in shaping the categories under which the world is ordered, experienced, changed. The senses are not merely passive, receptive: they have their own "syntheses" to which they subject the primary data of experience. And these syntheses are not only the pure "forms of intuition" (space and time) which Kant recognized as an inexorable a priori *ordering* of sense data. There are perhaps also other syntheses, far more concrete, far more "material," which may constitute an empirical (i.e., historical) a priori of experience. Our world emerges not only in the pure forms of time and space, but also, and *simultaneously*, as a totality of sensuous qualities—object not only of the eye (synopsis) but of *all* human senses (hearing, smelling, touching, tasting). It is this qualitative, elementary, unconscious, or rather preconscious, constitution of the world of experience, it is this primary experience itself which must change radically if social change is to be radical, qualitative change.

II

The subversive potential of the sensibility, and nature as a field of liberation are central themes in Marx's *Economic and Philosophic Manuscripts*. They have been reread and reinterpreted again and again, but these themes have been largely neglected. Recently, the *Manuscripts* served to justify the concept of "humanistic socialism" in opposition to the bureaucratic-authoritarian Soviet model; they provided a powerful impetus in the struggle against Stalinism and post-Stalinism. I believe that in spite of their "pre-scientific" character, and in spite of the prevalence of Feuerbach's philosophic naturalism, these writings espouse the most radical and integral idea of socialism, and that precisely here, "nature" finds its place in the theory of revolution.

I recall briefly the principal conception of the *Manuscripts*. Marx speaks of the "complete emancipation of all human senses and qualities"[3] as the feature of socialism: only this emancipation is the "transcendence of private property." This means the emergence of a new type of man, different from the human subject of class society in his very nature, in his physiology: "the *senses* of the social man are *other* than those of the non-social man."[4]

"*Emancipation of the senses*" implies that the senses become "practical" in the reconstruction of society, that they generate new (socialist) relationships between man and man, man and things, man and nature. But the senses become also "sources" of a new (socialist) *rationality*: freed from that of exploitation. The emancipated senses would repel the instrumentalist rationality of capitalism while preserving and developing its achievements. They would attain this goal in two ways: *negatively*—inasmuch as the Ego, the other, and the object world would no longer be experienced in the context of aggressive acquisition, competition, and defensive possession; *positively*—through the "human appropriation of nature," i.e., through the transformation of nature into an environment (medium) for the human being as "species being"; free to develop the specifically human faculties: the creative, aesthetic faculties.

"Only through the objectively unfolded richness of man's essential being is the richness of subjective human sensibility (a musical ear, an eye for beauty of form—in short, *senses* capable of human gratification, senses affirming themselves as essential powers of man) either cultivated or brought into being."[5] The emancipated senses, in conjunction with a natural science proceeding on their basis, would guide the "human appropriation" of nature. Then, nature would have "lost its mere utility,"[6] it would appear not merely as stuff—organic or inorganic matter—but as life force in its own right, as subject-object;[7] the striving for life is the substance common to man and nature. Man would then form a living object. The senses would "relate themselves to the thing for the sake of the thing. . . ."[8] And they can do so only inasmuch as the thing itself is objectified human *Verhalten*: objectification of human relationships and is thus itself humanly related to man.[9]

This outrageously unscientific, metaphysical notion foreshadows the mature materialistic theory: it grasps the world of things as objectified human labor, shaped by human labor. Now if this forming human activity produces the technical and natural environment of an acquisitive and repressive society, it will also produce a dehumanized nature; and radical social change will involve a radical transformation of nature.

Also of the *science* of nature? Nature as manifestation of subjectivity: the idea seems inseparable from teleology—long since taboo in Western science. Nature as object per se fitted all too well into the universe of the capitalist treatment of matter to allow discarding the taboo. It seemed entirely justified by the increasingly effective and profitable mastery of nature which was achieved under this taboo.

Is it true that the recognition of nature as a subject is metaphysical teleology incompatible with scientific objectivity? Let us take Jacques Monod's statement of the meaning of objectivity in science:

> What I have tried to show... is that the scientific attitude implies what I call the postulate of objectivity—that is to say, the fundamental postulate that there is no plan, that there is no intention in the universe.[10]

The idea of the liberation of nature stipulates no such plan or intention in the universe: liberation is the possible plan and intention of human beings, brought to bear upon nature. However, it does stipulate that nature is susceptible to such an undertaking, and that there are forces in nature which have been distorted and suppressed—forces which could support and enhance the liberation of man. This capacity of nature may be called "chance," or "blind freedom," and it may give good meaning to the human effort to redeem this blindness—in Adorno's words: to help nature "to open its eyes," to help it "on the poor earth to become what perhaps it would like to be."[11]

Nature as subject without teleology, without "plan" and "intention": this notion goes well with Kant's "purposiveness without purpose." The most advanced concepts of the Third Critique have not yet been explored in their truly revolutionary significance. The aesthetic form in art has the aesthetic form in nature (*das Naturschöne*) as its correlate, or rather desideratum. If the idea of beauty pertains to nature as well as to art, this is not merely an analogy, or a human idea imposed on nature—it is the insight that the aesthetic form, as a token of freedom, is a mode (or moment?) of existence of the human as well as the natural universe, an objective quality. Thus Kant attributes the beautiful in nature to nature's "capacity to form itself, in its freedom, also in an aesthetically purposive way, according to chemical laws. . . ."[12]

The Marxian conception understands nature as a universe which becomes the congenial medium for human gratification to the degree to which nature's *own* gratifying forces and qualities are recovered and released. In sharp contrast to the capitalist exploitation of nature, its "human appropriation" would be nonviolent, nondestructive: oriented on the life-enhancing, sensuous, aesthetic qualities inherent in nature. Thus transformed, "humanized," nature would respond to man's striving for fulfillment, nay, the latter would not be possible without the former. Things have their "inherent measure" *(inhärentes Mass)*.[13] this measure is *in* them, is the potential enclosed in them; only man can free it and, in doing so, free his own human potential. Man is the only being who can "form things in accordance with the laws of beauty."[14]

Aesthetics of liberation, beauty as a "form" of freedom: it looks as if Marx has shied away from this anthropomorphist, idealistic conception. Or is this apparently idealistic notion rather the *enlargement of the materialistic base?* For "man is directly a *natural being*; he is a corporeal, living, real, sensuous, objective being" who has "real, sensuous objects" as the objects of his life.[15] And his senses ("like those organs which are directly social in their form")[16] are active, practical in the "appropriation" of the object world; they express the social existence of man, his "objectification." This is no longer Feuerbach's "naturalism" but, on the contrary, the extension of Historical Materialism to a dimension which is to play a vital role in the liberation of man.

There is, however, a definite internal limit to the idea of the liberation of nature through "human appropriation." True, the aesthetic dimension is a vital dimension of freedom; true, it repels violence, cruelty, brutality, and by this token will become an essential quality of a free society, not as a separate realm of "higher culture," but as a driving force and *motive* in the *construction* of such a society. And yet, certain brute facts, unconquered and perhaps unconquerable facts, call for skepticism. Can the human appropriation of nature ever achieve the elimination of violence, cruelty, and brutality in the daily sacrifice of animal life for the physical reproduction of the human race? To treat nature "for its own sake" sounds good, but it is certainly not for the sake of the animal to be eaten, nor probably for the sake of the plant. The end of this war, the perfect peace in the animal world—this idea belongs to the Orphic myth, not to any conceivable historical reality. In the face of the suffering inflicted by man on man, it seems terribly "premature" to campaign for universal vegetarianism or synthetic foodstuffs; as the world is, priority must be on *human* solidarity among human beings. And yet, no free society is imaginable which does not, under its "regulative idea of reason," make the concerted effort to reduce consistently the suffering which man imposes on the animal world.

Marx's notion of a human appropriation of nature retains something of the *hubris* of domination. "Appropriation," no matter how human, remains appropriation of a (living) object by a subject. It offends that which is essentially other than the appropriating subject, and which exists precisely as object in its own right—that is, as subject! The latter may well be hostile to man, in which case the relation would be one of struggle; but the struggle may also subside and make room for peace, tranquillity, fulfillment. In this case, not appropriation but rather its negation would be the nonexploitative relation: surrender, "letting-be," acceptance...But such surrender meets with the impenetrable resistance of matter; nature is not a manifestation of "spirit," but rather its essential *limit*.

III

Although the historical concept of nature as a dimension of social change does not imply teleology and does not attribute a "plan" to nature, it does conceive of nature as subject-object: as a *cosmos* with its own potentialities, necessities, and chances. And these potentialities can be, not only in the sense of their value-free function in theory and practice, but also as bearers of *objective values*. These are envisaged in such phrases as "violation of nature," "suppression of nature." Violation and suppression then mean that human action against nature, man's interrelation with nature, offends against certain objective *qualities* of nature—qualities which are essential to the enhancement and fulfillment of life. And it is on such objective grounds that the liberation for man to his own humane faculties is linked to the liberation of nature—that "truth" is attributable to nature not only in a mathematical but also in an existential sense. The emancipation of man involves the recognition of such truth in things, in nature. The Marxian vision recaptures the ancient theory of knowledge as *recollection:* "science" as the *re*discovery of the true *Forms* of things, distorted and denied in the established reality, the perpetual *materialistic core of idealism.* The "idea," as the term for these Forms, is not a "mere" idea, but an image illuminating what is false, distorted in the way in which things are "given," what is missing in their familiar perception, in the mutilated experience which is the work of society.

Recollection thus is not remembrance of a Golden Past (which never existed), of childhood innocence, primitive man, et cetera. Recollection as epistemological faculty rather is synthesis, reassembling the bits and fragments which can be found in the distorted humanity and distorted nature. This recollected material has become the domain of the imagination, it has been sanctioned by the repressive societies in art, and as "poetic truth"—poetic truth only, and therefore not much good in the actual transformation of society. These images may well be called "innate ideas" inasmuch as they cannot possibly be given in the immediate experience which prevails in the repressive societies. They are given rather as the *horizon* of experience under which the immediately given forms of things appear as "negative," as denial of their inherent possibilities, their truth. But in this sense, they are "innate" in man as *historical* being; they are themselves historical because the possibilities of liberation are always and everywhere historical possibilities. Imagination, *as knowledge,* retains the insoluble tension between idea and reality, the potential and the actual. This is the *idealistic core* of dialectical materialism: the transcendence of freedom beyond the given forms. In this sense too, Marxian theory is the historical heir of German Idealism.

Freedom thus becomes a "regulative concept of reason" guiding the practice of changing reality in accordance with its "idea," i.e., its own potentialities—to make reality free for its truth. Dialectical materialism understands freedom as historical, empirical transcendence, as a force of social change, transcending its immediate form also in a socialist society—not toward ever more production, not toward Heaven or Paradise, but toward an ever more peaceful, joyful struggle with the inexorable resistance of society and nature. This is the philosophical core of the theory of the permanent revolution.

As such force, freedom is rooted in the primary drives of men and women, it is the vital need to enhance their life instincts. Prerequisite is the capacity of the senses to experience not only the "given" but also the "hidden" qualities of things which would make for the betterment of life. The radical redefinition of sensibility as "practical" desublimates the idea of freedom without abandoning its transcendent content: the senses are not only the basis for the *epistemological* constitution of reality, but also for its *transformation*, its *subversion* in the interest of liberation.

Human freedom is thus rooted in the human *sensibility:* the senses do not only "receive" what is given to them, in the form in which it appears, they do not "delegate" the transformation of the given to another faculty (the understanding); rather, they discover or *can* discover by themselves, in their "practice," new (more gratifying) possibilities and capabilities, forms and qualities of things, and can urge and guide their realization. The emancipation of the senses would make freedom what it is not yet: a sensuous need, an objective of the Life Instincts *(Eros).*

In a society based on alienated labor, human sensibility is *blunted:* men perceive things only in the forms and functions in which they are given, made, used by the existing society; and they perceive only the possibilities of transformation as defined by, and confined to, the existing society.[17] Thus, the existing society is *reproduced* not only in the mind, the consciousness of men, but *also in their senses;* and no persuasion, no theory, no reasoning can break this prison, unless the fixed, petrified *sensibility* of the individuals is *"dissolved," opened* to *a new dimension of history,* until the oppressive familiarity with the given object world is broken—broken in a *second alienation:* that from the alienated society.

Today, in the revolt against the "consumer society," sensibility strives to become "practical," the vehicle for radical reconstruction, for new ways of life. It has become a force in the *political* struggle for liberation.[18] And that means: the individual emancipation of the senses is supposed to be the beginning, even the foundation, of *universal* liberation, the free society is to take roots in new instinctual needs. How is this possible? How can "humanity," human solidarity as *"concrete universal"* (and not as abstract value), as real force, as "praxis," originate in the individual sensibility: how can objective freedom originate in the most subjective faculties of man?

We are faced with the *dialectic* of the universal and the particular: how can the human sensibility, which is *principium individuationis*, also generate a *universalizing* principle?

I refer again to the philosophical treatment of this problem in German Idealism: here is the intellectual origin of the Marxian concept. For *Kant:* a universal sensorium (the pure forms of intuition) constitutes the one unified framework of sense experience, thus validating the universal categories of the understanding. For *Hegel:* reflection on the content and mode of *my* immediate sense certainty reveals the "We" in the "I" of intuition and perception. When the still unreflected consciousness has reached the point where it becomes conscious of itself and its relation to its objects, where it has experienced a "transsensible" world "behind" the sensuous appearance of things, it discovers that *we* ourselves are behind the curtain of appearance. And this "we" unfolds as social reality in the struggle between Master and Servant for "mutual recognition."

This is the turning point on the road that leads from Kant's effort to reconcile man and nature, freedom and necessity, universal and particular, to Marx's materialistic solution: Hegel's *Phenomenology* breaks with Kant's transcendental conception: history and society enter into the theory of knowledge (and into the very structure of knowledge) and do away with the "purity" of the a priori; the materialization of the idea of freedom begins. But a closer look shows that the same tendency was already present in Kant's philosophy: in the development from the First to the Third Critique.

1. In the *First Critique*, the freedom of the subject is present only in the epistemological syntheses of the sense data; freedom is relegated to the transcendental Ego's pure syntheses: it is the power of the a priori by virtue of which the transcendental subject constitutes the objective world of experience; theoretical knowledge.

2. In the *Second Critique*, the realm of *praxis* is reached with the stipulation of the autonomy of the moral person: his power to *originate* causation without breaking the universal causation which governs nature: necessity. The price: subjection of the sensibility to the categorical imperative of reason. The relation between human freedom and natural necessity remains obscure.

3. In the *Third Critique*, man and nature are joined in the aesthetic dimension, the rigid "otherness" of nature is reduced, and Beauty appears as "symbol of morality." The union of the realm of freedom and that of necessity is here conceived not as the mastery of nature, not as bending nature to the purposes of man, but as attributing to nature an ideal purposiveness "of its own: a purposiveness without purpose."

But it is only the *Marxian* conception which, while preserving the critical, transcendent element of idealism, uncovers the material, historical ground for the reconciliation of human freedom and natural necessity; subjective and objective freedom. This union presupposes liberation: the revolutionary *praxis* which is to abolish the institutions of capitalism and to replace them by socialist institutions and relationships. But in this transition, the emancipation of the senses must accompany the emancipation of consciousness, thus involving the *totality* of human existence. The individuals themselves must change in their very instincts and sensibilities if they are to build, in association, a *qualitatively* different society. But why the emphasis on *aesthetic* needs in this reconstruction?

IV

It is not just in passing and out of exuberance that Marx speaks of the formation of the object world "in accordance with the laws of beauty" as a feature of free human practice. Aesthetic qualities are essentially nonviolent, nondomineering—qualities which, in the domain of the arts, and in the repressive use of the term "aesthetic" as pertaining to the sublimated "higher culture" only, are divorced from the social reality and from "practice" as such. The revolution would undo this repression and recapture aesthetic needs as a subversive force, capable of counteracting the dominating aggressiveness which has shaped the social and natural universe. The faculty of being "receptive," "passive," is a precondition of freedom: it is the ability to see things in their own right, to experience the joy enclosed in them, the erotic energy of nature—an energy which is there to be liberated; nature, too, awaits the revolution! This receptivity is itself the soil of creation: it is opposed, not to productivity, but to *destructive* productivity.

The latter has been the ever more conspicuous feature of male domination; inasmuch as the "male principle" has been the ruling mental and physical force, a free society would be the "definite negation" of this principle—it would be a *female* society. In this sense, it has nothing to do with matriarchy of any sort; the image of the woman as mother is itself repressive; it transforms a biological fact into an ethical and cultural value and thus it supports and justifies her social repression. At stake is rather the ascent of Eros over aggression, in men *and* women; and this means, in a male-dominated civilization, the "femalization" of the male. It would express the decisive change in the instinctual structure: the weakening of primary aggressiveness which, by a combination of biological and social factors, has governed the patriarchal culture.

In this transformation, the Women's Liberation Movement becomes a radical force to the degree to which it transcends the entire sphere of aggressive needs and performances, the entire social organization and division of functions. In other words, the movement becomes radical to the degree to which it aims, not only at equality *within* the job and value structure of the *established* society (which would be the equality of dehumanization) but rather at a change in the structure itself (the basic demands of equal opportunity, equal pay, and release from full-time household and child care are a prerequisite). Within the established structure, neither men nor women are free—and the dehumanization of men may well be greater than that of women since the former suffer not only the conveyor belt and assembly line but also the standards and "ethics" of the "business community."

And yet, the liberation of women would be more sweeping than that of men because the repression of women has been constantly fortified by the social use of their biological constitution. The bearing of children, being a mother, is supposed to be not only their natural function but also the fulfillment of their "nature"—and so is being a wife, since the reproduction of the species occurs within the framework of the monogamous patriarchal family. Outside this framework, the woman is still predominantly a plaything or a temporary outlet for sexual energy not consummated in marriage.

Marxian theory considers sexual exploitation as the primary, original exploitation, and the Women's Liberation Movement fights the degradation of the woman to a "sexual object." But it is difficult to overcome the feeling that here, repressive qualities characteristic of the bourgeois-capitalist organization of society enter into the fight against this organization. Historically, the image of the woman as sexual object, and her exchange value on the market, devalue the earlier repressive images of the woman as mother and wife. These earlier images were essential to the bourgeois ideology during a period of capitalist development now left behind: the period where some "inner-worldly asceticism" was still operative in the dynamic of the economy. In comparison, the present image of the woman as sexual object is a *desublimation* of bourgeois morality—characteristic of a "higher stage" of capitalist development. Here, too, the commodity form is universalized: it now invades formerly sanctified and protected realms. The (female) body, as seen and plastically idealized by *Playboy*, becomes desirable merchandise with a high exchange value. Disintegration of bourgeois morality, perhaps—but *cui bono?* To be sure, this new body image promotes sales, and the plastic beauty may not be the real thing, but they stimulate aesthetic-sensuous needs which, in their development, must become incompatible with the body as instrument of alienated labor. The male body, too, is made the object of sexual image creation—also plasticized and deodorized...clean exchange value. After the secularization of religion, after the transformation of ethics into Orwellian hypocrisy—is the "socialization" of the body as sexual object perhaps one of the last decisive steps toward the completion of the exchange society: the completion which is the beginning of the end?

Still, the publicity with the body (at present, the female body) as object is dehumanizing, the more so since it plays up to the dominant male as the aggressive subject for whom the female is there, to be taken, to be laid. It is in the nature of sexual relationships that both, male and female, are object *and* subject at the same time; erotic and aggressive

energy are fused in both. The surplus-aggression of the male is socially
conditioned—as is the surplus-passivity of the female. But beneath the
social factors which determine male aggressiveness and female receptivity, a *natural* contrast exists: it is the woman who "embodies," in a
literal sense, the promise of peace, of joy, of the end of violence. Ten-
derness, receptivity, sensuousness have become features (or mutilated
features) of her body—features of her (repressed) humanity. These female qualities may well be socially determined by the development of
capitalism. The process is truly dialectical.[19] Although the reduction
of the concrete individual faculties to abstract labor power established
an abstract equality between men and women (equality before the machine), this abstraction was less complete in the case of women. They
were employed in the material process of production to a lesser extent
than men. Women were fully employed in the household, the family,
which was supposed to be the sphere of realization for the bourgeois individual. However, this sphere was isolated from the productive process
and thus contributed to the women's mutilation. And yet, this isolation
(separation) from the alienated work world of capitalism enabled the
woman to remain less brutalized by the Performance Principle, to remain closer to her sensibility: more human than men. That this image
(and reality) of the woman has been determined by an aggressive, male-
dominated society does not mean that this determination must be
rejected, that the liberation of women must overcome the female "nature." This equalization of male and female would be regressive: it
would be a new form of female acceptance of a male principle. Here
too the historical process is dialectical: the patriarchal society has created a female image, a female counter-force, which may still become
one of the gravediggers of patriarchal society. In this sense too, the
woman holds the promise of liberation. It is the woman who, in Dela-
croix' painting, holding the flag of the revolution, leads the people
on the barricades. She wears no uniform; her breasts are bare, and her
beautiful face shows no trace of violence. But she has a rifle in her
hand—for the end of violence is still to be fought for . . .

Notes

1. See Murray Bookchin, "Ecology and Revolutionary Thought" and "Towards a Liberatory Technology," in *Post-Scarcity Anarchism* (Berkeley: Ramparts Press, 1971).

2. See Alfred Schmidt, *Der Begriff der Natur in der Lehre von Marx* (Frankfurt: Europäische Verlagsanstalt, 1962).

3. Karl Marx, *The Economic and Philosophic Manuscripts of 1844*, Dirk J. Struik, ed. (New York: International Publishers, 1964), p. 139.

4. Ibid., p. 141.

5. Ibid., p. 141.

6. Ibid., p. 139.

7. "The sun is the object of the plant...just as the plant is an object for the sun..." Ibid., p. 181.

8. Ibid., p. 139.

9. "For the sake of the thing"—an illustration:
In Yugoslavia, they sell wooden cutting boards which, on one side, are painted with very colorful, pretty flower patterns; the other side is unpainted. The boards bear the imprint: "don't hurt my pretty face, use other side." Childish anthropomorphism? Certainly. But can we perhaps imagine that the people who had this idea, and those users who pay attention to it, have a quite natural, instinctual aversion against violence and destruction, that they have indeed a "human relation" to matter, that matter to them is part of the life environment and thus assumes traits of a living object?

10. Interview with Jacques Monod, *New York Times*, March 15, 1971.

11. Theodor W. Adorno, *Aesthetische Theorie* (Frankfurt/Main: Suhrkamp, 1970), pp. 100, 107.

12. *Critique of Judgment*, S 58.

13. Marx, loc. cit., p. 114.

14. Ibid.

15. Ibid. p. 181.

16. Ibid. p. 139.

17. For the following see my *Essay on Liberation* (Boston: Beacon Press, 1969), pp. 36 ff.

18. The fight for the Peoples Park in Berkeley, which was met with brute force by the armed guardians of law and order, shows the explosion of sensibility in political action.

19. This dialectic is the center of Angela Davis's paper *Marxism and Women's Liberation* (not yet published). Written in jail, this paper is the work of a great woman, militant, intellectual.